BORDERED LIVES

HOW EUROPE FAILS
REFUGEES AND MIGRANTS

About the author

Hsiao-Hung Pai is a journalist and author of *Chinese Whispers: The True Story Behind Britain's Hidden Army of Labour* (2008), shortlisted for the Orwell Book Prize 2009; *Scattered Sand: The Story of China's Rural Migrants* (2012), winner of the Bread and Roses Award 2013; *Invisible* (2013) and *Angry White People* (2016). She has written for *The Guardian* and many Chinese publications worldwide.

Acknowledgements

Bordered Lives would not have ben possible without people wanting and being willing to share their stories with me. I would like to thank them all so much for their friendship and for the time they spent with me. I hope that this book will contribute to a case for their rights to be recognized and respected.

I would also like to thank the *New Internationalist* for publishing this book. My gratitude goes to my editor Chris Brazier, for his time and enthusiasm in shaping it and making it work. His direction and advice have been most valuable. I am very grateful to Eve Leckey for her brilliant and thorough copy-editing. Her experience in Italy and her proficiency in Italian have contributed greatly to checking the accuracy of the text. Her professionalism kept us in line with the schedule. I am very fortunate to have had Eve working on the book: she's the best. Also, many, many thanks to Daniel Raymond-Barker for making the book accessible and promoting it. Their time and effort are greatly appreciated.

I'd also like to thank Alberto Biondo, Daniel Trilling and many No Borders authors whose work enriched my understanding of the subject. Many thanks to Patrick Ward for sharing his experiences.

My sincere thanks go to my partner Dave Barkway, who was there to support and encourage me (and cook many lovely meals for me) throughout the research and writing of this book. Immense thanks to him for his time and patience in subbing my English in the first draft. Immense thanks to him for being the first reader – Dave's unbeatable.

BORDERED LIVES

HOW EUROPE FAILS REFUGEES AND MIGRANTS

HSIAO-HUNG PAI

New Internationalist

Bordered Lives:
How Europe Fails Refugees and Migrants

First published in 2018 by
New Internationalist Publications Ltd
The Old Music Hall
106-108 Cowley Road
Oxford
OX4 1JE, UK
newint.org

Editor: Chris Brazier
Cover design: Ian Nixon
Design: Juha Sorsa

Printed by T J International Limited, Cornwall, UK
who hold environmental accreditation ISO 14001.

MIX
Paper from
responsible sources
FSC® C013056

British Library Cataloguing-in-Publication Data
A catalogue record for this book is available from the British Library.

Library of Congress Cataloging-in-Publication Data
A catalog record for this book is available from the Library of Congress.

ISBN 978-1-78026-438-7
(ebook ISBN 978-1-78026-439-4)

Contents

Introduction

'Refugee crisis,' 'migrant crisis'. These are the terms used by the mainstream media to inform us about the situation of people without capital, fleeing conflicts, wars and degradation. These are the terms used to play the numbers game and plant the idea that 'Europe cannot cope' in the public mind. Ultimately, these are the terms through which the concept of 'us' and 'them' is maintained and strengthened.

When I first read this media terminology and heard the language used to address the arrival of refugees and migrants in Europe, the questions I wanted to ask were: Who defines it as a 'crisis'? Why is it a 'crisis'? What is the nature of the 'crisis'?

In the unequal world in which we live, where the Global North defines and writes history on behalf of the South, our knowledge of the world is disseminated and controlled via the powerful institutions of the ruling elites of the North, and our understanding of world events is often shaped and guided by these institutions.

Contrary to the mainstream perspective that looks at the arrival of refugees and migrants in terms of security and migration management, this book puts forward an alternative approach that places people at the centre of the picture. As someone not born in Britain and only having lived here since the age of 21, I have always understood what it's like to be an 'outsider' and how difficult it can be to bring your voice into the mainstream. Powerful ideological institutions, such as the media, ensure that the story of the 'outsider' rarely gets heard – and when it does, the story is often presented as statistics and data that strip away the humanity. Somehow, through the working of the media, the tragic reality of tens of thousands of lives lost at sea has hardly caused a ripple. Refugees and migrants are, at best, portrayed as victims. In the public mind, they have neither faces nor names.

The aim of this book is to tell the story through the eyes of the refugees and migrants – it recounts the true story of people who fled persecution, conflict and abject poverty, risking their lives to cross the sea, only to find themselves trapped in a system that is not designed to offer them protection but often seeks to profit from them and keep them marginalized. It tells the story of people whose lives and destinies have been shaped by Europe's borders. It follows their journey as they move from shelter to shelter, south to north, country to country, and documents their circumstances, their aspirations and their resilience. This is their story told from their own perspective.

More than 5,000 migrants lost their lives crossing the Mediterranean and Aegean seas in 2016 – they were drowned, suffocated or crushed during the crossing. More than 25,000 migrants have died in their attempt to reach or stay in Europe since 2000. And, halfway into 2017, we have seen thousands more lose their lives at sea on their journey to Europe.

For those who have made the journey across the sea and managed to reach Europe, their next phase of misery has just begun. You see it in the asylum reception systems across the frontline European Union (EU) states, caused by the wholescale outsourcing and privatization of facilities (see chapters 2 and 3). You see it in the 'hotspot system' imposed by the European Commission that only works as a measure to reject the greatest possible number and protect the fewest (see chapter 1). You see asylum-seeking migrants facing icy temperatures without shelters on the island of Lesbos, trapped in limbo, as a direct result of the EU-Turkey deal. You see migrants having nowhere to turn and sleeping rough in the streets, in the middle of 'civilized' Western Europe (see chapter 6).

With powerful institutions in place, it has always been difficult to challenge the mainstream perception of migration and correct its narratives about refugees and migrants – and increasingly so since the financial crisis. Far-right parties and groups have grown steadily, taking advantage of economic bad times. In the past decade, the EU's austerity policies have contributed to growing discontent, a great deal of it misdirected against the 'outsiders': in other words, refugees and migrants.

While Donald Trump's rise to power and his regressive anti-immigrant, anti-refugee policies have provoked global outrage, policies identical to his have already been propagated, debated, and practised across Europe. The same kind of state violence can be witnessed in the way EU countries deal with refugees and migrants.

Britain has always had a draconian immigration and asylum system in which people are processed into fixed categories of 'refugees' and 'economic migrants', a crude and unjust labelling system that ignores the complex reasons for people's movement across borders. Throughout the 2000s, I came across numerous Chinese migrants who lived a life in limbo as a result. Some of them had, literally, worked themselves to death in a hostile environment where there is no labour protection for those who are undocumented or for those awaiting asylum decisions.[1] They had often been branded as 'economic migrants' and 'bogus asylum-seekers', despite their individual political backgrounds. These people became numbers in the system that defines migrants according to the interests of the state – until they turned up dead, like the 58 Chinese migrants in the back of a lorry at Dover in June 2000, and the 23 Chinese cockle pickers who drowned in Morecambe Bay in February 2004. Only then were they given names again, as the father, mother, son or daughter of someone in far-away rural China.

Britain has always failed to fulfil its international obligations to receive refugees, avoiding its responsibilities even when much larger numbers of refugees were entering Europe in 2015. Following David Cameron's pitiful pledge to take only 20,000 Syrian refugees from the refugee camps by 2020, Theresa May retrenched further, not only arguing against rescue operations in the Mediterranean, calling it a pull factor, but also making life harder for asylum-seekers when they arrive in Britain, maintaining the outsourcing of asylum reception services to private companies, offering asylum-seekers inadequate financial support, and subjecting them to appalling living conditions. The Tory government continues to refuse to take part in receiving refugees: only three per cent of asylum applications in Europe were lodged in Britain. In 2016, Britain received only 38,517 applications for asylum, compared with 722,370 applications in Germany, 123,432 in Italy and 85,244 in France.

Anti-refugee, anti-migrant policies have become mainstream

throughout Western Europe. In 2016, Denmark passed a draconian law that allowed Danish police authorities to search and seize valuables (worth more than 10,000 kroner, or $1,600) from asylum-seekers, to 'cover their housing and food costs'. Worse still, Danish law also ensures that a refugee has to wait three years before being able to apply for their family to come to Denmark.

Denmark has always had a low level of asylum applications, ranging between 3,000 and 5,000 annually before 2014. Even when tens of thousands fled from Syria and attempted to enter Europe, Denmark only received 15,000 asylum applications in 2014 and only 6,000 people were granted a permit to stay. In 2015, when Germany was receiving around 800,000 asylum-seekers, Denmark had only 18,500 applications and only 10,000 were granted. In a country whose economic landscape has not been affected by the presence of a refugee and migrant population, fear of an 'invasion' is no doubt the result of political manipulation.

Martin Petersen, a Danish author who has written extensively on migration in Europe, said that he feels appalled and saddened that a majority in the Danish parliament voted these laws through. He researched the journey of refugees and their conditions in Lampedusa in the 2000s, inspired by Italian journalist Fabrizio Gatti, who conducted undercover work in order to reveal the wretched destiny of refugees in Europe. Petersen himself witnessed the subhuman living conditions and cruel treatment of refugees and migrants – such as beating and the use of racist language – in Italian reception centres, which he renamed 'the container park' in his novel *Exit Sugartown*.

He sees the arrival of refugees as a test for the conscience of Europe. 'A few years ago, very few people in Denmark knew or were interested in what was going on in Lampedusa, Malta, Greece, Italy, Spain,' said Petersen. 'But from the day in September 2015 when Syrian refugees were seen and filmed walking north along the motorways in southern Jutland, I think a great many people opened their eyes. And the reactions have been many. From the man who spat at the refugees from a bridge over that motorway, to people who drove down towards the German border in their cars and offered refugees a lift to Copenhagen, so they could get to

Sweden faster. Some Danes who helped the Syrians have been tried and will probably be fined for trafficking – which in this case was to transport Syrian refugees, without any pay, from the German border to ferries or the bridge to Sweden.'

Petersen is ashamed of what Danish policies are doing to asylum-seekers. 'The centre-right governing party, Venstre, supported by the anti-immigrant Danish People's Party (DPP) which wants to close the borders, has openly said that these laws are passed mainly to keep people – and to scare people – from seeking asylum in Denmark. Twenty per cent of Danes unfortunately vote DPP, and they like the law; some even want it to be stricter.'

In the Netherlands, the main far-right party, the Freedom Party (PVV), has grown in popular support in recent years. It is headed by Geert Wilders, who has said that Europe should close its borders, described the arrival of refugees as an 'Islamic invasion', and called Moroccan migrants 'scum'. Wilders supported Trump over his similar policies for the US. The Dutch mainstream political parties have aimed to vie with Wilders' refugee policies. The acceptance rate for asylum applications has always been low in the Netherlands: in 2014, only 12,550 people were granted asylum; in 2015, only 16,450 were accepted; in 2016, only 20,540 applications were approved, making the Netherlands one of the toughest countries for asylum-seekers in Europe. On 15 March 2017, Wilders came second in parliamentary elections, winning 20 seats. He did not have to win more votes – anti-migrant, anti-refugee policies are already dominant in the country.

In April 2017, during France's heated presidential election campaigns, the centrist candidate Emmanuel Macron and far-right Front National leader Marine Le Pen were the favourites. Six days ahead of the first round of the election, Marine Le Pen sought to mobilize her grassroots supporters by pledging to suspend all immigration and shield voters from 'savage globalization'. 'I will protect you,' she said. 'My first measure as president will be to reinstate France's borders.' She won loud applause and cheers from the crowd of 5,000 supporters, prompting them to chant the party's traditional slogan 'This is our home!'

Meanwhile, the neoliberal Macron, a former investment banker and a 'convinced European', was not soft on 'protecting borders'. He emphasized that he favoured strong external EU borders and a united, integrated European policy, which proved appealing to voters from a wide political spectrum. He summed it up when he called himself 'the voice of patriots in the face of the threat of nationalism'. While Marine Le Pen tried to dress up her anti-refugee, anti-migrant racist policy in more mainstream terms to lure the electorate, as neo-fascists have always aimed to do in the post-War period, Macron had more subtly covered the ground. In the wake of the blaze that destroyed La Linière refugee camp in Grande-Synthe (see chapter 6) just two weeks before the election, Marine Le Pen called for stricter border controls into France and commented that the fire was 'the sign of huge migratory chaos that has been rocking our country for years'. She called for 'the chaos' to stop, while Macron warned that France could no longer act as the United Kingdom's 'border guard'[2] and said he intended to reopen talks with Britain as part of wider negotiations over Brexit.[3]

The Paris attack in which a police officer was killed only days prior to the election added ammunition to the long-standing linkage between security and migration emphasized by the Front National – despite the assailant being French born and bred and having crossed no borders to commit the crime. On the eve of the first-round vote count, Marine Le Pen celebrated her ideals of identity and sovereignty, shared and embraced by her supporters – ideals that had long since been incorporated into mainstream politics in France. Over the past two decades in France much of the far-right's anti-migrant, anti-Muslim agenda has been taken on by the centre-right, which has promoted an aggressive assimilationist secularism, thus neutralizing a large part of the Front National's terrain.[4] Every migrant and asylum-seeker would have been deeply troubled watching Marine Le Pen get so close to power. Moreover, the state institutions primarily responsible for their experience of racism, the police forces, consist to a considerable extent of loyal voters and supporters of the Front National.

In Hungary, prime minister Viktor Orbán of the rightwing Fidesz party is openly a fan of Donald Trump. In addition to closing the border with Croatia in October 2015 and then establishing further police controls between the two countries, he proposed the detention of refugees in border container camps where their freedom of movement would be completely restricted.

Across Europe, far-right parties are making gains in elections and their advocates increasingly believe that the anti-migrant, anti-refugee views they preached for years have now become prevalent in society. They go on popular talk shows and claim that refugees bring terrorism. They can even talk about 'border police having the right to shoot dead migrants who cross borders illegally' and still be treated as moderates by the media. The ultranationalist advocates of anti-refugee attitudes across Europe are no longer seen as the extremist fringe and their ideologies are increasingly presented as 'common sense' nowadays. Never before have the Front National and Alternative for Germany (AfD) been more confident of winning over the electorate. Alongside these developments is the rising level of attacks on refugees and their shelters (see chapter 5). In early 2016, the neo-Nazi Swedish Resistance Movement (SMR), part of the Nordic Resistance Movement, hailed a racist mob that attacked migrants, including children, in Stockholm, as 'heroes', and warned of 'a year of violence' against refugees and migrants – and so it turned out. Far-right violence feeds on systematic state violence which takes the form of surveillance, control and enforcement of the border regime.

Minority writers and journalists face many difficult obstacles, particularly when reporting migration and truthfully representing realities. The first challenge is always to break away from – and often expose – the confines of mainstream media and dominant political discourse. Through asking certain questions – who defines a 'crisis', why is it a 'crisis', and what is the nature of that 'crisis' – my research uncovered the structural violence set in place by the elites of the North. Refugees and migrants caught up in the managed migration system of the EU are seen and dealt with as simply figures on the balance sheets of the asylum reception chain – their needs and aspirations often treated as irrelevant. The true crisis we are facing is the crisis of the EU's inability to respond to people from the South fleeing desperate circumstances to seek refuge and to survive. The true crisis is the EU's massive failing to protect displaced people – whether we call them refugees or migrants – and respect their human rights.

The names of some individuals have been changed to protect their identities, except for those who gave permission to use their real names.

1

Gateway to Europe

Exhausted. Since boarding at midnight, I had not been able to get any sleep, even though the sea was relatively calm on this October night. The discomfort of lying across three plastic chairs with arms in the middle kept me awake. In the lounge alongside, dozens of local passengers were watching *X Factor* on a big screen, in Italian. We were due to arrive in the morning just after daybreak and I was counting down the minutes.

The 13-square-kilometre island of Lampedusa in front of us when the ferry docked was a raw and bare piece of land, unspoilt except for being a downmarket resort for a regular stream of holidaymakers, mainly from Milan and other northern regions of Italy. The first sight my partner Dave and I had on arrival was a group of dozens of migrants sitting huddled together on the dockside at the ferry port. They had just disembarked from a rescue boat, wrapped in blankets, and were waiting to be transported to the refugee reception centre (Centro Accoglienza) referred to simply as 'the camp' by the migrants being housed there.

That first sight told another side of the reality of Lampedusa. The island's main revenue has been tourism for several decades now. But just half a day here shows that holiday-making is only part of the story. While tourists from Milan enjoyed couscous dinners on the soulless Via Roma, the main street filled with souvenir shops and over-priced restaurants catering for visitors, and while they occupied the sunny beaches at the end of the holiday season, nearly 1,000 migrants were rescued from the seas around the island in just one day. Some of them would be transported to the camp here.

Shortly after our arrival, I came across a group of four teenagers who looked Asian, wearing flip-flops, standing near one of the Bangladeshi mobile phone accessory street stalls, a frequent sight on Via Roma. They appeared to be just looking around but they seemed uneasy. I wondered if they were new here and decided to approach them. They didn't seem shy and we started talking straight away. Three of them appeared to be very close to each other and one of them told me they had come from a village called Jaldhup in rural Bangladesh.

'We're all staying in the camp now,' he said, with a childlike smile, revealing his white teeth. He looked about 15 to me and the others seemed no older. How did they end up here?

'Our village was very poor. We were very poor,' he said quite confidently, as if he were talking to an auntie in the village. 'Our families' farming income was very small, you know, so our parents decided to send us out to work.' He told me he was 16, and his name was Jahid. The shy-looking boy standing next to him, called Asif, was the same age. Asif and Jahid called each other cousins, although they told me later that they were not related. 'Cousin' is anyone who is close to you and your family. Another boy standing near, Saeed, was one year older and was their closest friend. Jahid spoke English better than the others, so he naturally began to tell their story on everyone's behalf.

'The people who organized our trip abroad came to the village to find people like our parents. They know our villages. They know how poor we are. They wanted to recruit us; they always recruit from young people in the villages. They approached our parents. Our parents wanted us to leave home to earn money for our families. They had to sell animals and land to pay for my trip. Our parents paid €5,000 [$6,000] for each of us to be smuggled to Libya, to work.

'We travelled on forged passports to Libya by plane, through Dubai and Sudan. When we arrived at the Libyan airport, the mafia [local traffickers] were there to meet us and immediately withheld our documents. It was very scary... They told us to shut up, and one of them slapped me. We were totally shocked at the treatment. We realized that our nightmare had just begun.'

During my time in Lampedusa I got to know the three boys better and heard the rest of their story. It was only later that I realized hundreds of underage migrants like them had arrived on the island after being rescued at sea. It gradually became clear that the nightmare Jahid revealed to me on the first day we met was the nightmare endured by thousands of migrants arriving throughout Europe.

But for 'Fortress Europe', they are the 'foreign other'. As Fortress Europe builds up layers of borders to fend off the unwanted from the wealthier states of northwestern Europe, the task of patrolling and defending the Fortress' external borders has fallen to the poorer, peripheral states of the EU, such as Italy and Greece. These peripheral states at the frontier have been tasked to deal directly with the 'foreign other'. The number of migrants attempting to cross the sea to reach Italy has increased steadily over recent years: in 2014, 170,100 migrants arrived in Italy by sea and in total since the beginning of 2014 Italy has hosted around 400,000 migrants who arrived by crossing the Mediterranean. In the first three months of 2016, migrant arrivals in Italy grew by around 80 per cent. Both the EU-Turkey deal made in March 2016 – part of the consolidation of Fortress Europe's third layer of borders with countries such as Turkey, Morocco and Libya – and the border closures in the Balkans in the same month,[5] have resulted in a higher number of people resorting to the Mediterranean route between Libya and Italy.

For several years now, this progressive closing of the frontiers of Fortress Europe has turned the Mediterranean Sea into the graveyard of Europe – and Lampedusa is part of the mass burial site. One disaster that shook the Lampedusans deeply was the death of 368 migrants, including many children, in a shipwreck near Rabbit Bay (facing the Isola dei Conigli) on 3 October 2013. Only 155 people survived to tell the world about the tragedy that they had witnessed and the

The Gate of Europe monument in Lampedusa

17

suffering they had experienced. But even before the victims were buried another tragedy struck the very next day, when rescuers found that another boat had capsized carrying mostly Syrian migrants. Thirty-eight perished and more than 200 were saved.

The double tragedy outraged the Lampedusans. When José Manuel Barroso, the European Commission president, and Enrico Letta, the Italian premier, visited the island, they were heckled by locals who felt let down by the EU for doing nothing to prevent the death of migrants.

Indeed, since the sea crossings began to increase from 2011, there had been no co-ordinated search-and-rescue operation in place in the Mediterranean. Instead, the EU was putting money into defending its borders. Between 2007 and 2013, the EU spent up to €2 billion ($2.4 billion) on fences, surveillance systems and border patrols, according to Amnesty International. This was the context in which those 2013 tragedies took place. As Italian investigative journalist Fabrizio Gatti pointed out, rescue efforts for the second shipwreck were delayed by confusion on the part of the Italian and Maltese navies over who was responsible. That year, as a result, Italy took the decision to launch Mare Nostrum, a search-and-rescue operation that would cover international waters; it cost the Italian government €9 million a month to run while other EU states offered no financial support. Later, in November 2014, it was replaced by a smaller operation, Triton, run by an EU agency, Frontex.[6] In April 2015, two boats sank and more than 1,500 people drowned within a week. But the EU Council's response was to set up Operation Sophia[7] and focus its efforts on tackling people-smuggling networks in North Africa. According to the Council, '[The operation's mandate] is to contribute to the disruption of the business model of human smuggling and trafficking networks in the Southern Central Mediterranean' by 'efforts to identify, capture and dispose of vessels used or suspected of being used by smugglers.'[8]

Indeed, tragedies have not ceased to happen. On 29 May 2016, more than 700 migrants lost their lives in three drownings. The majority of the victims came from Eritrea, Nigeria, Somalia and Sudan. One of the NGOs which took part in the rescue, Sea Watch, said that the horrific scenes of drownings were partly the result of Europe's failure to create a designated search-and-rescue operation. The NGO said there was no European operation with a clear search-and-rescue mandate.

On 3 October 2016, around 1,000 Lampedusans commemorated the 2013 tragedy three years on. They marched to the Gate of Europe, the landmark memorial built in 2008 on the island to commemorate the loss of lives crossing the Mediterranean Sea. The date, nominated National Day of Remembrance for the Victims of Immigration, was the first official day of remembrance for the migrants. Lampedusa's mayor Giusi Nicolini reminded participants of the march that the tragedies were not history: 'Between then and now, another 11,000 have died. Some 3,500 have lost their lives in 2016 alone', she said – and this was three months before the end of the year. That day, not only in Lampedusa, but all over Sicily, activists and campaigners organized workshops and talks to mark the Day of Remembrance.

The hidden camp

To those who ask why I want to write about these tragedies instead of the island's sunny beaches and beautiful landscape, I would say they should come to see Lampedusa for themselves. The tragic drowning of so many migrants is a heavy burden on the islanders, affecting their awareness of and relationship with the outside world; the Gate of Europe memorial is the physical symbol of their sorrow and respect. This gate can be seen from miles away on a ferry. The tragedy has become part of Lampedusa's past and present.

However, on the surface, the life of the islanders can seem unaffected. The ordinariness of everyday life here may seem puzzling. You can sit at the docks and watch fishermen preparing for their daily work. Or stand around the church in the town centre and watch local residents going in and out on a Sunday morning. Such normality may give the appearance that their world has no contact with that of the migrants, and it is true that not every Lampedusan is aware of what happens on their arrival. I asked around and found that not every Lampedusan knows where the Centro Accoglienza is – only that it is in the middle of the island somewhere. In fact, it was only 20 minutes away by foot from Via Roma, if you walk fast, along country lanes into the centre of the island. An ordinary walk, it might seem. But on the way there, as I wondered about the insignificance of migrants' whereabouts to local residents, a banner appeared in front of us on a school fence, with the slogan 'Protect people, not borders', a clear and strong reminder to passers-by of the lives lost at sea and that nothing can be quite that ordinary here.

Walking through miles of dry fields where only cactus and olives grow, a metal gate finally appeared in the distance. Well guarded by the army, the Centro Accoglienza resembled a detention centre more than a reception centre. More than 1,000 refugees from all over Africa as well as Bangladesh were detained there (at the time of my visit in autumn 2016).

This was the island's only refugee centre, known as a Reception Centre (Centro di Prima Accoglienza – CdA), and it had been operating since 1998 as Lampedusa gradually became the first point of entry to Europe for migrants from Africa, the Middle East and Asia. Since the beginning of the 2000s, people from Africa and the Middle East have attempted to come to Europe via Italy, as a result of growing political instability and poverty. By 2006, an increasing number, mostly from Ghana, Nigeria and Mali, were being smuggled from Libya to Italy, via Lampedusa. Following the Arab Spring of 2011 and particularly since NATO's military intervention in Libya, even greater numbers have fled to Lampedusa from Africa and the Middle East. By August 2011, at least 48,000 migrants had come to the island from Tunisia and Libya. Throughout that period, the camp (as all migrants refer to it) functioned as a Centre of Identification and Expulsion (CIE) and there were several protests by migrants as well as local people. Housing conditions at the camp came under criticism from the UN High Commissioner for Refugees (UNHCR) for its overcrowding in 2009, when the number of migrants being accommodated greatly exceeded the capacity of 850, reaching up to 2,000 people. It was even reported that some migrants had to sleep outdoors and in the rain. That February, the appalling conditions led to a riot during which a fire broke out, destroying a large part of the compound.

That year, when the Italian authorities ordered the opening of a new CIE, protests erupted. Around 700 people escaped from the camp, and when ultimately a group tore down the gates, it was left empty. They marched through town with local residents, many of whom fed them during their escape. The scale of the protests was so significant that the police and *carabinieri* took no action to contain them. They stood by as migrants marched towards the town hall, chanting 'Freedom!' 'Please help us!' They wanted to be set free and not deported to their countries of origin.

In October 2015, the camp on Lampedusa became the first of Europe's 11 hotspots, functioning as a pre-emptive frontier. The EU began implementing the hotspot system that year, first in Italy and then in Greece, the frontier states, with the aim of blocking migration at Europe's southern borders and reducing the number of asylum-seekers as much as possible. Italy yielded to pressure from the EU to comply with its migration management policies, embodied in its Dublin Regulation[9] which denies a person the right to seek asylum in a country of their choice. The hotspot system aims to 'filter' migrants from the first point of entry and put them into two separate categories: asylum-seekers and 'economic migrants'. Migrants who are identified as potential refugees are allowed to enter the asylum-seeking process whereas those identified by Frontex and police authorities as economic migrants are rapidly excluded from the reception system and the possibility of seeking asylum. Those excluded are then issued with an order refusing legal entry and giving them seven days to 'deport themselves' from Rome airport[10] by their own means, as Italy does not have readmission agreements, relating to detention and deportation, with the migrants' countries of origin. With neither cash nor means, many migrants vanish into the shadowy margins of society and must fight for their own survival.

The core mechanism of the hotspot system by which migrants are categorized is fingerprinting. Italy has followed the EU directive on fingerprinting for several years but, as campaigners have noted, both soft and hard measures[11] are used in the procedures to obtain them. The identification process is biased as it is based primarily on the migrants' country of origin, and separates them into a variety of groups with completely different rights and entitlements. Migrants from West African countries, for instance, are mostly excluded from asylum-seeking processes and are therefore immediately categorized as illegal, whereas migrants who come from countries with more than 75 per cent of international protection recognition, such as Syria and Iraq, might be eligible for relocation to other EU countries. In reality, even amongst those 'qualified' for asylum-seeking, few have been relocated to other EU countries. As Lampedusa's then mayor Giusi Nicolini put it, the hotspot system works to 'reject the highest numbers of migrants and accept the smallest number of refugees.' As the European Commission's data show,[12] the EU has relocated a pathetically low number of 8,162 people (only 6,212 people have been relocated from Greece; 1,950 from Italy), meeting just five per cent of its promised goal of relocating 160,000 refugees from Italy and Greece to other EU countries.

Many of those who are excluded from the asylum-seeking process – in other words, most migrants from West African countries – have come from a background of poverty and economic degradation caused by political repression, corruption and instability. Their situation and – often – desperation is discussed in later chapters.

The first of its kind, Lampedusa's hotspot was seen as an experimental model for the EU-imposed system. In Sicilian cities like Trapani and Pozzallo, hotspots were set up a few months after Lampedusa's. As I witnessed, the hotspot policy in Lampedusa has resulted in the immediate illegalization of a large number of migrants who have just fled wars and destruction, and has pushed them into an underground, exploitative world of undocumented labour. Lampedusa's hotspot therefore serves as both an immediate point of exclusion for migrants seeking asylum and as the gate through which Europe absorbs its abundant source of irregular, low-cost, undocumented migrant workers.

At the entrance to the camp, two soldiers came up to ask me what I wanted, and then got hold of a UN staff member to come to talk to me. From various sources before arriving in the island, I had known that it would be highly unlikely for anyone, especially journalists and media workers, to gain access to this place. As predicted, the UN staff worker told me to write to the prefecture in Agrigento to apply for permission to enter the site. When I asked how long the application process could take, the staff worker shook her head. As to the likelihood of gaining permission, she shrugged and admitted that 'the chance is slim'. 'Basically it's a NO,' she said.

The idea of detaining migrants deep in the interior of the island and away from the local populace wasn't a surprise. Britain has a well-established system of detention and removal centres which are always located in remote areas and the isolated location of this hotspot reminded me of those. For the migrants being kept in there, the sense of deliberate isolation was profound. 'Why are they keeping us in the middle of nowhere?' many asked me. 'What are they trying to hide?'

The 'King of Lampedusa' and the secret pirate

Back in the town centre on Via Roma, the lights did not go off until after midnight. Even at the local history museum at the end of the street, people sat around on benches outside, talking and watching the selected documentary of the evening on a large flat-screen TV. The history of the Second World War was part of the museum archive. To my surprise, someone named Sydney Cohen, a 22-year-old who had worked as a fabric cutter in London's East End, and who later joined the Royal Air Force as a sergeant during the war, was a bit of a celebrity here. In June 1943, Cohen's aircraft was running low on fuel and there were problems with the compass. He decided to land on Lampedusa, the nearest land, and his crew were ready to surrender. Unexpectedly, however, when they landed, the islanders rushed to the aircraft, thinking they were being invaded, and surrendered immediately to Cohen and his crew. Since then, Sydney has been nicknamed the 'King of Lampedusa'.

A local historian named Nino was in charge of the museum archives and was also known for his work with African migrants. He was, however, very modest about his role and said that all he did was receive the visits of many African youths. Every now and then, in the evenings Nino showed documentaries about migrants' drownings in the Mediterranean, which always drew interested locals, visitors and migrants. His arms crossed, Nino would walk up and down watching the documentary, though he must have seen it hundreds of times before.

Lampedusa is not only geographically closer to Africa than Europe – only 110 kilometres from the Tunisian coast – but it also has a strong cultural familiarity with Africans. The islanders' attitude towards newcomers is mostly positive. Some publicly welcome migrants and are well-known for their support to refugees and asylum-seekers locally. One such person is the optician Carmine Menna[13] who saved as many lives as he could during the disaster in October 2013 when at least 368 people died. I visited him in his premises on Via Roma to say hello. When he heard what I hoped to do in Lampedusa, he shook my hand warmly with both his own.

It's no exaggeration to say that, as a place of transit and with its collective experience of the tragedies, the island is developing its own distinct identity, different from any other part of Italy. In most cases, when a Lampedusan tells you about the island's past and present, they do not talk about migration in terms of 'us' and 'them', but rather as part and parcel of the island's development and shared destiny.

I distinctly remember the day when we visited the local cemetery: an islander named Carmelo was anxious to point out the migrants' gravestones. It was as if he wanted us to recognize and understand what had happened in the seas around his homeland. There were no names on these white marble gravestones, just dates and numbers of the dead in each particular drowning. Flowers were regularly placed there by local residents. Later, when Carmelo showed us around the island, he continually defined Lampedusa in relation to Africa. The sense of solidarity with refugees and migrants is most evidently demonstrated in the political stance of the island's former mayor, Giusi Nicolini, who is known for her resistance to Italy's immigration laws, brought in under Silvio Berlusconi. She has continued to critique the militarization of the EU's 'migration management' that has been imposed on Lampedusa by Operation Sophia.

One day, we walked past five or six abandoned and wrecked boats that had been used to transport migrants across the

Graveyard in Lampedusa for migrants who have perished at sea and been washed up on the island. The words by the poet Cesare Pavese translate as: 'Whatever world lies beyond this sea I don't know. But every sea has another shore and I will arrive.'

QUALE MONDO
GIACCIA AL DI LA'
DI QUESTO MARE
NON SO, MA OGNI
MARE HA
UN' ALTRA RIVA,
E ARRIVERO'.

CESARE PAVESE

One of the boats used to transport migrants on the perilous journey from North Africa to Lampedusa.

Mediterranean, now lined up in an empty car park right next to the town's floodlit football pitch. All the boats were small, and I imagined could accommodate no more than two dozen people each. Fifty metres away was a fish café, which overlooked the harbour with its hundreds of small fishing boats just like a picture postcard. We went inside to cool down from the midday sun.

There, we met the local fisherman-turned-restauranteur Giuseppe Sanguedolce, whom we revisited many times. Giuseppe was proud of his ancestry and of the long history of his family, which has lived on the island for centuries. He showed me a book in Italian titled *Isola D'alto Mare* (Island of the High Seas), in which a distant relative had written an essay titled 'The Secret Pirate'. This relative bears the same name, Giuseppe Sanguedolce, and was a well-travelled man of many talents who explored the history of Lampedusa's pirates hundreds of years ago.

Giuseppe could speak some English because he had married a North American woman and they had a child who was now 21 years old. 'But that's in the past. I'm now remarried to a northern Italian and we have a seven-year-old,' he told me. Giuseppe was proud of having been a fisherman and had decorated his café with sea themes and sky-blue-coloured walls. He himself never met the public without sporting a pirate bandana. But fishing and running the café wasn't everything to him. Every evening when he shut up shop, he would close the door and enjoy playing the piano in the corner of the room.

When I explained the reason for my visit to Lampedusa, Giuseppe immediately commented that the asylum hotspot that I had visited in the centre of the island was 'nothing but a prison'. 'The migrants are kept there for a short while and often sent away the next day, to other parts of Italy,' he said.

Giuseppe informed me that the conditions inside the hotspot were extremely poor, 'and that is why they don't allow anyone to see it.'

'The migrants are sent away from the port here at 8am,' he said, pointing to the ferry port yards away.

As we chatted, Giuseppe revealed his discontent with various authorities. 'The UN staff and the police are making gains from this [the situation of keeping migrants in the hotspot]... The government pays them a lot of money... You can see them going into five-star hotels and dining in posh restaurants like the one next door, while the migrants have nothing.' As he spoke, a few people strolled into the rival restaurant next door. 'She's from Frontex,' he pointed to one of them, 'I know these people.'

'The boss next door is a woman from Catania, with a mafia background,' he whispered, with a mischievous grin. 'But Lampedusa is very different from Sicilia: there's no mafia here, just four large clans.'

That evening ended well, with Giuseppe's homemade aniseed liquor, a Lampedusan version of raki.

'Migrants can't sit here'

I got up at 6.30am the next morning and walked to the harbour to wait for the navy ship to transport migrants from the camp out of the island. The management and transportation of refugees here has been completely militarized. The government in Rome launched its 'military-humanitarian' mission around the island, increasing sea patrols by the navy which runs the entire task of migration control. There was a heavy presence of the military and police in their vans coming to and fro even at daybreak. Meanwhile, local fishermen went about their morning routines, seemingly unaffected by all that was happening around them.

The connection between migration policies and militarization is an issue brought into the public debate by the Askavusa Collective, created in 2008 and also known as 'Barefoot'. Giacomo Sferlazzo, a Lampedusan artist, singer and songwriter, and an activist of the collective, once said: 'It's strictly linked to military policies and very often military spending and choice are justified by the emergencies or shipwrecks... Millions and millions of euros have been spent over the past 20 years on militarizing borders and penalizing migrants who, in the best of cases, find themselves in a situation of entrapment that offers them not a shred of dignity or self-determination.' Indeed, the EU's response to people fleeing conflict, persecution and poverty has been to patrol its borders at the frontline, with national border forces working with the EU border agency to police the gateway to Europe.

On this particular morning, the transportation of refugees that I expected did not occur. Near the transportation point was a large noticeboard, awkwardly worded: 'Hello journalists. Respect the suffering and do not destroy the economic achievement that Lampedusans have built over the years.' It seemed apparent that local people have felt the pressure of international news coverage of the migrant drownings and the impact it has had on tourism, upon which the island's livelihood depends.

Perhaps this was all part of the rationale behind the 'keeping quiet about it' attitude evident from not only some of the local residents, but also the authorities – it is better if the existence of the newcomers remains hidden. It is a strange limbo-land where those who have tragically perished at sea are denied the right to their own names.

Back in town, migrants from Senegal were selling cheap jewellery and other merchandise on Via Roma. They had been settled on the island for two to five years. There were also several Asian sellers from Bangladesh, who travelled from Rome to Lampedusa simply to sell goods during the summer and autumn while the holiday season lasted.

And then I started to come across more migrants who were staying at the camp. They were in small groups. It appeared they had sneaked out for a stroll. Down at the harbour one evening, I got talking to three young men in their twenties from Bangladesh. They had arrived from Libya just the previous week. They were staying in the camp, and they expected to be transported to a camp in Rome some time the following week. I invited them to sit down to talk at Giuseppe's café and they happily said yes. One of them, named Koyes, said they had travelled all the way through Iran to Libya and then were smuggled across the sea before being rescued and brought to Lampedusa.

However, to my surprise and great disappointment, Giuseppe became worried at the sight of the Bangladeshi men. While they were sitting at the table outside the café, Giuseppe asked to have a word with me inside. He said that he was concerned about 'problems from the police'. He told me the owner of the restaurant next door was well-connected to the police, adding, 'I'm very sorry... These guys can't sit here.'

It troubled me to see that Giuseppe was so worried about possible prejudice from the authorities affecting his business, that he was not prepared to serve the Bangladeshi men in his café. The perceived prejudice from the police no doubt said much about the fact that asylum-seeking migrants were seen as potential criminals and a problem for the community and were therefore shunned.

The men in suits were going to the restaurant next door again, much to Giuseppe's annoyance. It was too difficult to explain to the three men from Bangladesh why they could not sit outside the café. The incident certainly changed my impression of Giuseppe.

Nightmare in Libya

Jahid, the teenager from Bangladesh whom I had met previously, told me about the traffickers he had dealt with before leaving Libya. 'The guys [traffickers] in Bangladesh work with Libyan businesses and factory bosses. They recruited us, lied to us, and got us to work free in Libyan factories. We knew nothing about Libya or Libyan factories at that time.'

The three teenagers were sent to work in a ceramics factory, for which they received no wages. Asif asked for their pay, and the company immediately had him put in a prison. He was beaten and tortured repeatedly, and he had no idea how long they would keep him there. When recalling this horrific ordeal, Asif lifted up his arm to show me his injuries from the beatings. The dark bruises had not gone away after all this time. All three of them said they had lived through hell in Libya.

'It was the worst time of my life. Nothing is worse than Libya,' said Jahid, still looking frightened as he recalled what had happened, almost running out of breath as he spoke, so overwhelming was the memory of his fear. 'It's the biggest mistake we made to go to Libya.'

Eventually, after a month, Asif managed to escape from the Libyan prison with friends who were jailed alongside him. He then joined Jahid and Saeed, who ran away from the factory. They found a local smuggler, which was easy, because all Libyan smugglers sought out Bangladeshi youth in the same situation – most factory workers here came from Bangladesh. The local smugglers knew they could make a profit from these youths as they were desperate to escape from Libya. The three boys asked their families to help them and managed to pay the smuggler €1,000 each to be transported to Europe by boat, alongside Moroccans and other Africans.

The state of lawlessness in Libya has been one of the major factors that has pushed tens of thousands of people to flee to Italy. The background to the chaos that has developed in Libya can clearly be seen in the events that have taken place there since 2011. That year, in the wave of popular protests known as the Arab Spring, Libyans took to the streets demanding change. The then dictator Muammar Qadafi set out to suppress the people's revolt. In response, the Western coalition led by NATO established an arms embargo against Libya and bombed Qadafi's military positions. The military intervention aimed at regime change resulted in the overthrow and death of Qadafi and subsequently the formation of a transitional government. Since then, Libya has spiralled into civil war and the collapse of any order as militias fight for control. The situation has gone from bad to worse in recent years, leaving migrants who are caught up in the dangerous chaos no alternative but to flee.

'The boat capacity was 30 but they took 65 people,' Jahid recalled. 'The motor broke down halfway... We had to row the boat with our hands. Luckily we were rescued and put in the camp in Lampedusa.' At this point, he stopped, but I was certain that he had gone through a lot more than he was saying and later he did talk about the sea-crossing, as we will see.

Here in Lampedusa, all three of the boys were fingerprinted when they had arrived a week earlier. Unfortunately, they had no idea where they were going next, nor when. A deeply uncertain future awaited them.

When they arrived, they were taken aback by the conditions inside the camp: as many as 25 people were put in one room – more a 'sleeping space' than anything else, there were three layers of bunk beds and Jahid and Asif were given the bottom layer, which was simply the concrete floor, without even a mattress to sleep on, or a blanket for warmth.

They were given three meals a day, but these were completely inadequate. Not only was the quantity insufficient, but the quality of the food was so poor that they could barely swallow it. The problem was not that it was Italian food that they might have needed time to get used to, but that it was not even properly cooked. It was stale and sometimes only half-cooked.

Is this what the asylum camp expected migrants to get used to? The boys often asked this question among themselves. 'Is this what they think we deserve?'

Besides the poor conditions in the camp, there were also rules that all the migrants considered unfair and unreasonable. 'We have no freedom to go out the way we choose – we are not allowed out through the front gate,' Jahid told me. 'So we have to climb the fence at the back of the compound to get out, just to get some fresh air.'

The three boys treasured the short time they were out each day. They would walk around Via Roma and the surrounding lanes and alleyways, curious to find out more about this place. All they knew was that these people seemed to eat nothing much except pasta, the same poor diet that they experienced in the camp. Jahid told me that he didn't know where Lampedusa was, even after their arrival. They certainly did not know the island was part of Italy. They found it difficult to explain to their families where they were when they managed to speak to them on the phone in the camp, and therefore their parents had no idea where they were. The more they found out about the island, the more they felt secure. When told that they had travelled 11,000 kilometres to date, they all went quiet, as if it didn't mean anything to them.

After wandering for two hours or so, the boys would quickly head back to the camp, fearful of creating problems with the staff there. I looked at their young faces and thought how vulnerable, innocent and defenceless they all seemed. I wondered what destiny awaited them. Asif said he had a relative in Palermo and planned to join him. Jahid wanted to join his relatives in France in the near future, and Saeed would follow him. They would start their asylum application process when they were transported to the next camp – it could be in Agrigento, Jahid said – but they had no idea how many weeks that might take. And at that point, they feared that it could take more than a few weeks.

The boys were totally on their own. It was difficult for them to contact their families as they did not have phones and had to rely on the camp to let them make calls.

Impact of trauma

One afternoon at the harbour I noticed there was a convoy of police vans. Two men in their twenties walked past me and, as I approached them to talk, they became very guarded and nervous. One was holding the other's hand tight, clinging on to him, as if frightened of some potential harm. 'I'm sorry to trouble you,' I said, and explained why I wanted to speak to them. They both looked confused, still holding on tightly to each other. As I talked, they seemed slightly more relaxed. Suddenly, one of them asked me: 'Can we have some water to drink, please?'

It was boiling hot in the mid-afternoon and they must have been walking around in the heat for a while. Not having a penny to buy themselves some water, they must have been terribly thirsty. I took them to a café across the road and bought them some cold drinks. They sat down, still physically shaken, as if unsure what might happen next. 'Please drink something,' I said. They sipped their drinks, looking up at me, thankful yet anxious.

I asked where they came from. 'Bangladesh,' one said timidly, 'speak English something.' The other one, with a shaven head, was still shaking. He could barely utter a word when I spoke to him and left his friend to speak for him. His speech was like a whisper, almost voiceless, as if he was dumb. The only word he kept saying was, 'yes, yes,' to everything I said, as if to seek approval. He stared confusedly, his eyes revealing much sadness and anxiety. It was as if he'd never been spoken to properly. I had the feeling that he was traumatized by what he had experienced on his journey. He was in such a terrible state that it would probably take a very long time to recover. Yet they were abandoned in this camp in the middle of nowhere.

They, like the other migrants from Bangladesh, had been smuggled first to Libya, and had been tortured in a prison there.

The one who spoke some English showed me an injury on his stomach. During the first half hour of our conversation it felt like they were both trying to hold back their tears. There was too much to tell, but no language to tell it in. All they could do was stare and try to make sense of what I was saying.

Mental health among migrants who have fled wars, conflicts, and situations of trafficking, torture and rape, is an issue that Europe's asylum reception system does not appear to have taken into account. Hotspots in Italy, in particular, do not provide mental-health services at all. According to Flavia Calò, a researcher at Doctors for Human Rights (MEDU), 80 per cent of migrants arriving from North Africa have suffered from physical assault or torture en route to Italy. She said that many migrants in reception centres showed signs of depression, post-traumatic stress disorder (PTSD) and other mental-health problems without access to any therapy or professional help. I also observed these issues among several migrants.

The two young men had no idea where to go or when they were to leave Lampedusa. Everything was in someone else's hands and, as had happened throughout their journey, they had no control over their destiny. Here on this island, they felt completely cut off from the world, and that isolation made them frightened of everything. As we sat there, I noticed stares from some Italian tourists. Suspicious stares.

Migrants climbing back over the fence into the camp in Lampedusa.

My partner Dave and I walked them through the winding country lane and cactus fields, back to the camp before 6pm, for dinner. Like all the migrants, they had to return through the degrading 'back door', climbing over a fence at the back of the compound. It was a much longer walk than going to the front gate, and I could imagine easily getting lost in the middle of the fields after dark. There was no lamp-post and you needed a torch. When we reached the fence, they waved goodbye and walked off into the distance. I watched them climb up the fence and turn back to wave goodbye until we were out of sight.

The local activist group Askavusa Lampedusa commented on the situation in November: 'After the summer in Lampedusa, people living within the hotspot can go out on the streets of the island using a hole in the fence. But in the summer, the hole in the fence is manned by the police so as to avoid the exits. This is [so they do] not interfere with the tourist season. Many tour operators and tourists have requested this kind of practice...'

When we met the two men again the next day at dusk, they brought a friend, also from Bangladesh, who spoke a bit more English. He came from the same village as them and he explained to me that the two men had gone to Libya to work as cleaners, but had ended up receiving no wages.

They had been staying in the camp for ten days. They had not received enough clothing from the camp staff. One of them pointed to his white T-shirt and said that it was the only piece of clothing he had. His friend was also wearing the only clothes he had.

Askavusa Lampedusa said: 'The hotspot is definitely a place where the dominant principle is profit. These days there are long queues in front of the church to receive some clothes from the few active volunteers in the parish. Clothes should be guaranteed by those who manage the hotspots but instead are not distributed or they distribute clothes that are not suited to the current weather conditions...'

Apart from the poor conditions, these young migrants also felt very alone and alienated from the surrounding, parallel society. They spent all of their time together and were fearful of leaving the camp alone. They didn't know what to expect of the local community. And why would they? They'd never had any contact or even a brief exchange of words with any local person in Lampedusa. When we sat together in a café on a second occasion they again received hostile stares from tourists – possibly from northern Italy. Were we disrupting their holiday as they sipped cappuccino and nibbled *cannoli* under the sun?

The first time I saw the two young Bangladeshis laugh was when Dave tried to talk to them about cricket. They certainly understood when he tried to explain 'Bangladesh has beaten England for the first time.'

Sea crossing

A windy day. I went to the coastguard station and asked for an interview. I was soon surrounded by five or six officers and one of them told me that, as they were part of the navy, I must seek authorization from Rome. The officer gave me an email address for the press office there, but I later discovered that it was not valid: my email bounced back. The coastguard station officer also told me that, even if an interview with their chief was granted, I would not be allowed to quote anything he said.

I decided not to go back but to talk instead to officers on the crew of two coastguard ships moored in the harbour. One team member told me that they had rescued 2,000 people in the past month and 100 people the previous week. But there had been no rescue this week, due to poor sea conditions – it was already mid-October, after all. When I attempted to talk further, he referred me to his team leader, Marius, who led me onto the ship and offered me coffee in the cabin. The six team members stood around me, watching and listening to the conversation. The leader explained apologetically that the headquarters in Rome had given orders that they should never speak to the press or anyone from outside about rescue operations. 'We're part of the military and must follow the rules,' he said. He admitted that any interview application to the Rome headquarters was pointless as it was very unlikely I would get permission. He didn't know the rationale behind the orders but just apologized sincerely. 'I really regret that I can't speak about our work.'

I met with Jahid and Asif that afternoon, on Via Roma. We sat in a café as it was too hot to stand in the street. The waitress greeted us with hostile stares, and when she brought the cold drinks, she didn't respond when I said 'Grazie'. She was obviously uncomfortable with the presence of Jahid and Asif. Where was the hospitality I was expecting from the locals?

For some of the local residents, the refugee camp was simply another world, even if it was only a few kilometres away. Some were not aware that these people were enduring appalling conditions on their island. Biased media coverage about the 'refugee crisis' over the last decade has planted the seeds of resentment.

In mid-June 2017, Giusi Nicolini lost the mayoral election to Totò Martello, a former mayor who argued for a shift of policy focus back to issues concerning the islanders. This is seen as a demonstration of local feeling concerning the lack of assistance from the rest of the EU in receiving refugees. The election result came a few weeks before Italy's interior minister, Marco Minniti, called on other EU countries to open up their ports to migrant rescue ships.

At the time I met Jahid (October 2016), there were in total 600 migrants in the camp, half of them from Bangladesh. Around 400 were actually underage. Most Bangladeshi migrants were teenagers under 18. Adults lived alongside unaccompanied minors, and the staff appeared to have no understanding or consideration that they were dealing with children. This was inexcusable, especially as the number of minors crossing the sea to Italy is known to have grown fast. In the first seven months of 2016, 13,700 children crossed the Mediterranean, double the amount for the same period in the previous year. Over 25,000 unaccompanied minors arrived in Italy in 2016 – almost twice the number recorded in 2015.[14]

The three boys seemed relaxed with me. I believe that they liked to be able to talk about their situation to someone who would listen. They were very unhappy with the living conditions in the camp and it was one of the issues they talked about most.

When talking about their life back in the village, I asked their birth year and date, and, to my surprise, Jahid said they didn't know because their parents never remembered their birthdays. 'They were too busy working on the farm and growing rice,' he said, smiling.

'My parents sold everything to send me out. I'm the eldest son and have a duty to go abroad to earn money for the family. Half of the people in our village send their children out to work.'

They knew they were fortunate survivors of the journey who, in the future, would be able to help their families. They often recalled the horrific experience on the boat to Italy. 'I saw the number of people boarding the boat was double the capacity, but we couldn't turn back because the smugglers carried guns with them and were pushing people to board. I feared that we would be shot if we disobeyed,' said Jahid.

'Throughout the 52 hours on the boat, we were standing. There was not a moment of rest. And there was no water after the first six hours. No food.

'We prayed and prayed when the waves rocked the boat... When I felt that we were going to drown, I just felt so scared and angry. Angry with the smugglers. When I felt I was going to die, I thought of my parents and how sad they'd be.

'We were very lucky to be rescued by the Italian coastguard, near Malta, before the boat sank.' Jahid sighed, and then laughed. 'When the rescue boat approached us, I saw "Guardia Costiere" [Coastguard] written on the side. I didn't understand what it meant. I thought it might mean "Costa Rica", and I got worried that we might be sent there.'

Even when they were rescued and finally arrived at Lampedusa, they had no idea how far away they were from home.

But at least now they knew they were safe, although their ordeal in Libya made them very fearful of any Libyan migrants who were now staying in the same camp as themselves and tried to avoid them.

What was awaiting them felt daunting. Jahid said he had an uncle in Milan who he believed would be able to pick him up in Sicily once he arrived there – if Jahid wished to join him. Asif, at this stage, felt unsure about staying in Italy although he didn't know where he wanted to go yet. There was too much uncertainty and too little information. It was all too confusing.

Another day in the camp

On a sunny day, we decided to walk westwards, for about four kilometres, until we reached Cala Greca. Beyond the harbour area the island is pretty barren. Barrenness embraced by the sea. While, in the middle of nowhere, we were struggling to walk back, Giuseppe drove past in his small car and offered us a lift to the town. So we ended up having dinner in his café that evening. A dozen navy officers dined there that Friday evening, while police officers frequented his rival restaurant next door all night, their vans parked outside.

Giuseppe offered us a red-coloured liqueur named 'heart of friendship'. I ordered my favourite dish 'spaghetti with calamari' using Google to translate on the mobile phone. He offered to drive us around the island the following afternoon.

Something caught my eye as we left Giuseppe's café: a lively and noisy local wedding party was celebrating. People were dancing to music and dining in a large restaurant with open windows. A dozen migrants, out of the camp for an evening stroll, were fascinated by this scene of joy. They stopped and watched the wedding party through the restaurant windows, their eyes glued to this happy spectacle. They were outsiders observing a community to which they did not belong. They were just onlookers, observing the scene as if they were watching a film, a foreign film that they did not understand – a film that was totally removed from their lives, without even subtitles.

When I met with Jahid, Asif and Saeed again, I realized that the conditions at the camp had become unbearable for them. They were angry and frustrated with the way they were being treated. 'More and more people are brought in – now we have 50 of us in one room,' Saeed said. The facilities were not properly maintained; for instance, the toilets were always filthy as too many people were sharing one. Living in these conditions he had begun to feel unwell.

By now Saeed had managed to get himself a cheap mobile phone from the Bangladeshi street trader and shared it with many other migrants in the camp. He was approachable and people began asking him to take calls for them. While we spoke, Saeed answered many calls that were for other migrants. He joked that he had practically become everyone's personal assistant. He managed to call his uncle in England – this was the first time he had mentioned an uncle. Saeed asked me if I could speak on his behalf and explain that he was in a camp in Lampedusa, as his uncle didn't know where the island was and was getting very worried. He dialled the number and his aunt answered. She spoke English. Saeed eagerly passed the phone to me. On hearing my voice, she thanked me repeatedly and asked me to look after Saeed. I reassured her and told her he was all right and would soon be sent to Sicily.

The boys told me again that the food was very poor in the camp. Saeed said their breakfast consisted of only two small slices of cake, and there were six hours between meals, 'So we often go hungry,' he said.

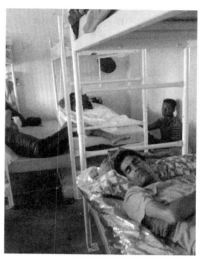

Inside the camp in Lampedusa.

'They gave us half-boiled rice. How can we eat that?' said Jahid. 'When we complain to them, the staff say, "take it or leave it". And most days we are given only a small portion of pasta.'

He continued: 'They serve us pork. They don't consider that there are hundreds of Muslims in the camp. When they serve us pork, we just push it aside and eat only the chips.'

Jahid asked me: 'Do you think we should talk to them about it?' He was worried as to whether it would be the right thing to do. I said they definitely should tell the camp. I wrote a note for him in Italian, saying 'We are Muslims and we don't eat pork. Do you have other types of meat that we can eat?' I told Jahid to give the note to the staff.

'Would you like me to speak to the staff with you?' I asked.

'Don't worry. We'll deal with it,' Jahid said.

Medical care was also generally lacking in the camp. 'With any health problems, they give us just paracetamol, as if paracetamol would cure anything,' Jahid said, making everyone laugh. 'You have a cold? Take paracetamol! You have a tummy ache? Take paracetamol! The two doctors are no use.'

As to religious practice, the camp clearly didn't consider those needs at all. There was no prayer room, and they had to pray in front of everyone else in the shared room.

Alongside the appalling conditions was the purposeless waiting. They had been told that they would leave the camp in two to three days. 'I live every day thinking I am likely to leave the next day,' said Jahid. But he had already been there for two weeks.

Inside the 'Jungle' camp in Calais

In France during the same period, the Calais migrant camp known as the 'Jungle' was making headlines due to its planned closure and demolition at the end of October 2016. Three kilometres away from the town of Calais, the former camp was a world of desperation kept segregated from French society. If you walked there from the town, you would see pretty gardens, suburban cottages, and even a school for training dogs along the road. You couldn't imagine the destitution of that camp was just a short distance away. When I visited it in spring 2016, the tension was high as people were constantly faced with the threat of its closure.

When I arrived, I was invited to sit down with a group of Sudanese migrants. One of them, Abdullah, made a cup of black coffee for me. He was 28 years old, and had been through a hellish journey via Libya before reaching Italy and then France. He showed me the tents where they slept on mattresses. He shared his tent with two other migrants from Sudan – there was no private space, just this shared sleeping area.

Like everyone else in the camp, Abdullah was waiting for the next chance to get himself onto a lorry – he had tried many times. It was obvious that he was extremely stressed. I passed him a cigarette, but he put it behind his ear, saying, 'I'm saving it for later; I can't afford to buy cigarettes.' A younger Sudanese man introduced himself as Salah. He looked thin and malnourished. He could not speak as much English as Abdullah, but his sorrowful eyes said everything.

Politicians had been treating the camp as a political tool, while for a long time local residents had argued for its closure. In February 2016, a petition by charities to stop the planned demolition of the southern half of the Calais camp was rejected by a French court; the French government received approval from the court to evict 1,000 migrants from the camp. During the evictions in March, workers under heavy police guard began to demolish shacks in the camp. Police clashed with migrants and activists from the No Borders network.[15]

Patrick Ward, an activist and journalist, witnessed what happened to the camp on 9 March 2016, when its southern section was being torn down. He saw how the actions of the police and authorities impacted on the migrants living there at the time. He recalled the event as follows:

'Do not take a photo or use my name!' the teenage boy told me with playful urgency, covering his face with his hands so that only his smile remained. He was crouched against the wall of a wooden hut near the entrance to the Jungle camp, surrounded by a group of other young men and children, who were taking a rest after a game of football. They were covered in mud, everything was covered in mud. After conferring with his peers for a few minutes, he settled on allowing me to use the name 'Ahmed' (he had previously decided to use 'Johnson', but changed his mind after his friend suggested it might confuse people to hear about a boy from Afghanistan with a name like that). This cautious friendliness was typical of the dozens of people I spoke to at the camp in Calais... This wasn't paranoia. The police, local government officials and fascist groups were all operating in the area – it paid to have your wits about you.

Ahmed had travelled to Calais alone. Even with his chosen pseudonym, he was still cautious about telling me his background, other than that his family was still in Jalalabad. 'I lived in the mountains but I don't like the mountains – they are dangerous,' he said, recalling 'difficulties' with the Taliban. 'But the Jungle too is full of problems, it's very difficult to live here.' Now, on the day the southern section of the camp was set to be torn down by the authorities, his entire focus was on reaching the UK. He was sick every day, he said, and only had old clothes to protect him from the bitter cold, for which he relied on donations from solidarity campaigners. His house was cold, damp and rat-infested, and he regularly suffered the effects of teargas canisters tossed by police into the densely populated camp.

He had lived like this for six months. 'The Jungle is finished; where do we go?' he asked. 'That's the big problem.'

Patrick described how the police behaved:

> The booze-cruising Brits, the English pubs and the overpriced cafés were replaced by row upon row of towering razor-wire fences. Police vans stood on every corner, and officers prodded and kicked at bushes to smoke out anyone trying to reach the ferry terminal... Two young men, in their late teens, darted out of some bushes ahead of me. 'We tried to go under the fence,' one of them said, pointing to some nearby bushes, 'but the police grabbed me and hit me with sticks.' He gestured to red marks on his face and shoulder.
> In the camp itself there was an eerie sense of calm and normality on that grey day. The main road through the camp – a well-worn path thick with mud – was lively with makeshift shops, cafés, barbers and first aid points. Shopkeepers sat cross-legged on the ground, rolling cigarettes from large sacks of tobacco. Others poured tea and Nescafé. People sat watching Arabic-language music videos over rice and vegetables, charging their phones and attempting to dry their damp clothing. Dozens of international volunteers mingled among the residents, taking details, organizing food distribution, offering legal advice, and, in some cases, agitating. Young men played football in an already-cleared area near the entrance to the camp, under the watchful eyes of police. Children ran up and down the street, as children do, shouting and smiling despite their wet, muddy clothing. People crammed into the huts of those who had all of a sudden become community leaders, trying to hatch ever more desperate plans to escape the camp. Expectations and enthusiasm rose, only to fall moments later when the insurmountable scale of their plans became apparent.
> Abu Omar was one such community co-ordinator, who registered the names and details of Syrians entering and leaving. He was friendly, freely offering tea and coffee to visitors as they poured in asking for help every few minutes. On display in his small shelter was a framed sketch of his

face, adorned with a UK postage stamp and the words: 'Let your smile change the world, but don't let the world change your smile.' Today, though, he was visibly angry. *'Liberté, égalité, fraternité...* for who? For me? Bullshit,' he said. 'There are no human rights here because there are no human beings.' One of his priorities at the time was attempting to ensure that at least some of the 450 unaccompanied children living in the camp were taken care of. 'I have so many boys who lost all their family in Syria,' he said. 'They have one dream, to go to the UK to live with sisters, brothers, uncles. They lost all their other family members in Syria. And I do this job to show you who I am, and who we are, because we are human beings, not animals, and so we work together.'

Apart from Syrian and Afghan migrants, Patrick also spoke to people from Egypt, Palestine, Sudan, Ethiopia, Eritrea, Kuwait, Saudi Arabia, Iraq, Iran and Somalia. He described:

Many now wished they could return home, but having spent their life savings on their journey so far, had little option but to stay and hope Britain would open its border to them. 'I would never have made my journey had I known this,' said Rafi, a 30-year-old teacher from Afghanistan. 'Even the war is better than this. In war, you live or you die – here you never die, but you never live either.'

As I sat in one of the camp's cafés writing up some notes, a group of local government officials marched in. One of the men behind the counter turned down the music volume, as a stern-looking woman in uniform informed him about the dismantling of the camp. They had an arrogance about them – barging in to inform them of a decision that had already been made. They wore black bomber jackets with the words *'Liberté, égalité, fraternité'* printed on the back, like a sick joke. With this sort of interaction, confusion reigned – was the threat real, or just an attempt to disorientate? In place of trustworthy facts, rumours spread rapidly. Many of those who feared eviction tried desperately to gather their meagre belongings to move somewhere else (to where?); others felt this was yet another attempt at sowing confusion and disregarded the rumours. Many of them would be homeless by nightfall.

As the light began to wane, the police lined up, the bulldozers approached and the fires started. Thick clouds of black smoke began to rise from around the camp, and people scrambled to extinguish them. No one seemed to know who was starting the fires. Some people said that they were started by residents in a gesture of defiance, others maintained that they were the work of fascists and police. Defenders of the government actions would often claim that they were the work of 'activists'. Whatever the truth of it, the reaction of the authorities was telling. For the hundreds of police tooled up and masked, in line after line as they protected the bulldozers as they did their work, there were only two fire trucks that I could see. In any other densely populated area of France, you would expect fire trucks to arrive by the dozen. Not here.

I joined a group of volunteers as they filled pots and buckets with water, throwing them against the walls of burning buildings. This particular group was trying desperately to save a structure next to the children's play centre. We threw water against its hot wooden walls as the fire approached. As I carried a large rubber container of water over to the building, a small child – perhaps ten years old – started silently hitting it with a nail-studded stick. He was expressionless, other than a look of blank concentration. It is small incidents like this that were used by some of the media to prove the 'real' nature of these refugees – dangerous, violent... uncivilized. I don't know anything about who this child was, but he had most likely spent much of his young life travelling from country to country, border to border, escaping who knows what, to reach this place. It would be more astonishing if he had emerged from such experiences with anything other than deep trauma. At the time, the popular press was reporting, with gleeful horror, stories about children in the camp throwing stones at journalists. The fact these children were able to function in any way whatsoever was to me astounding.

Groups of residents and volunteers were taking apart homes and loading them onto rickety trailers in a race against time as the lines of riot police edged ever closer. Behind them, a muddy wasteland, punctuated by skips of debris and bulldozers struggling through the mud and over what remained of someone's meagre belongings. All around us new fires were starting, engulfing structures that were, until then, what passed for a neighbourhood. 'I want to take down one of the homes!' shouted a young man at the police, pointing to where the bulldozers were. The police gave no response. It was an eerie chaos. It was quiet, with the residents and their supporters working around those destroying their property like birds repairing their nests after high winds. It was almost normal.

Behind all this, the spires of the beautifully crafted wooden church cut through the toxic smoke against the grey sky, watching over the violence below. Seemingly oblivious to the mayhem engulfing him, a young child rode a small bicycle through the mud, a man behind him carrying a sack of belongings. The man occasionally glanced back over his shoulder, before looking forward once more and encouraging the boy to keep moving. Toys, clothes and large dead rats stuck from the mud. Some people were leaving the camp for nearby woodland in the search for somewhere else to go. But now they would be more isolated in smaller groups – low-hanging fruit for the fascists.

I have reported from refugee and displacement camps around the world, in places like Palestine, Tunisia and Nepal. What I think made this different was that this camp was stuck between two of the wealthiest countries in the world, and it existed purely to appease the selfish desires of those whose ignorance of the situation was gleefully fed by the media and cowardly, opportunistic politicians on both sides of the Channel...

On the day that I left the Jungle, a small piece of graffiti caught my eye under the road bridge near the entrance, which encapsulated the situation in just a few words: 'Maybe this whole situation will just sort itself out.' But would it?

By the beginning of September 2016, there were around 10,000 people – Kurdish Iraqis, Sudanese and Eritrean migrants and others – still living in the Jungle camp, although, according to No Borders activists, around 3,000 migrants had left by mid-October, most of whom had been fingerprinted according to the Dublin Regulation. They did not want to be transported to reception centres in rural parts of the country where they would be isolated. Among those who left, many had headed to Paris. They had nowhere to stay but in the streets and along the canals. Alongside the migrants who had arrived in Paris from outside the country in the previous year,[16] the newcomers from Calais set up tents in the north of the city and joined the homeless population. In mid-October 2016, their total number reached over 1,400.

Meanwhile, Paris, unequipped to cope with refugees and asylum-seekers, was preparing to set up its first two camps. The first, located on Boulevard Ney in the north of the city, was to cater for single men. It was to open in mid-October and was expected to provide temporary accommodation for 600 people by the end of 2016. The second camp, which would cater for 350 single women and families, was set to open at the end of the year in Ivry-sur-Seine, a wealthy suburb south of Paris. This camp had already received opposition from local residents, who believed the presence of refugees would bring harm to their safe and protected community.

Other migrants who left the Calais camp before the closure had stayed in the area and were trying to set up new camps, before attempting to get to Britain again.

Among the thousands who remained in the Calais camp until the closure, over 1,000 were minors who might apply for asylum in France. Prior to the demolition, the first group of migrant children from the Calais camp arrived in Britain. Under the Dublin Regulation, migrant children with close relatives in Britain were entitled to seek asylum there even if they had claimed asylum elsewhere. Fourteen of these migrant children, many of them from Sudan and Syria, arrived by coach on 17 October 2016 at the British Home Office in Croydon.

Their arrival was watched by the whole country and received much hostile press. Popular British media have not hesitated to demonize these migrants from the first day of their arrival. 'First "child" migrants who claim to be aged between 14 and 17 arrive in UK from Calais Jungle', said *The Sun*, on 17 October. The

Daily Mail adopted a similar tone in its headline: 'The first Calais "children" arrive in Britain: migrants who claim to be aged 14 to 17 are reunited with their families in the UK as French prepare to demolish jungle camp.'

In the following days, the British press continued questioning the migrants' age. The *Daily Mail* criticized the authorities for not carrying out dental checks on the migrants. The *Daily Express* ran this headline on 19 October: 'The Home Office has refused to medically age-check "hulking young" migrants from the Calais Jungle posing as children to claim asylum in Britain because dental tests are considered "intrusive".'

Getting to know Asif, Jahid and Saeed

Jahid said our meetings had been a consolation to them, but every time we met, I felt their anxiety growing about their stay in the camp. They had arrived in Lampedusa on 5 October 2016, and it was now 16 October. Other migrants I met had been there for over three weeks. This was clearly a situation shared by many. Out of desperation, Saeed and Jahid asked if I could talk to the staff at the camp to express their concern about the long period of waiting and try to see if the process of transfer could be speeded up. I promised that I would visit the camp and try to speak to the staff, although I was certain that I would not be able to help them.

The boys had been doing their best to get on with everyone during their stay in the camp, in difficult circumstances. The staff soon found that Jahid could speak English better than many of the migrants there, and asked him to act as an interpreter for some of the Africans during their interviews with police officers. Italian police officers monitored by Frontex staff performed identification procedures in the camp. 'We were given four questions to find out about our status: "Do you come here to look for work? Do you come here for international protection? Or to join your relatives? Or for other reasons?" I was asked to interpret these questions for the African migrants,' said Jahid. 'All the Africans answered, "I come here for work".' Were any of the migrants aware what the questions actually meant? Were they aware that these questions would contribute to determining their status? Jahid said no. When you answer 'I come here for work', even if you are also needing protection, you will be classified as an 'economic migrant'. Jahid said that he himself didn't understand what the questions were for, and had answered 'I'm looking for jobs'.

It has been reported by groups protecting the rights of migrants that Italian police often filled in the documents on their behalf. Following the questionnaire, migrants were kept in the camp for a while, in most cases much longer than the 72 hours established by law, before they were sent to various locations in Sicily or mainland Italy. In fact, all the migrants I met on the island were kept at the camp for longer than a week.

Fingerprinting was also an issue for the migrants here. Some do not wish to claim asylum in Italy and fear that fingerprinting will keep them stranded there. However, if they refused to be fingerprinted in Lampedusa, they would, in effect, be held there indefinitely. Between November 2015 and January 2016, a group of 250 Eritrean, Somalian and Sudanese migrants refused to give their fingerprints because they demanded their right to choose where to seek asylum in Europe. Many of them had relatives in northern Europe. As a result of their refusal, they were not allowed to leave the island.

This is a common situation for migrants who resist the procedures of fingerprinting in Lampedusa: they cannot be transferred off the island and are trapped in a situation whereby, unable to enter the asylum system, they are effectively in a state of detention. Ironically, the right to choose a place of asylum has led to confinement in a prison-like camp. Similarly, the hotspot system that the EU wants to use to fast-track and 'filter out' the unwanted is simultaneously the mechanism by which many migrants become stuck, 'jamming up' the system.

There had been several migrant protests against this situation in Lampedusa in the past two years, the most notable of which occurred in December 2015, organized by the migrants from Eritrea, Somalia and Sudan mentioned above. Some of them had been detained on the island for over a month just because they refused to give fingerprints. They challenged the Dublin Regulation and the relocation system. They demanded the right to travel to other EU countries where they have relatives, and to claim asylum where they choose. Outside the island's town council, they held up signs saying 'We are refugees. No fingerprints!' Meanwhile, the European Commission demanded that, if required, Italy should use force to take fingerprints of migrants on their arrival. The island's mayor at the time, Giusi Nicolini, strongly opposed the entrapment of migrants and had urged the authorities to accelerate the relocation of refugees. She told the press that 'Lampedusa can't be used as a prison,' and 'imprisonment of refugees is violating human rights'. However, it would seem that the establishment of the hotspot system, and its eventual impact, is not up to the people of Lampedusa.

On this evening the boys told me that their dinner the previous night was two eggs and some vegetables. It was a tiny portion and was near its expiry date. 'It smelled bad,' Saeed said. 'The potatoes were half-boiled, given to us in a box. I believe all the camp food is processed by machine.'

Jahid couldn't even have a quiet meal. 'The Libyan boys jumped queue at dinner time. They asked me for a fag and pulled up my collar. They fought with others a lot.'

Jahid and Asif were finding it more and more difficult to sleep on the concrete floor as the weather got colder. Jahid took a couple of pictures of the sleeping area to show me. The tiny square metre of the concrete floor was all the two of them had to sleep on. The two bunks of bed above them at least had thin mattresses. Jahid and Asif had been asking for blankets for two weeks. 'What do you expect?' Jahid said. 'Even when we asked for sandals, we waited for three days. We just had to walk about barefoot.'

The boys tried to spend more time outside the camp. They dreaded going back. One day they walked all the way to the other side of the harbour, to the tourist beach where people were sunbathing. 'Those tourists looked at us as if we were from outer space!' said Jahid. They never returned to that beach again.

Saeed spent a lot of time on the phone. He told me he had an older sister in Birmingham. By 'sister', he did not mean specifically a blood-relation, but someone close to his mother. He passed me the phone and asked if I would speak to her. She told me she was very worried about him, and thanked me again and again for my 'help'. How could I even begin to help?

The next evening, we met with the boys again. Saeed presented me with a gift from all of them – a bracelet with little sea turtles on it. (Sea turtles are the symbol of Lampedusa.) I knew they had no cash on them, and was very moved that they were so thoughtful. They had put together the few coins they had and bought me this bracelet from the Bangladeshi street seller on Via Roma.

The three youngsters were among the sweetest people I have ever met, yet they had such distinct characters. Jahid was innocent, sincere and always trusting – a nature that has sometimes landed him in dreadful situations that he has found it difficult to get out of. Jahid was the tallest of them all, and easily seen at a distance. He always wore a long T-shirt from Bangladesh and said he didn't want to look European. It was the only T-shirt he had and he was not interested in material possessions. Saeed seemed to look after his appearance much more, and was always in his clean sportswear, his hair carefully combed even just for a walk outside the camp. He said he was puzzled by the word 'Ciao'. 'Not good, not bad, but they say "ciao",' he said. He was keen to use the words he had learned and greeted every Italian on the street with 'Ciao'. He wanted to understand the language. He was soft-spoken but outgoing, which made him popular with most people. Asif, on the other hand, did not always vocalize his emotions. On the surface it looked like he was simply following the other two and keeping quiet, but on getting to know him, you realized that he was the cleverest observer of the three. Asif never spoke much, but he had a good sense of humour. He laughed when his friends said things that he considered over-sentimental or childish and mimicked their facial expressions, making fun of their sensibilities. But then they would all laugh at themselves. Asif was also a natural rebel, even when this put his safety at risk – as when he demanded wages from a Libyan factory boss. The boys complemented each other and were a great team.

To return their lovely gesture of friendship, I took them to a local cafeteria for some delicious Lampedusan home dishes. Among the colourful variety of local cuisine, such as *arancini* (stuffed rice balls) with different fillings, *pasta alla Norma*, seafood in a tempura-like batter, *sfincione* (a thick pizza) and *caponata*, to name a few, the only thing that caught their eye was grilled chicken and rice – properly cooked meat was something they had not had for a long time. Jahid said the last time they had eaten meat was three months ago in Bangladesh before they left home on their journey. After tasting the rice, Saeed said, 'this is cooked the way it should be and it is good'. They ate in silence – they must have been hungry.

When he had finished, Saeed looked up from his plate and said, 'All is fair and lovely!' He explained that this was a popular catchphrase from a Bangladeshi TV advert for skin-lightening cream manufactured by the transnational company Unilever (there is a series of well-known adverts that portrays an Asian family with a middle-class European image). We all laughed. As we left, Saeed shared the catchphrase with the local chef, who probably thought Saeed was praising his cooking. From then on, 'fair and lovely' became a code we used to express a bit of optimism.

As I had promised Jahid, Asif and Saeed, the next morning I went to speak to the staff on their behalf, about how long they had been staying there. A doctor came to talk to me, but when I explained myself, he said I could only talk with the staff if I had authorization.

Looking over the gate, I could see the three boys sitting far away in a corner, waving at me. They were prevented by the guards from approaching the front gate. After a few minutes, they were told to go back into the building. It depressed me to see the prison-like confinement they were stuck in. They could not have visitors. They could not even go out through the front door. And worst of all, they were being denied the right to know what would happen to them.

Meanwhile, a bus drove past, with a crowd of migrants waving at us from the windows. Several police vans and military vehicles were behind it. Those migrants were being taken to the ferry port, to go to Sicily.

Saying farewell

In the chaotic situation created by the demolition of the Calais Jungle, it was now very difficult to know how to advise Jahid, Asif and Saeed. Given the conditions in the camp in Lampedusa, they were concerned that life as asylum-seekers in Italy would be difficult. But going to France might not be a sensible idea, although Jahid had relatives there. At this stage, they didn't have any information about alternative options.

When we met the boys in the evening, Jahid told me that the camp had offered them bedsheets and a T-shirt for the first time since they had arrived two weeks before. Coincidentally, I had got them a T-shirt each from the museum, with 'Everyone loves Lampedusa' written in Italian on the front. I decided that we would have a pizza dinner, a proper sit-down meal, as we would soon be leaving. The boys had never had any proper food in the camp, and they had no idea what Italian food was really like. Jahid liked the seafood pizza in particular, saying while chewing it, 'this is really good food, like good naan bread with seafood on top'.

After dinner, we walked to a spot overlooking the harbour. They had never seen the sailing boats lit up in the dark and stood watching for a long time. Saeed started singing songs in Bangla, with Jahid joining in. They were waving their hands as they sang, as if they were a popular boy band. 'I want to be a singer,' said Saeed, changing from song to song. Asif was always the self-conscious one and hesitated when he was asked to join in. He did eventually, once. Then he quickly backed out and just stood watching the other two from the side. Every time Saeed and Jahid raised their voice to a higher pitch, Asif giggled.

Jahid said he had thought about it and wanted to go to join his two uncles in Paris. One of them worked as a builder, the other one a street seller. He had no plans or ideas as to what he might do in Paris, but he was certain that his uncles would be hospitable. His arrival in France would be at a time when many were applying for asylum, including those who had been fingerprinted elsewhere. Perhaps he had a chance of getting his asylum claim accepted.

Jahid was also thinking beyond asylum in France. 'Eventually, I want to go to England, to join my sister,' he said. 'One day, I want to make money to support my family in Bangladesh... I want to help my parents and my relatives.'

When we returned to Via Roma, we stopped in front of the history museum. Nino was at the door talking with a visitor.

A documentary about migrant drownings was being screened outside. We all sat on the bench to watch it. It really caught the boys' attention and they followed the film in silence. Saeed gave out a deep sigh when the documentary showed photographs and belongings of the victims. It was the tragedy of the mass drownings in 2013 and inevitably he was deeply upset as the memories of their horrible sea crossing came back. 'After the rescue, you know, I felt I had a second life,' he said quietly.

We walked them to the top of the lane that led to the fence at the rear of the camp. It was pitch dark, near midnight, but they said they could find their way back all right. They had done this many times before. But Asif still had a cut on his hand after falling from the fence a few nights ago. They looked sad and were trying to hold back their tears. It felt wrong to leave them behind – they were still trapped there, and so desperate. Unfortunately, I had to keep to my schedule and return to Palermo in Sicily. I gave each of them a big hug and promised to keep in touch.

The following morning, Carmelo picked us up and drove us to his place. He wanted to show us the apartment he wanted to rent the next time we were there. We met his son, who was in the Air Force, and his builder friend who had built his whole two-storey house. He picked fruits from the cactus around his house for us to eat. It was a sweet and delicious breakfast.

As the ferry departed and the island became smaller and smaller, fading into the distance, I regretted leaving behind Lampedusa and the boys. What would happen to them now? Would they survive the inevitable hardships along the way? Would they eventually join the army of undocumented labour in Europe? Would they make it to where they want to be, start a new life, and manage to send money home to support their families?

Shortly after, I received a text from them: 'We miss you guys. We are alone without you. May Allah bless you. You came into our lives like angels. We love you very much. Our wish is to meet you again.'

2

The business of asylum reception in Sicily

Never has the blueness of the sea filled me with hope and joy as it did in Sicily. It hugged the rail line all the way to the northwest of the island, never letting go. Through the train window, humidity following the brief showers of a late summer day made the vast green fields appear misty. Following a 13-hour overnight rail trip from Rome, finally Palermo[17] came into sight. It felt good to step out of the train. It was a sunny 28 degrees centigrade.

This 2,700-year-old capital city of Sicily was, at first sight, not quite as 'rough and ready' as its reputation implied. It appeared to be dozing in a leisurely siesta, languid and exhausted. The history of Palermo being a hotbed of the Sicilian Mafia[18] lies hidden behind this calmness. Mafia activity ravaged the city between the 1950s and 1980s, bringing with it the deep-seated corruption that is still so ubiquitously present here. The Mafia's criminal activity may have lessened in recent years, but their control remains.

Throughout my time here, it appeared that the city's warm and eclectic mix of cultural influences offered a pleasant distraction for visitors, diverting attention from any nastiness, be it Mafia control or corruption, that might affect the everyday life of ordinary Sicilians. Palermo's history, its buildings and monuments, reflect the successive and mixed civilizations that have settled here since its foundation in 734 BCE by the Phoenicians. They named it Panormus, which means 'sheltered port'. Between 831 and 1072CE, the city fell under Arab rule, when it became the capital of Sicily. The Arab rulers changed the Greek name into Balarm, which is the root of Palermo's present-day name. Following the Norman reconquest, Palermo became the capital of the newly established Kingdom of Sicily between 1130 and 1816. Eventually, Sicily was united with the Kingdom of Naples to form the Kingdom of the

Two Sicilies, until the unification of Italy in 1860.

Sicilians are proud of their history, and of the ancient civilizations that have shaped its identity and destiny. Most Sicilians today are accustomed and proud to receive people from outside. Since the 1980s, Sicily has become one of the gateways into Italy, and into Europe, for many migrants who, in turn, have become part of the life of the island. Palermo is emblematic of this recent history, with a diversity of cuisines, peoples and cultures evident around every street corner.

We stayed in a cheap hotel in a dreary room. People seemed to arrive and leave all night into the early hours, and it took a while to get to sleep. I had already sent a Google-translated message in Italian to my first contact here, Alberto Biondo, to organize a meeting. Alberto was a missionary who gave up his job in 2009 to work with Borderline Sicilia, a non-profit organization founded in 2008 that monitors and reports on the situation of migrants in Sicily. Alberto said he wanted to work with migrants, as they are the people most in need in society. Since then his work had been to monitor reception centres and shelters for asylum-seekers and migrants, following all stages of the reception process in Sicily. His work covered Palermo, Trapani, Agrigento, Catania, Syracuse and Messina in particular.

Alberto contacted two friends and colleagues, Donata and Veronica, who kindly agreed to help with interpreting for me. I arranged to meet him outside the church of Santa Chiara, which was known for offering help to some of the refugees who have ended up here. This was located in the middle of Ballarò, the oldest, liveliest food market in the city, with its stands assembled daily in the neighbourhood called Albergheria. The streets of Ballarò were lined with stalls loaded with every kind of fish under the sun – my favourite being a giant swordfish dramatically displayed – fresh vegetables, fruits, sweets, colourful marzipan cakes, and all the household items anyone could ever need. Sellers were busy touting their wares. It was hard to imagine that the area around the market, now so populous, was once almost empty as most of the historical centre was left to crumble after the bombings of the Second World War and the activity of the local Mafia.

In the late 1980s, the low cost of housing in the poor area around Ballarò drew migrants who arrived from Bangladesh, followed by Africans, gradually filling up the deserted neighbourhood. Over the past decade, the local estimate was that the migrant population had grown steadily to around 30,000, making Ballarò the area with the greatest concentration of migrant communities in Palermo.

Alberto Biondo and I walked to a nearby café called Moltimotiv, which worked with asylum shelters (referred to by migrants as camps) in the area providing meals to migrants.

There, Alberto gave me an introduction to how Sicilian society sees refugees and migrants.

'Generally, people in Sicily are more welcoming than in mainland Italy. Unfortunately, recently, due to distortion and the criminalization of migrants – portraying them as potential terrorists, for instance – in the media, some of the local communities are becoming suspicious or fearful of people from outside, worrying that migrants are taking things from them.'

His friend Veronica said: 'In Palermo [unlike in mainland Italy], people are more used to migrants because they live alongside them and it's easier to share the same social space, to be in the same school or the same football team.'

Donata added: 'The difference also exists between town and country, in my opinion. In my village Castellana Sicula [which is 70 kilometres southeast of Palermo], with only 3,000 residents, the situation is different from Palermo... It's more difficult for migrants to get involved in local communities if the project [in reception centres] doesn't have an integration aspect. If the [reception] centre doesn't get migrants involved in doing things with the local communities, then the local residents are more scared... because the contact with migrants is very limited in the villages.'

However, Alberto reminded her that racist incidents occur more frequently in cities, such as Palermo. This situation was provoked by increasing – and largely negative – media reportage on the 'refugee crisis' that has been stirring up and heightening public fear. 'Migrants are portrayed as a menace to society,' he said. 'Europe's news reports about migrants and refugees have increased by 85 per cent; some years ago you read in the news that 8,000 people crossed the sea and four drowned... Now you read in the news that 8,000 people crossed the sea and ten were arrested because they were steering the boats...' This change represents the media's attempt to vilify migrants who risk their lives to cross the sea to Europe.

Alberto objected to Europe's approach to refugees and migrants. 'Europe doesn't concern itself with saving lives. The fundamental thing for Europe is that these people don't reach their continent... Therefore, for them, it's been important to sign agreements with borderline states, such as Turkey, North African countries, so in this way we don't get to know about the numbers. It's left to these countries to manage the situation, and it's their responsibility. These countries are then able to do whatever they want [with people who want to cross borders] because they don't have the human rights laws that we have.'

The first thing Alberto had to say about the asylum reception system here was that the reception centres and shelters were operated purely as businesses. 'It's built not with the intention of making the system work for migrants, but for Italians to make a living out of it,' he said.

'As a result of the commercial nature of how the reception system is operated and the level of profitability it involves, it becomes easy for the Mafia to get in and try to make a profit themselves, like everyone else. As the system has illegalized migrants and created invisible people who are caught up in the world of the informal economy, it then creates the opportunity for criminal networks to exploit that situation and thrive. The Mafia then get to profit from migrant labour by involving them in agriculture, drugs and prostitution... The worst situation is in agriculture, where migrants who live in shelters in squalid conditions are sent to work in the fields... The state is aware of this.

'And it's important not to make the direct link between Mafia and migration,' Alberto said. Contrary to media reports, the Mafia has not been a natural part of migration management; it is simply exploiting the situation.

Alberto also talked about the role of the church in the asylum reception system. 'The church is heavily involved, but it is not always playing a positive role... The churches, like the Mafia, make a lot of money from the reception business.' The state allocates €35 ($42) for each migrant per day, which is paid to the shelters and camps, some of them run by the churches. 'This money is supposed to be spent not only on food and lodging, but also to provide support, medical care, counselling, legal aid and all other services to the migrants, which the shelters and camps have not done. They simply pocket the cash from the state.' Throughout my time in Sicily, I continually witnessed the state of affairs that Alberto described.

A woman in her thirties walked past and Alberto called out her name. 'Yodit!' She is the manager of one of the SPRAR (Sistema di protezione per richiedenti asilo e rifugiati / System for Protection for Asylum-Seekers and Refugees) shelters in Palermo. SPRAR is the second level of shelter in the reception system that provides support services to facilitate integration. This level is intended to offer training and internship to migrants in order to involve them in the job market and help them prepare for an independent life. Alberto took the opportunity and introduced Yodit to me, asking if she could take me to visit the shelter. Usually it is difficult to gain access to these centres due to their political sensitivity. It requires 'connections' to get into them. Alberto himself spent a long time trying to get access in order to report their conditions to the outside world. Fortunately, thanks to Alberto's personal connection with Yodit, she agreed to help me.

However, two days later, Yodit's colleague Lucia contacted me to say that she would now be responsible for showing me around the camp, but she was not available at that moment as, in her second job, she was currently occupied with receiving hundreds of migrants who had just arrived on a rescue boat. Indeed, in just two days, more than 10,000 migrants bound for Italy had been rescued in the Mediterranean Sea in a series of more than 70 operations led by the Italian coastguard. During those 48 hours, 28 bodies had been recovered, while three babies had been born, with the assistance of Italian doctors, on a ship heading to Catania in Sicily.

Facing such tragic loss of lives day after day, week after week, hopelessness prevails. Alberto Biondo said that Europe needed to change its perspectives. 'I'm speaking as a European... If we could change the way we perceive people, if we could stop seeing these people as a source of income but instead as human beings, like you and me, who are entitled to rights, then maybe we could start changing things.

'If tomorrow my daughter or son want to go to Turkey, they can just go with a ticket. But people in Tunisia or Morocco cannot do the same. This means we have two types of citizen, and it's Western countries that get to choose who is what. Europe's choices are only based on economic concerns. Europe went out and colonized Africa and the rest of the world. Europeans went out there to take their raw materials and stole from them. Today Africans are here because Europeans were there.'

Palermo's 'African Quarter'

One day, I went to the Moltimotiv café in Ballarò and stood looking around for a seat. The waiter asked a middle-aged African man with a baseball cap to get up and move to the bench outside the door. He quickly got up and politely insisted that I should have his seat. 'Don't worry, I'm part of this,' he said, smiling.

'You're part of this?' I didn't understand.

'Yeah, I am part of the system here,' he said. It was only later I realized that he meant he used the facilities at this café regularly as a refugee.

This tall, broad-chested man introduced himself as Banta. He was from Gambia, like several friends who were with him at the café, though he looked older than them. Palermo was their first point of entry to Italy, and they had all been here for over two years. They were staying in a camp managed by Centro Astalli.

Centro Astalli Palermo is a shelter for non-EU migrants, refugees and asylum-seekers and is part of an international network, the Jesuit Refugee Service (JRS), which offers protection to people escaping from war and persecution. Centro Astalli was established in Palermo in 2003 and started out as an Italian language school. In 2006, it developed into a SPRAR shelter in the district of Ballarò, with the aim of assisting migrants to lead an independent life in the future.

Centro Astalli's shelters across Italy accommodate over 8,700 people, including families. The services they provide are intended to meet the basic needs of the residents, by supplying food, clothing, medical care, legal advice, employment training, an Italian language school and, according to the charity itself, 'listening and offering psychological assistance'. The shelter's stated aim is also to facilitate integration by 'allowing people to live the social life of the centre', running an after-school club for children and teaching computer skills.

However, in the following weeks and months it became clear that many of these stated aims have not been realized – if indeed there had ever been any intention to do so.

According to Banta and his housemates, instead their freedom was limited and the facilities were very basic. At the time of meeting them, they were all waiting for their asylum documents to be processed by the authorities – and already two years had passed. I asked Banta if we could meet again and he happily agreed.

Located next to the church of Santa Chiara was a school compound and an asylum shelter run by Centro Agape, which is associated with the charitable organization Caritas. Caritas International is a confederation of over 160 members globally; its work is to respond to humanitarian crises and offer support to the vulnerable. This particular centre was classed as an emergency camp, but when I met Salif, another Gambian, he told me he had been living in this camp for three years now, a totally unreasonable amount of time for an 'emergency' camp. Salif was now quite

Migrants at the entrance to the Caritas camp in Palermo.

dispirited about his life there, which was hardly surprising. He was 29 years old, and had been a soldier in Gambia, but when his superior was arrested he believed his life was in danger and that he had to escape as political oppression at the time was rife.

Salif was very unhappy with the living conditions at his camp. He had to share a room with two other people, and there was no personal freedom. The front gate was always locked after dark. 'I cannot even bring friends back to the place. I have to always ring the bell at the front door when I return in the evening. It's more like a prison than a shelter.'

When asked the reasons for such a long period waiting for his documents, Salif said he didn't know. 'Caritas' lawyer is no good. I'd like to find a private lawyer to work on my case,' he said. He believed there was corruption going on among those who were managing their cases. 'The longer I stay there, the longer Caritas is getting the money.

'Money comes from the government, but is not spent on us... Food and a bed is all we have. There are no other services for us,' he added. No work was available, and life had been put on hold. He simply felt isolated and hopeless.

He walked over to the Senegalese Association opposite the shelter, and watched several Senegalese men playing chess outside the Association office. He chatted with them, patting them on their shoulders, and offered to introduce me to them.

Salif told me that his parents had passed away and his sister was now his only family back home. 'My future is in Italy. But I will have no future here before receiving my documents and being granted regular status.'

Getting to know Banta

In the afternoon, I met with Banta again, back at the Moltimotiv café where we met the first time. He walked me to the camp run by Centro Astalli, situated near the church Casa Professa, where he lived at the time. On the wall opposite the gate to the camp was a peculiar painting with a half-bird, half-human figure on it. Banta didn't know its meaning, but said that sometimes people came to take pictures of it. I was not allowed into the camp building but only to the front yard, which had a table football machine in the middle. There was a tranquil yet quite mysterious atmosphere to the place. Unfortunately, Banta said that the manager was there that day and we would have to wait for a day when she was absent.

This was a SPRAR shelter that housed 25 asylum-seekers, mainly from Gambia. Banta shared a room – a tiny space of about two square metres – with one other man. There was no kitchen, just a common room where they could watch TV. It was a former military building. Banta said the manager used to be a police officer, and she never smiled. The rules were that you had to return to the building by 9pm every day, otherwise you had to sleep outside. It was a puzzling rule, since this was a second-stage shelter where migrants were supposed to be taking part in an 'integration' process where they equipped themselves with skills and experience to 'integrate' with the local community and eventually to live independently. These house rules seemed to contradict the way in which SPRAR should be operating.

Banta said he had been locked outside the building twice and had had to sleep by the door until it was opened again the next morning. The manager treated migrants like children. As in other camps, migrants were not allowed to receive visitors in their rooms and were not even permitted to hang pictures on the walls.

The first place Banta had stayed in was a camp in San Giuseppe Jato, a village some 25 kilometres south of Palermo. He had been transferred to Centro Astalli two years before. Although dissatisfied with Centro Astalli, he was not willing to ask for another transfer, in case it complicated his asylum application process. However, things seemed to be getting worse: when he had recently received the leave to remain documents that he was waiting for from the lawyer, the Centro Astalli manager had withheld them. And what was the reason given? The manager said it was because Banta was 'stubborn'. 'I think she meant that I probably wouldn't know what to do with my freedom if it was granted,' he said, shaking his head. He believed that he was being kept there, and his documents withheld, because the camp wanted to use him to squeeze more profits out of the system. This sounds like a serious allegation to make, but unfortunately Banta's situation wasn't unique. Many migrants found themselves in the same position: either their documents were being withheld, or they were kept waiting for documents for a seemingly indefinite period of time.

In the meantime, the centre arranged for several of the migrants to work outside the camp, but they received only half the wages. Where did the other half go? Apparently, the camp kept it and I later discovered that this practice was quite common among asylum camps in Palermo and in Sicily in general. Migrants were recruited to work in restaurants, clean or undertake other types of menial work in the towns or cities, and the camps or centres retained at least half the wages.

I was told that there was another SPRAR shelter just five minutes down the alleyway, within Ballarò, run by Casa San Francesco. It was a grim-looking building, of exposed grey concrete, where 25 migrants were housed, two to a room. One of the occupants claimed that some of those who were working did not receive any wages from the camp at all. The employers paid migrants' wages to the camp management, which then withheld the money entirely. Back in Moltimotiv, I met a 19-year-old boy who was living in the Casa San Francesco shelter and who confirmed that he too had been sent to work in a restaurant by the camp but only received half the wages, while the other half was kept by the camp. His housemate shared the same experience.

This situation of desperate waiting and exploitative casual employment has led some asylum-seeking minors in Palermo's camps to run away. Banta said, 'I know of these young kids, one of them as young as eight years old, he ran away from the camp and went to Germany on his own.' Such drastic action is not uncommon among children in Sicily's asylum shelters.

Banta walked me through the streets of Ballarò, past the African barbers, food stores and cafés where authentic Gambian food was served, into a tiny alley. At the top of it was his favourite place, 'Kalacutta', an African café and a hangout place for many migrants here. It was run by a Nigerian man married to a Tunisian-Italian woman. Banta commented that the man's Italian connection made it easier for them to run a business in the Mafia-controlled neighbourhood. Banta often came to this café in the evenings, when the manager would host a DJ to play his favourite African music mixed with US hip hop. Banta enjoyed Fela Kuti the most, and he didn't care whether he had company to share it with or not. He would just sit at a table with a bottle of beer, offered to him free of charge by the Nigerian manager, and tap his fingers to Fela's music. This was about the only time he really relaxed.

It was here that Banta started telling me about himself. He was born in Banjul, the capital of Gambia; he and his family later moved to Serrekunda, 13 kilometres away – the most populous city (337,000 people) in the country. He recalled his childhood as a happy one, living in an area called Dippakunda. His father worked hard selling salt and was able to buy a compound for the family, which was Christian. When Banta was young, he used to do a lot of carrying and loading to help his father. He has two sisters, one living in Sweden now whom he doesn't get on with, the other married to a Muslim. Neither of them has been in contact with him much.

Banta remembered his hometown as a lively place where the cultures of different tribes coexisted and were freely expressed in a great variety of activities. 'You don't feel lonely there,' he said. And he had fond memories of always going to the nearby beach where many of his friends worked in bars. It was a great place to grow up.

In the past decade, however, the political situation in Gambia had become increasingly unstable and unpredictable. The dictatorship made people fear for their future; work opportunities were scarce and many young people in Serrekunda chose to move to the capital; some sought employment in the seaside towns and resorts where jobs in the hospitality industry were available. In March 2014, when future prospects didn't look good under the dictatorship, Banta left home and travelled to Senegal. 'But after a week, I found that Senegal wasn't easy, so I checked out the situation in Mali, as it is supposed to be easier for foreigners to survive there. Mali turned out to be not too good, either, so I only stayed there for three days, and then moved on to Burkina. Within two days, I understood that the economy in Burkina wasn't good.'

Eventually, Banta moved on to Niger, where the near-Saharan climate was too tough for him. 'It was the first time I went there.

I found the culture – and food – so different from ours. I stayed there for the week. Then a friend said, let's go to Libya – there's work there. Let's go. I said, OK, let's go, no problem.

'So we travelled from Agadez in Niger, into the desert, and spent four long days crossing the desert, in order to reach Libya. It's a very dangerous journey because you could run into criminals anywhere along the way... We were packed into trucks like goats. They normally overload people, so it was hard to breathe... When the driver knows the way, it takes you a maximum of one week; but if the driver isn't familiar with the route, then it could take two weeks or more, which means you'll die of thirst and hunger. Each person was allowed to carry 5-20 litres of water and one kilogram of food for the entire trip... I survived the journey because I was praying all the way.'

Banta eventually reached Qatrur, a village in southern Libya, at the end of the trip across the desert. There, he waited for three days for the pickup man to fill up his vehicle with new arrivals, to be transported to Sabha, an oasis city in southwestern Libya, 640 kilometres south of Tripoli. Banta saw Sabha as the most dangerous place in Libya, where kidnapping and human trafficking is endemic. 'There's gunfire in the streets, so foreigners aren't supposed to go out... Even going out to the supermarket to buy food is risking your life,' he said. He had to spend two weeks there, waiting for the connection [transport arranged for him by the smuggler] to go to Tripoli. 'The connection I joined had a partner in Tripoli, who'd welcome me when I reached there and take everyone to the next destination, provided that you had the money to pay him.

'Libya is a country at war... There's no law. Everyone carries guns. Tripoli turned out to be similar to Sabha. You can't just go out to find work when you want. Because when you go out, they can kidnap you. A lot of kidnapping is happening all of the time. Every now and then boys in their sports cars roam the streets, looking for someone to catch and sell... They can kidnap me and sell me on to someone else, to work for free... When you're on the streets looking for a job, you have to look out for the passing cars... When you see that a car stops and the driver is a young man, don't go near when he calls you. Don't answer him. If he starts walking towards you, you have to run, or he will catch you and sell you for a few hundred dinars...'

There's no such a thing as permanent work or a full-time job in Libya. Getting work in Tripoli depended on pure luck. Having casual work on the odd day was seen as fortunate enough. 'Some honest people came to the place where we were camping and took some of us to work... Or sometimes you might get lucky and bump into an elder in a car who offers you work...' he said. 'Sometimes they pay you for your work; other times they don't, but just give you food. There's nowhere to report these things because there's no law.' Banta felt lucky enough to be able to get some stacking and loading work for a shop, for which he was paid.

'To go to Libya is easy, but to get out is the problem... In fact, throughout the whole journey, you can only keep moving on. You cannot turn back. It's a long, long way back.'

Every single day of his three long months in Libya, Banta knew that he couldn't stay and had to do something to get out. He kept his head down and tried his best to earn and save money for the sea journey to leave the country. 'In any country you can meet some good people, too. Me and a man from Mali were working for a Libyan. He told us, "It's not safe here, you can't stay here," and he got both of us onto a boat... Because we were introduced to the smuggler through this Libyan man, our boat trip only cost €800 each. If we had contacted the smuggler directly, it would have cost over €1,000.'

Before departure, Banta realized that they were boarding a small boat with 100 others. But he couldn't turn back – the smugglers had guns with them, pushing them onto the boat. Your fate is sealed from the moment you see that boat, and you have to make the trip. Here too there is no turning back – only moving on.

Banta spent four days on the boat. 'I had a small bottle of water on board, but no food, because they don't want you to carry food – it would add to the weight of the boat which is always overloaded. I didn't sleep for four days. There was no space. We were all standing. Women and children, too. When you sat down, the water would enter the boat, you see. When we were rescued, we were able to sleep on the deck.

'I thought about whether I was going to die all the time. Some people were crying. It was a small boat. After a few hours at sea, problems started – water started to come into the boat. And people started crying, men and the only two women on board. It felt like you're just a dead guy and there's only God to help you...

'The front of our boat was broken... The engine soon broke down. If you force the engine, the boat will simply go down. We were crying for help. On the fourth day, we were sure that if we didn't get rescued that night, we would die. We were bound to go down... People started praying; me too. We had no idea where we were, in the middle of the Mediterranean Sea. There's no life around. Only you, God and the water.

'Around 7pm, we saw something in the distance. When it came closer, we saw that it was a boat; we all started shouting. Luckily, a man came out onto the deck of the ship and saw us waving. He waved back at us. It was complete chance. He immediately went inside, and raised the alarm to let us know that he saw us. It was a Singaporean ship on the way to transport cars to Africa. They came alongside, and threw ropes to us...

'They rescued us and gave us dinner. They said they couldn't take us to Lampedusa, but they could take us to Sicily. We kept hearing them say the word 'Palermo'. We had no idea where that was.' Banta and the others spent another two days at sea, on the Singaporean ship, and on the third day, they reached Palermo. The sense of relief was immense. That was 9 July 2014.

'Although, some were vomiting, because of the smell of the fuel and the sea for all that time.'

Following interviews with immigration officers, Banta and his fellow migrants were separated into groups and bussed to different camps. Banta was sent to the camp in San Giuseppe Jato, where he was fingerprinted after two weeks. He lived there for two years, until he was transferred to his current location run by Centro Astalli, where he was interviewed for his asylum claim. Then, after six months' waiting, he received a six-month residency permit. When the six-month permit was up, he had to visit the police station for another interview to repeat the process. By now, he had been granted refugee status, but although his documents had been received two months before, they were still being withheld by the camp management. When I asked how long they would keep his papers, he said with a smile, 'When they're happy, they'll give them to me.'

Each month, Banta received €45 from the state. 'I spend €10 on calling my family in Gambia... My worry is my mum... She needs support, and so I send her €20 to €30 a month. The rest of it I spend on tobacco.

'I want to be free one day,' he said thoughtfully.

Banta said this with a self-deprecating smile but this was no joke – right now his life was limited to a walk to and from his camp, the Moltimotiv café where he had his meals, and Kalacutta. 'I don't usually move beyond this quarter,' he said. One reason was that he feared hostility from local people. This was due to a frightening incident he had heard about: in 2015, a young Gambian man was murdered for his 'different appearance'. And his favourite social space – Kalacutta – wasn't exempt from racism; the café had previously been in the centre of town, but it had moved to the current location in Ballarò because local youths frequently attacked it.

Banta was also very aware of suspicious looks from people. He had little interaction with the local community. 'If there's any interaction between black and white people, it usually happens at work. Socially, white people don't mix with non-whites. In the church I go to, when some white people see a black person, they tend to change seats and move away.'

In the early evening, Banta walked me out of Ballarò and into town where I met up with my partner Dave. The introduction was awkward at first as Dave was the first English person Banta had ever talked to, and Banta was certainly the first Gambian that Dave had ever met. Besides, Banta rarely left Ballarò, let alone went out to explore the town. It was still warm, and so we walked to Piazza della Indipendenza and had a cold drink and some ice cream together. Banta said he'd never done this in Italy before – in fact he had never sat down for a beer anywhere outside Ballarò. He was too aware of people staring. But he felt comfortable in our presence, and seemed relaxed in this new environment. He told me stories about his interactions with local people. An older man, a neighbour, always ignored him when he said 'good morning' every single day, for over a year. But recently, the older man had changed, and had started to return his greeting.

When we headed back to where we were staying, Banta walked with us for quite a while, and then turned right towards the shortcut that would take him back to the 'African quarter' of Ballarò.

Pact with the Mafia

Several evenings later I met up with Banta again at Kalacutta. A group of young men was gathered in a corner of the café, chatting. Banta said they were from Gambia and Nigeria and were living in one of the camps. They came here because the drinks were cheap, although most of them did not order any. 'They come to listen to Fela Kuti, just like me,' he said.

Some men – Italians of Tunisian origin – came in and were greeted warmly by everyone. A bit later, a couple of local white men came in to buy weed, though Banta said these were normal everyday dealings here and, as far as hard drugs were concerned, there was no policing around Ballarò. Ballarò is run by the local Mafia, as everyone quietly acknowledged. One of the local residents said: 'There's no policing here because the police made a pact with the Mafia some 15 to 20 years ago, and allowed them a free hand in this area as long as their expansion isn't too noticeable. So this is the Mafia's territory.' The authorities accepted this as a compromise in order to contain and control the influence of the Mafia in Palermo. Since then, the criminal network has consolidated its dominance in Ballarò. This has coincided with more migrants being drawn into the area because of the cheap rent – you can rent a studio flat for €150 per month around here – and thus their lives fall within the control of the Mafia. Migrants have therefore had to learn to co-exist with the local criminal world.

Banta said it was not safe to talk about the Mafia in public places, as it could cause suspicion if anyone overheard, so we developed a code for us to use every time the subject came up.

Banta had clearly built up a circle of his own in Ballarò, but not in the wider society. I asked if he liked life in Italy and whether he intended to stay here. 'Whether or not I have a future in this country depends on my work opportunities here,' he said. The first thing he had to do was to claim his documents from the camp and leave this state of limbo behind.

The following day, Banta said he could show me around his camp, because the manager was away. On our way there, we came across one of his friends, a young man in his twenties, who lived in the same centre. He told me that his documents had also been withheld, and he had become angry with the management. It seemed that as a result of his protest he had recently been offered some work and he believed that was an attempt to appease him. His wages, as with others, were shared half and half with the camp.

Another of Banta's housemates was an 18-year-old boy, who was also unhappy with conditions there, saying that the camp management made rules without any willingness to take migrants' feelings into account.

As Banta led me up the wide marble stairs on the other side of the front courtyard, the place felt a little cold. And the stairs went on and on. 'It goes deeper. It keeps us deep inside,' he said. It certainly felt like where we were going was further and further from public view. I followed him through an unlit corridor – it was dark during the daytime, with so little sunlight reaching inside. I could only see the words 'Centro Astalli' printed large on the bare wall at the far end. There was a simple harshness about the place and, as Banta kept reminding me, this used to be a military building. On our left was another long corridor but there we were stopped when one of the staff members approached us.

Banta asked me to wait for him in the common sitting area overlooking the front yard below. I saw him limping a little as he walked towards the staff worker and went into a room to talk with her. Five minutes later he came out again, and told me that he wasn't allowed to take me to his room. No visitors. He had told her that I was a friend, but she had said 'No' and he always followed the rules, never talking back to the staff. CCTV was installed all around the building, so it was impossible to break the rules in any case.

We sat in the common area for a while, looking out at the view outside. 'That one is my room,' Banta pointed to a window on the

*Banta in the unlit corridors
of the Centro Astalli camp.*

opposite side of the building, just across the yard. He told me he had no key to his own room and he always had to ask for it. Although he had so few belongings, there was no place where he could keep them locked safely. I gave him two small jars of mustard as a gift, but he was not sure where he could keep them. The centre did not even have a fridge that the residents could use.

Banta walked me to the 'highway', a word he used to refer to the main street that connects the edge of Ballarò with the town centre. We said goodbye for the time being.

Detour to Agrigento

Agrigento is a city on the south coast of Sicily, best known as the site of the ancient Greek city of Akragas, one of the leading cities of Magna Graecia. Besides being an ancient heritage site, Agrigento is also where one of Sicily's asylum hotspots is located. After a two-hour train journey from Palermo, the tiny town of Siculiana is another 15 kilometres from Agrigento.

The Villa Sikania camp, which was once a hotel, is situated on the side of a busy road leading to the village of Siculiana, which can be seen rising in the background. The 24-hour security was heavy. When I arrived at the gate, all I could see were police vans and police officers standing around. From outside the gates, I could see the former hotel's swimming pool in the distance, now lying empty.

At the time, the camp housed some 300 migrants, mostly from Senegal and Eritrea. They lived three to a room. Sixty minors with families were living upstairs. The majority of migrants at this camp had been there for one to three years, waiting to be transferred. Even the police officer I talked to at the gate shook his head when he told me how long the migrants were being kept there. I tried to persuade the officer to let me into the site, but as expected, there were no favours or exceptions made for anyone.

A woman was sitting near the gate. I approached her and tried to have a conversation. She was from Gambia, and had arrived the day before, transported from Lampedusa with 6,000 others, some of whom had been distributed to other towns in Sicily.

As the next group of police officers came on shift, I was asked to leave the premises altogether. As we walked along the external boundary, heading towards the village, I saw that the camp was surrounded by military vehicles, while armoured cars were arriving from a distance. Altogether it was an intimidating sight – clearly this military presence had become a dominant feature of the asylum reception system in Italy.

We climbed up to the hilly village, following the steep, twisting road, in the midday heat. Everything seemed arid and dry, except for the valleys far below the hills. The humidity and heat were overwhelming. During the afternoon siesta, nothing except a newsagent and a bakery were open. A dog barked in the distance, breaking the silence. It was almost surreal to be here, in the middle of this tiny village that had fallen asleep, high above the heavily policed, overcrowded camp where hundreds of refugees were crammed into a former hotel building.

Banta wrote to me that evening: 'I walked from the camp to the café, and then to Kalacutta, and then back to the camp. It was raining the whole day and the place is a bit cooler. Right now I'm sitting in my room, thinking about my future and when I'll be free from the camp.'

A camp in the village

On our return to Palermo Dave and I booked into an old apartment on Via Roma, just five minutes' walk from Ballarò. Around the corner from us was the Grand Hotel Et Des Palmes, where the legendary summit between the US Mafia and Sicilian Mafia took place in 1957. It was here that, allegedly, the agreement was reached by which the Sicilian Mafia took over the export of heroin to the US market.

We had a lot of catching up to do with Banta, so that afternoon we went back to the ice-cream shop on Piazza della Indipendenza. The waiter greeted Banta like an old mate – the only one of us who could speak Italian. He said that the Italian lessons given to him over the past couple of years had done him some good. As I ate my favourite pistachio ice cream, Banta told us he had finally received the documents withheld by the camp. He was now able to apply for the UN identity card which he could use for two years while he applied for a Gambian passport. As for an Italian passport, that would require quite a few more years of residence in Italy. He was pleased that he had received the documents – at least this was one step in the right direction for him.

Banta wanted to go to Germany, to find out what work was available there – maybe Berlin, or Munich, somewhere multicultural. His plan was to go with his room-mate. He had now decided not to stay in Italy, due to the lack of employment opportunities. Banta also did not have any confidence in Italian society in general, as a result of what he had seen and experienced in Palermo. He often spoke about how powerful the Mafia networks were and how they still controlled businesses there. He knew of someone who had to pay protection money in order to keep his bakery open. 'Now there's less street crime around only because the authorities have made some sort of a deal with the Mafia and that's why "guns are put away" at the moment.'

The next day we joined Banta for lunch in his regular café Moltimotiv, which had contracts with the camps in the area to provide food for the migrants. It felt a little awkward that, while I was able to order my Afghan meat and rice dish from the menu, Banta had no choice and was served the same food that he had almost

Ballaro: the 'African Quarter' of Palermo.

every day. There was no variety and Banta and his housemates were only ever served two different dishes on alternate days with no other choice. I glanced at the food on his plate across the table – some meat with sauce and a helping of rice. He said it was peanut sauce, a proper Gambian dish so at least the café was catering specifically for people from different countries. That was not the case in most of the camps.

Banta greeted everyone loudly, touching hands with them as they approached him. His housemates came and ate their lunch with us too. One of them, in his early twenties, told me that he had been working as a mechanic, a job organized by the camp. 'I haven't got paid, though,' he said dispiritedly. 'And, to be honest, I don't know if I'll ever get paid.' He had been doing the job for six long months. He took out a picture of himself in his work uniform, posing for the camera. It was clear that he was proud of his work, yet he hadn't been rewarded for his labour.

Banta's other housemate, Austin, walked past and greeted us. He and his wife had brought their baby son with them from Nigeria a year ago. Banta loved the sight of the child and always held him in his arms, cuddling him. He encouraged the little boy to drink the cola we had ordered for him and, to everyone's amusement, he gulped it down and then asked for more.

The next morning, Banta took me to his first camp in Italy, in the small village of San Giuseppe Jato, in a hilly region of Palermo's hinterland. It's surrounded by vast fields of olives, grapes and corn. The camp is a SPRAR and is owned by a member of the Mafia, which also owns several other camps in the region.

When we parked a few steps from the camp, a woman from the bakery opposite called out to Banta: 'You're here! What's brought you

Common room in the San Giuseppe Jato camp in Sicily.

back? It's been a long time!' She came over to shake Banta's hands warmly, and called her daughter to come out of the shop to greet him. Banta told me there was a story behind their friendship. When he was living in the camp here, the migrants were upset with the food provided. 'It was porridge with bits of meat, soggy and stale, and no one was able to swallow it,' Banta recalled. 'This woman who runs the bakery... She'd never seen a black person in her life. She was curious and fascinated by the sight of us... She started talking to us. She's a kind-hearted lady and she cried when she saw the food we had... Her daughter was sick when she saw it. The woman felt very angry with the way we were treated. So she started preparing food and brought it to us every day. Sometimes she even did a barbecue for us. The local people all got to know about this, and everyone wanted to help. They kept bringing us food...'

Shortly after, everyone's anger boiled over and there were protests every day. Eventually, Banta called in the *carabinieri* and reported the problem of poor food. He also showed them pictures of the food that he'd taken as evidence. The problem was so grave that the authorities had to act: the *carabinieri* ordered the camp management to improve the migrants' diet, obliging them to take action. Since then, the food has been prepared by chefs at the San Giorgio camp in a village called Piana degli Albanesi and is transported to San Giuseppe Jato. Banta smiled when he recounted the experience of resisting this maltreatment. It is a bitter-sweet tale of solidarity: solidarity among migrants, and solidarity between them and the local residents.

The locals had also protested on behalf of the migrants against the camp rules which decreed that they had to return to the site before 10pm. 'They're not prisoners and should be respected,' local protesters said at the time. As a result, the management had to change the rules and since then the migrants have been able to leave and return to the camp freely at any time.

This camp housed 60 migrants, mostly from Gambia. Banta's arrival was greeted warmly by his former housemates, who had been there much longer than him. Banta said they were like family to him and the day he was sent away to Palermo because the camp was becoming overcrowded, he had cried as he said goodbye to them.

Banta had not been back to San Giuseppe Jato since then: he couldn't afford the transport. But he didn't need to inform people here about his visit in advance – this was family so you could turn up at their door any time. He just walked in and along the corridor, going into each room and sitting chatting on his friends' beds like he had never been away. They sat around him, asking questions – there was just so much to say.

The camp was overcrowded, with four or six people to a room, sometimes even eight, and the largest room, around six square metres, had nine. People sat talking on their bunk beds as no other sitting area was available.

In the common room at the front of the building, several Gambian and Ghanaian migrants were playing table football. A man from Morocco was sitting alongside on his own, smoking. He told me he was from Casablanca, and left home 'to avoid prison', but he couldn't explain further in English. All he could tell me was that he left his family behind and fled to Libya, where he got on a boat to Italy.

The Moroccan man got up from his seat, offered it to me and went out to get coffee for Banta and me. It was the habit of hospitality that he had brought from home.

On the walls of the common room were phrases written by the migrants themselves, such as 'Diversity of cultures is something to be valued, not feared'. National flags and maps of African countries were painted in all colours on the other side – Senegal, Mali, Gambia, and others.

This was where their first interviews took place, where they were asked about their reasons for coming to Italy. They were sent to Palermo for the day, for the second interview, where they were questioned along the same lines in various ways, to examine and assess their asylum claim.

They were all waiting for their documents, which everyone believed were being delayed by the camp so they could profit from the state funding allocated for each migrant per day.

In the morning, migrants from the San Giuseppe Jato camp were often picked up by farm employers to go to work in the Corleone area – picking vegetables, grapes and apples on land owned by the

Mafia. For this they were getting paid an average of €35 for a full working day. Although this was not officially organized by the management, farm employers always knew how to find migrants to work for them and their low-paid, and exploitative, employment was common knowledge.

A second-level camp in Palermo

Lucia, from the shelter on Via la Loggia, eventually responded to my request and said she would meet me in the café on Piazza della Indipendenza for a chat. Unexpectedly, she turned up with Yodit, the camp manager I had tried to meet before, and asked me to get in their car. Life is full of surprises when you don't speak the language.

We headed off into the outskirts of Palermo, a ten-minute drive to the shelter which was located on an estate in the middle of a row of run-down apartment blocks. Lucia told me the shelter was a former mental hospital, and pointed to the graffiti all around the walls. The building was in a pretty derelict state, with paint peeling off the walls and gaps where the plaster had fallen off – walking through the grim, unlit corridors gave me the creeps. You could easily have thought this was an empty, disused building with no one in it. Somehow nothing had been done to make it look more acceptable and pleasant as an asylum shelter.

This shelter was a SPRAR, the second-level camp, and started operating in July 2014. (SPRAR accommodation can be a shelter that houses 30 people, or a self-catering apartment, or something in between.) There were only eight people here: seven young African boys and one middle-aged Syrian man. Most of them had been transferred from minors' camps and they were all waiting for their documents. Lucia introduced me to the Syrian, who was called Joseph. In his forties, he was quite humorous about his origin and said, 'Many people are surprised to find a Syrian here, so they take pictures of me.' Indeed, I was told he was one of only four Syrian refugees in Palermo.

Italy was a transit point for Joseph when he first arrived by sea a year ago. He attempted to reach Germany via Holland, but was detained for six months there and then sent back to Italy, where he had given his fingerprints when he first arrived in Europe.

Joseph had now come to accept the reality that he would not reach Germany. He accepted that he would settle in Italy and expected that his wife and six children would be able to join him here in a year's time – it was a long time to wait, but he recognized that his situation could be a lot worse.

Joseph's long-term wish was to set up his own business making bespoke furniture, which was his trade back in Syria. He would like to do that in Palermo but said he could not even think about his career options until he was reunited with his family. In the meantime, he was trying to prepare for the future, by learning Italian, for example – and getting used to Italian cuisine.

This shelter was run by a co-operative named CRESM (Centro de Ricerche Economiche e Sociali per il Meridione) and was a non-profit organization that worked with socially disadvantaged groups and communities. Apart from this centre, CRESM also ran a shelter for asylum-seeking women and girls which was a self-catering apartment.

Lucia had been working there since the place had first opened. The other half of her time, around 15 hours per week, was taken up working in a medical centre for undocumented migrants. Her interest in working with migrants started when she was at university, studying languages in Milan, part of which was a course in 'cultural mediation', which had concerned the relations between migrants and local people. It was encouraging to find a qualified professional in the reception system who had a firm knowledge and interest in issues concerning the welfare of migrants. She was only 27 years old, but was one of the most amiable staff I had met in the shelters. She enjoyed working with the six other staff members, proudly calling it a 'multicultural workforce'. She cheerfully showed me around the place, leading me into the shared kitchen and telling me that migrants could cook for themselves as well as do their own laundry. We visited the room where various workshops were held and shared with people from other camps in Palermo.

Lucia said there were seven other second-level camps in Palermo, all of which had started operating around the same time as this one, although they varied in capacity and facilities. One of them had 'special category' status: it had only four people and catered particularly for migrants with mental-health issues. Another had nine people; two other camps had 30 each. They were run either by co-operatives or charity organizations.

As a SPRAR, their job was, ideally, to prepare migrants for the labour market, for a self-sufficient life, and to become part of society. Activities in the form of workshops took place regularly, such as one with European visitors to discuss 'prejudice', while another had been held in co-operation with a local artists' association on 'street art'. The migrants also took part in theatre workshops with the schools they were attending and they were encouraged to choose the topics they wanted to discuss and study.

In addition, training programmes were provided; for example, teaching restaurant and catering work. At the end of their training, the participants were assessed, following which they would be awarded a certificate. Although they were not permitted to work before they received their immigration documents, sometimes employers would make contact with them and try to get them to work, but they were asked to report these cases to the shelter staff. The migrants here, Lucia said, needed to seek advice in such situations. Advice and information about future employment was also given to migrants, including those who preferred to leave Sicily and go to bigger cities. 'Many of them want to go to Milan after this,' said Lucia, 'because they see Milan as a city connected with the world and so offering greater work opportunities.'

Joseph came back into the room with two cups of mint tea, for Lucia and me. He seemed to feel at ease with the staff here. He sat down with us, exchanging pleasantries, and I had a feeling that he probably found the other residents a little too young for him to socialize with, as he was old enough to be their father. In the daytime, apart from learning the language, Joseph often went out cycling around the city. Meanwhile, the young boys from Gambia kept themselves to themselves, watching TV in the common room, which seemed to be their main leisure activity. Despite the run-down external appearance, the place was more spacious than elsewhere, each bedroom being shared by two people.

That evening, Dave and I met with Banta and walked around the local Sicilian street festival called 'Ballarò Buskers', a music, dance and art festival that takes place every year in the district. However, when we sat among local youth watching a performance in front of the church of Santa Chiara, I noticed that Banta did not feel part of the Sicilian culture at all. He felt more like an observer than a participant, and did not seem to relate to the festival activities – he remained an outsider. 'They don't include people,' he commented. We sat around the church square for a while, and then he suggested we took a walk and headed back to Kalacutta. That was where he could really relax.

The next day, as usual, we met with Banta at Moltimotiv. After his lunch, we suggested that we visit the cathedral together as it was a sunny day. He had never been there since coming to Palermo and, seeing that he enjoyed visiting the interior, we spent a long time walking around. We then climbed up to the roof of the cathedral, to get a view of the city. 'That's Ballarò,' he said, pointing out a mass of terracotta rooftops in the distance.

Following that, we walked towards Porta Nuova (New Gate), in the direction of the café on Piazza della Indipendenza, for some more delicious ice cream. Just outside the *carabinieri* headquarters in front of Porta Nuova stood the monument to General Carlo Alberto Dalla Chiesa. He became the prefect of Palermo in 1982, tasked with the mission to end the violence of the second Mafia war (1981-83) which led to over 1,000 homicides. He did not last long in the job. Only three months after his appointment, he was killed in a machine-gun ambush in Palermo, along with his wife and driver, on the orders of Mafia boss Salvatore Riina.

At the café, Banta returned to his favourite topic of conversation: the criminal networks in Sicily. He talked about Giovanni Falcone (1939-92), an Italian judge and prosecuting magistrate who spent most of his professional life trying to overthrow the power of the Mafia. He was eventually killed by the Corleonesi Mafia in May 1992, near Capaci, on the motorway from Palermo airport. Following his death, his best friend Paolo Borsellino took over Falcone's job, only to be murdered himself a few months later. The murders of these two men led to a huge public outcry and to mass protests previously unseen in Palermo, which finally pressurized the authorities to act against the Mafia. Violent street crimes by the Mafia are no longer common; however, traces of their ruthlessness could sometimes be seen unexpectedly on street corners, where graffiti threatening individuals were painted on walls, reminding people of the horror of those brutal Mafia murders.

A local source, who did not want to be named, told me that the owner of the camp in San Giuseppe Jato (where Banta lived) is a Mafia boss by the name of Giovanni Bovi. Bovi owns five camps, including the San Giorgio camp in Piana degli Albanesi. 'I know his brother,' Banta whispered. When he was living in San Giuseppe Jato, his camp manager used to send him to help with interpreting in the San Giorgio camp, where he got to know the family.

Corleone

When I met Banta the next afternoon, he was furious. 'No water,' he said. Everyone at the Centro Astalli camp was supposed to receive one litre of water per day, usually supplied by the café Moltimotiv. But there was none and Banta's housemate became angry with the café manager, who referred him back to the camp.

The next morning, we had thunder and rain and it felt like autumn was coming. It was the last day of the Sicilian street festival, so we met with Banta in Ballarò, grabbed a beer and listened to some live Ivory Coast drumming.

Then, at the end of the evening, we heard the news about more deaths. A Norwegian boat, the Siem Pilot, rescued 2,400 migrants off the coast of Libya; 17 bodies were discovered, including that of an eight-year-old. The officers were in the process of transferring 1,000 migrants from a boat to the Siem Pilot when rubber dinghies suddenly appeared with migrants who desperately tried to reach the rescue ship; dozens of people jumped into the water to swim towards the ship, forcing the captain to pull back to deter others from doing the same. Safety boats from the Siem Pilot later pulled them out of the sea, while a Médecins Sans Frontières (MSF) vessel picked up the bodies. Tragedies like this were routine occurrences in the Mediterranean.

We all got up early the next morning, heading to Corleone, a small village with a population of 12,000 in the province of Palermo.

Many migrants worked in the surrounding farms and I wanted to talk to some of them who lived in the area. It was a 45-minute drive through vast tracts of farmland along the way. Banta wanted to join us; he seemed intrigued by the idea of Corleone, the place where several Mafia bosses have come from and which gave the characters in *The Godfather* their name. In Corleone, 153 people were murdered by the Mafia in four years between 1944 and 1948, the highest murder rate in the world. The local Mafia clan, known as the Corleonesi and the most violent, instigated the second Mafia war in Sicily, and led the organization in the 1980s and 1990s.

The town appeared quiet when we arrived and the locals all seemed approachable – a town seemingly going about its daily business. However, the Mafia world is never too far beneath the surface of everyday life. In summer 2016, following an investigation by Italy's Ministry of the Interior, Corleone's town council was dissolved by order of the national government in Rome because it had been infiltrated by individuals with Mafia connections and public contracts had been awarded to Mafia businesses. This means that, to this day, the Cosa Nostra still has a considerable grip on what goes on in local politics.

While walking around Corleone, I received a call from Saeed and Jahid, the Bangladeshi boys we had met in Lampedusa. They told me that the three of them had been transported from Lampedusa to the camp in Siculiana, in southern Sicily. They sounded desperately upset. 'Please help us,' Jahid said. 'We want to leave the camp!' This plea for help was very sudden and I could not understand what had happened to them.

'It's so horrible here. We want to run away from the camp and come to Palermo,' he explained.

'But what are you going to do after you get to Palermo?' I asked.

'We will go to Milan, and then to France,' Jahid answered.

'But you've been fingerprinted... You might get sent back to Italy.'

'We'd like to try... try to claim asylum in France,' said Jahid, at the same time discussing with Saeed in the background.

I did not feel in a position to advise them either way, not knowing the whole situation, although I really wanted to help them. I felt the best thing to do was to ask them to consider everything before coming to a decision. After all, any decision they made at this point could determine the direction of their young lives.

'Are you sure you don't want to wait to be transferred to Palermo?' I asked.

'It may take three to four days... We've asked the camp,' said Jahid, anxiously. 'We can't wait. The situation here is so bad. It's so overcrowded, dirty, and the food was the most horrible ever. Everything's even worse than in Lampedusa.'

I tried to reassure them and asked them to think it over. Jahid said they would call me that night to tell me their decision. Most under-age migrants run away from their shelters for three main reasons: the conditions are poor inside the shelters; the waiting time for documents to be processed is unreasonably long; and they are not given sufficient information about what will happen to them and how long they will have to wait. I had a feeling that the three boys would run away from Siculiana and it was a thought that worried me for the rest of the day.

As we walked towards the edge of Corleone, several young Africans walked past us carrying plastic bags, as if returning from shopping in town. I decided to walk along with one of them, as I guessed he must have been returning to an asylum shelter. He stopped to answer me, telling me he was indeed living in a camp, at the top of the hill. It was a former hotel named Hotel Belvedere (meaning 'beautiful view'). The front of the three-storey building had balconies with clothes hanging over them to dry. Several migrants were standing around talking outside the entrance.

Chatting with them, I found out that this camp had 63 migrants from Gambia, Nigeria and other countries. An 18-year-old Nigerian boy who looked tired and depressed got talking to me. 'I haven't had enough water to drink,' he told me. 'They don't give us enough water.' I was puzzled – how was it possible they had no water to drink? Hoping to find out more, I followed him into the building and he led me into the common room, where his housemates were sitting. When I explained my reason for being there, they were all eager to express their frustration and anger with the conditions in the camp.

The lack of a basic water supply was the number-one problem here, they said. 'The water is only switched on twice per day, only 30 minutes each time,' one of them explained. He introduced himself as Amat, from Gambia. 'There's no hot water, so we have to boil water.' Later he showed me the gas cooker they used – outside.

'We are only given one litre of drinking water every two days. It's not enough, so we all have to go out to buy water ourselves, using the little money we save up. And we have to save our drinking water all the time.'

Even so, Amat had fetched a glass of drinking water for me. It was from the bottle of water he had saved for days.

Amat and others showed me their rooms. Without water most of the time, they couldn't even flush the toilets. I tried to use the tap in the washroom and not a single drop of water came out. How did the camp management expect people to live like this?

Three to four people shared a room there, and the camp management still wanted to put in more people. 'We're not animals, we cannot live like animals. We told them so,' said Amat. Clearly, the issue at stake for those who ran the camp was how much profit could be made from each arriving migrant.

The migrants here had all worked on the farms nearby, picking tomatoes and fruit during the season. Farm employers would come to pick them up from the camp in the morning and they would earn up to €20 ($23) per day for a full day's work. One young Gambian told me that he earned €2 per hour harvesting tomatoes. He pointed to the farms a few kilometres in the distance, 'over there,' he said.

'Corleone people are very bad,' one of them said to me. Of course, as the employers and camp managers are the only people they're in contact with in Corleone, that was bound to be their perception of local people.

Those who oppose migration have always argued from an economic viewpoint that 'migrants are bad for the country's economy' and 'migrants are a drain on resources'. I do not believe in arguing for migrants' rights on the basis of their 'economic worth', as if those with lower economic productivity do not deserve the right to move across borders.

However, as the economic argument is prevalent in society, this falsehood must be corrected with some facts that show migrants are neither a drain on nor negative for the economy. Indeed, the opposite is true. Nearly 80 per cent of the migrants arriving in Italy from around the world are of working age. All over Sicily and the entire country, migrants, many of whom are kept in limbo, denied their official status, have joined the army of labour that the industries of an ageing Italy thrive on. The total contribution of migrant workers to Italy's GDP in 2015 was 8.8 per cent ($139 billion), according to a report titled *The Economic Impact of Immigration* by the Leone Moressa Foundation. Their contribution to the economy, however, depends on them remaining in a subordinate economic position at the very bottom of the wage ladder and without any labour protection. Their 'economic worth', therefore, comes from their invisible (and in many cases, state-less) existence.

At the Hotel Belvedere camp, each migrant received €75 ($87) per month from the government, most of which they spent on buying water and food. As regards the food provided, everyone was outraged: the quality was so poor that most migrants simply threw their meals away. Amat and others led me to the back of the Belvedere where the hotel swimming pool lay empty. Piles of packed meals that had been discarded were stacked next to it: inside the plastic wraps were some dried potatoes, threads of carrots, and a stale piece of chicken. 'We just can't eat these,' one said.

On the other side of the pool was a gas stove which they used to cook their own food. They would walk all the way down the hill to buy the low-cost ingredients in town, and cook here at the stove together. Usually it was rice with a homemade stew – simple but tasty. The management was fully aware that the migrants were cooking their own food, yet nothing had been done to improve the diet provided by the camp.

The lack of water, poor food provisions, and the increasingly overcrowded conditions meant that this shelter was entirely unfit for purpose. Amat told me that many migrants housed here had chosen to run away because of the conditions. They had subsequently become homeless as they had no means to support themselves. It is well known that the EU-imposed hotspot system has created conditions that have driven many migrants into

Inside the camp in Corleone...

...and a sample of the food given to the camp's inmates.

homelessness and destitution. But it is less known that migrants continue to suffer appalling conditions at all levels of the asylum reception system, as in this camp in Corleone, and many have become homeless as a result. In Palermo itself, for instance, the situation had become so severe that charities for homeless people had now extended their services to homeless migrants. Hope and Charity is one such group. Their three centres near the railway station had reached their capacity of 1,000 people.

Those who choose to remain in camps have had to develop their own way of dealing with the conditions. For instance, could they report the situation to the *carabinieri* who, in some cases, have put pressure on the camps to improve the situation? But Amat said that was impossible in Corleone. 'The camp is owned by the Mafia, who work with the police,' he said. 'The police here will not listen to us.' The entire system was milking the migrants.

That afternoon, we went to Piana degli Albanesi, a village which had given shelter to a large group of Albanian refugees in the late 15th century. Banta wanted to show me the San Giorgio camp where he used to be sent to help with interpreting. It was a pleasant drive through the green valleys and fields, stunning as they embraced lakes in bright sunlight. It was a sharp contrast to all the misery that I had witnessed. How much more misery was hidden in this land of beauty?

The San Giorgio camp was also located on the outskirts of the village, up a hill, and away from public view. It was yet another dingy former hotel, this time like a 1970s angular, concrete public building. The common room looked like an old hospital waiting room, with nothing but plastic chairs and noticeboards on the bare white walls. Two boys from Gambia came up to greet us and talk to Banta. They had turned 18 seven months ago, and were then transferred here from the camp for minors. However, their asylum documents had been withheld and no reason given, although it seems obvious as – Mafia-owned or not – the practice is so common among the camps in Sicily. The two boys told Banta how unhappy they were, but there was nothing they could do.

When we returned to Palermo in the evening, I talked to Jahid on the phone, to find out what they had decided. They said they had thought about it and decided to run away from the Siculiana camp before daybreak and take the bus to Palermo at 7am. They wouldn't listen to my concerns. 'We're so happy that we will see you tomorrow,' Saeed said innocently. But I was desperately worried for the entire evening. Where would they go from here? Could their decision be the beginning of their lives as the *clandestini* of Europe?

Meanwhile in Calais…

On the morning of 24 October 2016, the evacuation of the Calais camp began. Most of the migrants there were being sent to 451 reception centres across France. Three in five of these centres were located in towns with populations larger than 30,000. Bed space was in extremely short supply. The number of beds available in France totalled 7,585.[19] Sixty per cent of France's reception centres had space for fewer than 20 migrants. In Calais, hundreds of migrants were choosing to stay in the area. Many minors were waiting to be relocated, but in the days following the evacuation, some of them were still sleeping rough around the camp site. Volunteers from the charity Help Refugees were giving out food and blankets to the stranded children.

Asif, Jahid and Saeed bid to escape

Saeed, Jahid and Asif, along with one other young boy, another villager from Bangladesh, left the Siculiana camp in the early hours of the morning and walked for seven hours to reach the nearest bus station, finally arriving in Palermo at lunchtime. It was moving to see them again. They looked so much more tanned – and more tired – than when I had last seen them in Lampedusa. The fellow villager who ran away with them had an uncle in Palermo, who made a living selling mobile-phone SIM cards on the streets. He kindly brought the boys a Bangladeshi lunch, wrapped in plastic. Jahid couldn't wait to eat this home food, which he had not enjoyed for three long months, and finished his lunch within minutes. 'I'm fine now,' he said.

The villager's uncle also organized bus tickets to Milan for the boys, paid for by Jahid's uncle in Paris. It was to involve a 19-hour bus trip. They had only just got off one bus, and now had to board another one. But I saw only determination in their eyes. All they wanted to do now was to get out of Sicily and head north, to Paris, where they had no idea what might be awaiting them – but they didn't want to think about that yet. They would deal with it when they got there.

Saeed told me that he had a younger brother (not a blood-related brother but a close family friend he referred to as brother) who was staying in a minors' shelter in Agrigento. He said his sister in England was so concerned that she wanted to ask me to help him. He called her and then passed the phone to me. She said anxiously, 'Please help Saeed's brother, he will give you the address.' Saeed explained that his sister wanted me to get his younger brother out of the minors' shelter and take him to Palermo. I had to explain to him that I couldn't do that because he was a minor and it was best for him to wait for the transfer to a minors' shelter in Palermo. Saeed took the advice, and I found out a few weeks later that his younger brother did get transferred to Palermo, although he ran away from the shelter soon after and got on a bus to Milan, hoping to join Saeed in Paris.

Asif also had an uncle in Palermo, and he came to pick him up from the bus station. Not long after, Asif's uncle put him on a bus for Milan, too, to join the others in Paris.

Jahid and Saeed were getting the bus in an hour's time, so we only had time for a cold drink together. They told me all about their past few days: 'After all that waiting, we were only given one hour to get ready for the ferry that took us from Lampedusa to a Sicilian port [Porto Empedocle],' said Jahid. 'On the ferry, we spent ten hours sitting on the chair with nothing to eat but two eggs and potatoes.

'Things were really bad at the Siculiana camp. There was no shower and not even doors to the washrooms. They crammed us in the camp like animals. It was so bad in there that we had to run away.' Jahid said now he felt free, and at last he felt like he was in Europe.

He said they would be staying in Milan with his relative for just one night. He couldn't stay longer because the host was not a close relative. 'I'll be all right to stay with the uncle in Paris because we're blood-related.'

Many young migrants, including those under age, are able to move from place to place and reach their destination via family and social networks, which are strong enough to cut through and overcome the barriers of borders. When the boys left, I had no idea how things would turn out when they got to Paris, whether they would be granted asylum or would simply go underground. But as they left, they reassured me that they would be all right during the journey to Paris. We hugged each other farewell. 'We will meet again, in France. *Inshallah*,' said Jahid.

Racism's tentacles

One afternoon when I walked past the Senegalese Association in Ballarò, I stopped to watch a group of people playing chess outside the entrance. There I got talking to a social worker by the name of Lamine, who came from Senegal and had settled in Palermo some 17 years ago.

He told me about his career and experience working with migrants. He had been a civil servant in Senegal and arrived in Palermo in 1999 to join his cousin. Since then he had settled here and made it home, marrying an Italian woman. They now had two boys. 'Palermo is where I'd like to bring up my son until he's 18,' he said. 'That is my responsibility as a father.

'Then I'll be free to go where I want... Maybe the United States, England, or anywhere else... The world is my home. At the moment, maybe this is better than Senegal. I feel this is home and I'm happy here.'

Lamine had found himself living in a multicultural community in Palermo. The largest African immigrant communities in Palermo were Mauritian, Ghanaian and Nigerian. In the past two to three years the fastest-growing migrant groups had been from Ghana, Nigeria and Gambia. The Eritrean community was also growing and was now bigger than the Senegalese, he said, although ten years ago, there were only ten or so Eritreans in Palermo.

Lamine said: 'The Senegalese communities are becoming more established now. They are more self-sufficient and are able to rely more on the older community of Senegalese immigrants – around 200 of them, mostly traders – as their social networks from which they get help and advice. You can get food and be hosted, free of charge, for six to seven months [when you first arrive]... Their hospitality is in their culture... They don't tend to look to churches or any other organizations outside their own community.'

Lamine had worked continuously with migrant communities for 16 years. He started his career interpreting for African and Asian adult migrants. 'There was great diversity, with people from all cultural backgrounds... It was very emotional and challenging work,' he said. He was part of Sicily's first project to provide training for professionals working with migrant minors, begun in 2007 – the concept of providing care for migrant minors was unprecedented in Sicily at the time.

Lamine talked specifically about the endemic problems of the asylum reception system in Sicily. In his entire career working with both adult and minor asylum-seekers, he said he had never come across 'a good centre, shelter, or camp, one that could be described as well managed.' He did not hesitate to name the worst ones: 'The worst camp for adults is Partinico, in Palermo, run by the co-operative Sol.Co; they have more than 100 migrants there. No facilities, poor diet. The worst camps for minors that I've seen are San Giorgio [in Piana degli Albanesi], San Francesco, and Bocca di Falco in Palermo.

'All the camps have problems of delaying asylum procedures. This is due to bureaucracy, corruption and profit-making,' he said. He went straight to the heart of the matter: the fundamental problem was that the state played no role in regulating the shelters and camps.

The state allocates €45 ($53) per day for a child and €35 per day for an adult to the shelters, which can allocate and use this money in whatever way they like. There are no rules to be followed. In almost all the shelters the staff are not trained and are not required to receive training. Migrants, including minors, do not receive any advice, help or counselling because the shelters prefer not to spend the funds on such services.

Lamine talked about the issue of integration and pointed to 'a society where compassion for other human beings is a rarity.' He believed that the problem of integration lay with the receiving country and its structures. When he went to speak about migration in schools, he said, he found pupils were unconcerned about migrants' tragedies. 'Some students were looking at their mobile phones and were unaffected.

'The system has not equipped migrants with what is needed to live independently and become part of society, even when they receive their documents.' With his long experience, Lamine identified racism as a huge obstacle whereby migrants are seen as a problem. 'Integration' is simply a nicer word for assimilation when the context is racism. Racism also means that people of African origin are ruled out as possible providers of services and care – they are ignored as a part of providing 'solutions'. Thus, when staff are employed within the asylum reception system, racial discrimination is commonplace. Even when they are well qualified, people of African origin are not usually employed by the camps. 'It's because people of African origin are seen as inferior and only able to take on menial jobs. So they'd rather give those jobs to white people who aren't capable of working in these camps,' he said.

Lamine paused, sighed and said that one way to detect how penetrative racism could be, is when the police talk to a non-white person using the informal 'you' ('tu' as opposed to 'Lei' in Italian). He himself had experienced this and challenged the police officer about the way he was talked to.

Word had spread that I was talking with Lamine, and this had annoyed Banta. He said there were conflicts between Senegal and Gambia and people from these two countries tended not to get along, even in Italy. He described a competitive relationship between the two communities, although I have seen Gambian and Senegalese migrants communicating and making friendships. Perhaps it is more accurate to say that some members of those communities felt competitive towards each other – perhaps as a result of the pressure to do well in the 'host country'.

Banta seemed to feel insecure a lot of the time. Given the amount of time he'd spent in the camps, he had struggled to maintain his sense of purpose. He didn't seem able to trust people easily and this distrust of others was most likely a result of his traumatic experiences on the journey to Europe – as well as what happened afterwards. He had been able to trust very few people on his journey, which was a tale of endless betrayals, the last one almost costing him his life at sea. Sadly, what happened to him after setting foot in Europe had not allowed him to put the trauma behind him.

On Via Roma one evening, a middle-aged man stopped to talk to me. He seemed to know me, and kept saying, '*La casa, la casa!*', as if to remind me of something. It took me a few moments to realize it was Joseph, the Syrian man at the shelter on Via la Loggia that I had visited a short while ago. I had not recognized him because I couldn't distinguish him from the local people, and he could have been taken for an Italian man. He was wandering around town at dusk, on his own, without a purpose. With no more than a few words in Italian, he could not really strike up a conversation with locals, either. Watching him slowly disappear into the crowd, I could only imagine his isolation and loneliness: what it must be like to have to accept what is given, instead of choosing where you want to be; what it must be like to have to make do. I only hope that he did not have to wait longer than a year to be reunited with his family.

That evening, Banta told me some terrible news: several of his neighbours from Gambia were feared to have drowned in the Mediterranean on their way to Italy. Four of them were confirmed dead. He showed me their pictures: an 18-year-old girl, and three men, one of whom had left three children behind. That Friday, a Save the Children rescue boat docked in Catania, bringing in 20 bodies, including those of his neighbours, and 290 survivors.

Meanwhile in Britain...

On 25 October 2016, the Calais police commissioner said that a total of over 4,000 migrants had been transported out of the Calais camp in the previous two days. The camp would be fully demolished by Friday, he said, and only about 200 migrants were expected to stay in the area. A total of 372 unaccompanied minors were taken to temporary reception centres set up within the Calais camp.

Around 200 minors from the camp had been brought to Britain by this point, some under the Dubs Amendment (to Section 67 of the Immigration Act 2016). Alfred Dubs, a member of the House of Lords (and once a child refugee brought to Britain from Czechoslovakia on one of the Kindertransport trains in 1939), had pushed for the draft law to be amended and it became law in May 2016. This enabled a 'specific number' of vulnerable children to be considered for refuge in Britain. However, because of the unspecific content of the amendment, the government could decide on the actual number of child refugees after consulting with local authorities, which, mostly as a result of limited budgets, were not always willing to take in child refugees. As the Help Refugees charity said: 'There is a real risk that with limited funding available, very few councils will step up to welcome these children[20] and that the process will move so slowly that many desperate children who stand to benefit will end up in the trafficking networks of Europe instead. If each constituency offers refuge to just five unaccompanied minors, then 3,000 children will be brought to Britain.'[21]

Elane Heffernan, a London-based activist and professional who has worked with asylum-seekers for nearly two decades, said that a complex and toxic mix of reasons makes local authorities reluctant to take in asylum-seeking children. 'Grant funding from central government only meets about 50 per cent of the cost of actually fostering asylum-seeking children – they get £95 [$125] a day for those under 16 and about £70 for over 16s, but the cost is more than this in many areas, especially where 16- and 17-year-olds are in foster care and even more when care leavers are aided to exercise their right – if in education – to stay in foster care beyond their 18th birthday. There is no funding at all for a proportion of care leavers in every local authority who arrived as unaccompanied minors... The leaving-care system has been especially difficult as most asylum-seeking young people leaving care are in education... and this requires additional funding... It might require remaining in foster care rather than hostels.'

However, not everything is down to costs. Elane also pointed out racism as one of the main reasons behind the reluctance. 'Newham, for example, seeks to avoid taking [asylum-seeking] children not just because of cost but because of hostility towards newly arrived migrants, as do many other areas... The belief that it's immigrants that put a burden on public services is very pervasive. Also, lots of local authorities believe that their population is more hostile to asylum-seekers than they are, and don't want to risk what they believe will be a backlash.'

The children's shelter

'In Sicily we have a constant feeling of total despair in relation to the practices of institutional actors, those who are meant to protect people, particularly minors, in line with national and international regulations,' wrote Alberto Biondo of Borderline Sicilia.

'Not a single day passes in which we don't receive a dozen calls for help by teenagers who have found themselves abandoned and frequently treated badly, above all on a psychological level. Thanks to the conditions into which these minors – victims of a total indifference – have been "welcomed", they end up considering themselves unworthy of help or attention, living out a kind of degradation and undervaluing which quite easily accompanies them all the way into the hands of further exploiters.'

He continued: 'The intolerable Italian system of reception continues to be affected by the chronic lack of legal guardians, as well as of cultural-linguistic mediators who might offer psychological support which could alleviate the minors' suffering during the interminable waiting period for obtaining the leave to remain set by the bureaucratic process, and above all the lack of activities organized within supporting projects and courses which might make their presence more acceptable within these complexes (whether of first or second level, both housing communities and SPRAR centres) for month after month. All too frequently we have heard about the "hell" without end when told about the long stays within the various centres.'

I wanted to visit some of the minors' shelters in Palermo and asked Alberto Biondo for advice about how I could get access. He suggested that I visit the city's department of social policy on Via Garibaldi and talk to the secretary to ask for a permit. 'I'm sorry that there are no legal alternatives,' he said. With this information, I headed for the address, only to arrive at a firmly locked door. It said 'Department of Social Policy' on the door, but no one answered. It was obviously closed – at 4.30pm and I then discovered that it only opened on certain days, including Mondays from 9.30am-12.30pm. How does an important department like this function only part-time? I decided to give the authorities a miss.

That day, Dave and I went to have lunch with Banta at Moltimotiv café. He had his meal of meat and rice with peanut sauce, while I enjoyed a plate of Sicilian pasta. Malian migrants were sitting at another table, separate from the Gambians.

One of Banta's housemates, the 18-year-old boy called Jabril, also from Gambia, was sitting near us and said he would take me to see a minors' shelter called the Centro di Mondo. Jabril's friend, whom he knew from school in Palermo, was living there. Jabril therefore led the way out of Ballarò, followed by Banta and me. We walked up to Via Roma, where the shelter was located in a shabby-looking block of flats with a 1920s-style cage lift. We climbed the stairs slowly to a residential front door. A middle-aged man, the staff worker, opened the door and let us in.

Nine under-age migrants were living there when I visited. Jabril's friend was a very shy 17-year-old from Gambia, and was pleased to see us – he rarely had visitors. He welcomed us into the six-square-metre sitting area, where the others were quietly watching TV. The interior arrangement was simple and modest; the furniture needed replacing. Three people shared a room of about five to six square metres, which was tiny for that many. The teenagers didn't seem to have much to do all day, except when they went to school to learn Italian. This seemed a very confined space for young people. The staff worker was friendly and talked about London to me: 'A friend of mine told me that people are cold in England.' That made everyone laugh.

Jabril then took Banta and me to the bus that headed towards northern Palermo. It was a part of town that I'd never seen. There were no landmarks in this ordinary residential landscape and there was quite a distance to walk through the streets after we got off the bus. This was where Jabril's first camp was located, on Via Abruzzi, when he was still a minor. He was there for ten months and was extremely unhappy. Ironically, the shelter was called 'Gandhi'. It housed a dozen child migrants from Africa, including one from Egypt.

The only staff worker was a woman in her twenties who never let us out of her sight from the moment we walked in. Jabril later told me that it was because she didn't want us to talk with the children there. The place was utterly bare, with little furniture or facilities except for a TV in the empty common room. It looked more like a dentist's waiting room than an asylum-seeking children's shelter. On the white wall, all the children's names were written on pieces of coloured paper, which was the only thing that caught my eye in this unstimulating space. Down the corridor, Jabril showed me a box-room-sized bedroom where he used to live. As always, three children shared that tiny room.

Jabril said that when he was living there, the owner of the shelter had pocketed their entitlement of €2.50 each per day. 'She only gave us €16 a month and kept the rest for herself,' he said. 'Good camps would give the minors up to €100 [$116] per month.'

Jabril believed that the camp is simply a money-making venture for the owner, who has another camp elsewhere. 'For each minor, she's been allocated €700 [$812] by the government. Not much out of this has been spent on the kids,' he said, shaking his head.

One of the major issues there was the lack of care. Children's basic health needs were being ignored. 'There was no medical care for us in the house. I was only sent to a doctor if I became very ill,' he said.

Jabril was also angry that there were never any facilities for the children; the camp staff never organized any activities for them, which meant that they spent a large amount of their time hanging around town and doing little. This was a common problem in minors' camps. A friend of Jabril's, a minor, was living in a nearby shelter when I visited. He was so lonely that he walked miles every day to visit friends living on the other side of town and only returned to the shelter late at night. He called himself 'governor' – 'governor of the poor', he said.

That evening we heard the news that 200 people had drowned off the Libyan coast. Another 97 were missing. Only 29 people were rescued.[22]

The next morning, we went to Casa Marconi, an emergency camp that received migrants who had just been rescued at sea, including many children. There were six emergency camps in Palermo, all known to be overcrowded. Casa Marconi was a former hotel and was notorious for being controlled by the Mafia. The building looked like a down-on-its-luck business hotel in a run-down estate. A few metres down the street, posters of victims of past Mafia murders were displayed on the door of an anti-Mafia charity, warning people about the violence. Several security guards were standing outside Casa Marconi. As predicted, I wasn't allowed in, but two young men, Christopher and Isaac, from Nigeria, stopped to talk. They had only arrived at this camp three days before. They felt a little dazed, and had received no guidance or advice from the camp about anything – not about the city or the area, their whereabouts, or where they might go in the next few days or weeks. In fact, they didn't even have a map to go out for a walk, so for a while they had wandered around town blindly and then decided to return to the camp.

They said overcrowding was the biggest problem, with three people sharing a room. They had given their fingerprints at the camp, but didn't know when they would be transferred or where to. There was nothing I could do for them, except offer to drop by with a couple of maps the next day. However, when I came back the next morning, the security guard and staff workers asked me many questions before they said they would pass on the maps to the two youngsters.

Alberto Biondo wrote this in June 2016 about Casa Marconi: 'Via Monfenera is defined by everyone (by both the residents and the workers, who remain there only for a few weeks at a time) as a hell, in which there are currently more than 270 minors. The building consists of six floors of a former hotel, in which a single worker – without any experience, and in the absence of the means of communication, i.e. mediators – takes responsibility for each floor. Here, might makes right. There is no bedside table to place your belongings in, so everything has to be carefully and systematically conserved, otherwise the pervasive theft 'will turn on you too'. The centre, even though brought to the attention of Save the Children, is the scene of continuous "psychological maltreatment".' (I was to hear confirmation of this situation later from the minors living there.)

That evening, we took a walk with Banta, through the backstreets and run-down estates that Banta called 'the Mafia-infested area', to reach the seaside. The colour of the sky was strangely dark-blue, as if before a storm. We stood watching several migrant youths playing football in the park right next to the sea. Coconut trees were waving in the background, in the sea wind and for a moment the scene was almost carefree.

By Sunday 30 October, 3,800 lives had been lost in the Mediterranean so far in 2016, during which around 156,000 migrants had reached Italian shores.

Forgotten teenagers

In every Sicilian town and city you will find migrants either hanging around or sleeping rough at the train stations. In Palermo, in the square in front of the central station, groups of teenage migrants gathered at all times of the day. This was where I met 17-year-old Alaji and 18-year-old Suma, both of whom were from Gambia.

They looked nervous and timid when I first approached them, probably because no one ever tried to talk with them. They soon relaxed, and opened up to tell me about their situation.

Alaji said he was an only child and left home to join his dad, who had migrated to England, where he had a new family. Suma was an orphan. The two boys came from the same village and had decided to travel together to look for work in Libya. There, Suma was imprisoned by the company that employed him but eventually he was able to escape, with the help of several kind local people.

The two soon found a smuggler who got them onto a boat heading for Italy. There were many teenagers like themselves on board. 'The boat was overcrowded. I was standing the whole way... I could hardly breathe,' said Alaji. They were rescued and eventually sent to Palermo. 'We were lucky. The boat that set off before us had sunk.'

In late October 2016, Alaji and Suma had already been at the Casa Marconi for seven long months without knowing where they might be sent next or when. This situation remained the same for the next seven months, despite Alaji's attempt to get more information about their future.

The conditions inside Casa Marconi were intolerable, according to the two boys. Both adults and minors were housed there. Overcrowding was once again confirmed to be a major issue. 'Five people share a small room, with bunk beds of three layers,' Alaji told me. The food provisions were poor: rice was always half-cooked, pasta always stale. 'It's so terrible that we often throw away the food, except when we are starving,' he said.

There were no facilities for the young people inside the camp. The only thing they did was go to school to learn Italian and when there were no classes the two boys would walk around Ballarò, or go to hang out around the central station. At the time we met, they knew no one outside the camp, not even other people from Gambia, although they had already been in Italy for seven months.

Casa Marconi never provided migrants, even those who were under age, with any clothing. The two boys had to purchase their own clothes with the little cash they had – they were given €15 ($17) every 15 days and had to spend most of this on buying clothes. Some of the migrants went to the market area of Ballarò at the end of the day and looked through the dustbins to see if any suitable clothes had been discarded by the shops there and occasionally they were lucky.

Even when December came, the boys told me the camp did not provide any winter clothing. They also had no heating, and always felt cold in bed during the night. Alaji and others complained to the camp manager and the staff many times, but the excuse was always that no one spoke English. Eventually, they reported the situation to an English-speaking staff member, but she seemed unable to report it to the management. When I called her on the boys' behalf, she simply put the phone down on me – twice. Throughout the winter, Alaji and the other migrants did not see any improvements.

Alaji and Suma were not the only teenagers who were caught up and suffering in the failing asylum reception system.[23] Many teenage migrants, including those under age, were idling their youth away on the streets of Sicilian towns and cities. The lack of adult guidance or any level of advice and help in the asylum reception system often put them at risk of harm and abuse in the outside world.

Despite the fact that the existing asylum reception system was corrupt and badly managed, the government still opened a hotspot in Palermo in June 2017, to the fury of campaigners. The new hotspot, situated in a 260-square-metre space in Via Oreto, had the capacity for 150 migrants, both adults and children, including unaccompanied minors. It was a piece of land that had been confiscated from the Mafia family called Graviano.

While I was talking with Alaji and Suma, an Asian man called out to me and approached us. It was the uncle of Jahid and Saeed's fellow traveller. He was pleased to see us and greeted us warmly. He was holding lots of SIM cards in his hand, and probably he had been busy selling on the streets. 'How's business?' I asked. He shrugged, looking for a reply, and then told me the news that Jahid and Saeed had just reached Paris. He did not know Asif, and as Asif did not have a mobile phone, I was not able to find out what had happened to him. Soon afterwards, Saeed got in touch with me from a new phone number, a French one. I was so pleased to hear from him but it sounded as if he and Jahid were surrounded by relatives and couldn't talk freely.

We said our farewell to Banta at a local diner on Via Roma. He said his eldest sister who lived in Sweden had invited him to join her there, but Banta wanted to be free from her control. He seemed to feel the pressure from family members to do well and to prove to his sister that now, at the age of 40, he was also able to send money to support them. The responsibility of being the breadwinner and improving living standards for the family is a heavy burden on every migrant's shoulders. 'When I talked with my sister on the phone, she tried to turn on the video and show me their Hallowe'en party... But I switched off the video. I didn't want to watch.

'I will go visit her and the kids soon enough. The kids haven't met their uncle yet,' he said. 'But it's unlikely that I will move to live in Sweden.' His ideal place of residence remained Germany. Stuttgart, capital of the southwestern state of Baden-Württemberg and a large manufacturing city, was the best option for him because his closest friend was there. We toasted to his future.

3

Going underground

The next time I met with Lamine, the Senegalese social worker, he was more relaxed as he had time to spare before he began work. He told me about the relationship between migration and the criminal world, and how migrant youth get caught up in the exploitative underground world.

'There are many young Nigerian women and under-age girls in Palermo who don't want to be here and didn't even know they were coming here. They're trafficked. And they're out in the streets working as prostitutes. The largest network of African traffickers are the Nigerians. But they can't work in Palermo without the local criminal networks. This is one reason why it's been difficult for the authorities to combat them – the networks are vast and linked up.'

Police operations in 2016 have revealed the presence in Italy of several Nigerian gangs, such as the Black Axe, the Vikings, the Buccaneers, the Eiye and the Maphites. They are known to be trafficking women and girls. According to the UN, 80 per cent of the 3,600 Nigerian women and girls who came to Italy by boat in the first half of 2016 would be trafficked into prostitution. Over the years, the number of Nigerian women and girls who have travelled the route from Libya to Italy has risen from 1,454 in 2014 to 10,624 between January and the end of November 2016, partly as the result of increased trafficking activities by these gangs.

Lamine was familiar with this situation due to his work. He used to work on a project offering food and water to women and girls selling sex in a forest area near Palermo. The Nigerian women and girls who have been trafficked had been recruited from villages, in some cases with the complicity of their parents and village chiefs, who had been paid. Some of the women and girls were controlled psychologically through 'witchcraft', which made them conform to any work arrangement and made them believe that they would be punished if they did not follow the rules. In the early 2000s the women and girls were mainly trafficked via the route through Senegal and Côte d'Ivoire; nowadays, they were mainly travelling through Niger, Tunisia and Libya.

According to 'Inter/rotte: Storie di tratta, poercorsi di resistenza',[24] a report based on interviews with 100 Nigerian women detained in the Ponte Galeria CIE (a centre for identification and expulsion) in Rome, published in April 2016 by the co-operative BeFree, violence and exploitation were commonplace while crossing Niger and in Libya, where the women were detained before travelling by sea to Italy. The report said that Nigerian women passing through Niger are brought to Agadez, to connection houses where they are often raped and forced into prostitution in order to continue their journey.

According to Lamine, during the journey, the women and girls would be housed, picked up and transported by link men along the way. 'My daughter's sick and so I have to go but someone else will come and pick you up', is the sort of excuse used by traffickers when they change hands, to avoid the women and girls becoming suspicious. Many do not know that they've been trafficked until they reach Libya.

Libya is where thousands of women and girls have their first sexual experience violently imposed on them: they are raped or gang-raped and then forced into prostitution. They are placed in dormitories by the Nigerian traffickers, who know the women and girls will always stay silent and not run away, because they fear the risk of rape outside. Eventually, they are trafficked by boat to Sicily, and placed in the camps for adults and minors.

These women and girls are told to call a trafficker based in the local area when they reach Sicily, and from then on they are under the control of this person, even during the time they are in camps. Lamine revealed: 'They would have a certain number of girls in one camp, others in another camp... In one of the Caritas shelters located in the suburbs of Palermo that I was working for three years ago, there were 25 girls, aged 15 to 16... They were in that shelter for a week... I accompanied them to the hospital. Some of them had infections from the sex work they were doing... They were sent to the Partinico camp after that.'

When questioned further, Lamine revealed that the particular Caritas shelter he was talking about was the house of the priest Don Sergio Mattaliano, who is the director of Caritas Palermo. He provided shelter for under-age girls and boys in his own house. When providing shelter for the Nigerian girls that Lamine had met, Don Mattaliano was aware of their situation as victims of trafficking. However, they were offered no help or advice and the situation was certainly not reported to the authorities. These women and girls should not even have been processed in the reception camps. They should have been sent to specialist shelters to receive professional advice as victims of sexual exploitation. (Non-protection of victims of sexual exploitation is a situation prevalent throughout the camps in Italy. The training provided to staff by the International Organization for Migration (IOM) to identify victims of trafficking, is at an elementary stage. Most camps are not equipped to do this.) I asked Don Sergio Mattaliano to comment on the above situation but he did not respond.

When the camps were beginning to get overcrowded in Palermo, Don Mattaliano wanted to help and started to set up shelters himself, for which he was paid by the state – a sum of €35 ($42) per day for each adult migrant. He offered only accommodation, while the Catholic NGO Caritas provided food for the migrants. He housed up to 50 migrant boys and girls in his own house. During his time working with the shelter, Lamine saw that six or seven Nigerian girls were sharing a single room. Don Mattaliano had also run four other camps under Caritas, housing 60-200 people in each place.

This revealed the dubious role played by the church, as a provider of support as well as a beneficiary of cash from the state. Don Mattaliano has made a very healthy profit from migrants while offering them help. Churches in general have profited a great deal from the asylum reception system. 'One of the churches even changed the rules and started to charge migrants a fee for joining their congregation when it used to be free,' said Lamine.

'It didn't used to be like this,' he said, 'The previous priest was different. He was the best priest of Santa Chiara. He was hosting migrants... When his mum passed away, I went with many migrants by bus to attend her funeral... He was pushed out because he denounced and reported cases of child abuse by VIPs that took place with the complicity of their parents, near Santa Chiara. When he reported it to the police, those men, the VIPs, were stronger than him, and they got rid of him.'

Trafficked into the sex trade

The trafficking of migrant women and girls was not uncommon here, said Lamine. Nothing was done to lift them out of the situation, because the asylum reception system depended on migrants to make money and consequently no one in the reception system offered them any help. Their cases remain unreported. The majority of these women and girls do not have documents, and are often, eventually, lost in the asylum system.

During my time in Palermo, and Italy in general, I had rarely met single migrant women or girls. Most of the women I met were married and had come here with their families. Complex reasons lie behind female migration. An IOM report,[25] providing a socio-economic profile of migrants arriving in Italy, offers some explanation. The report is based on interviews conducted with migrants based at all levels of reception centres in several regions of Italy between April and July 2016. It points out that the reasons that drive people to migrate change dramatically according to gender. 'There is a striking difference in the percentage of women versus men that left for family or friend-related reasons (37.8 per cent versus 17.8 per cent),' it said. 'Many women report leaving to avoid abuse within the family, forced marriage or to follow a partner.' The report also points out that 82 per cent of male migrants made the decision to leave primarily on their own, versus 59 per cent of women, which means that, in two cases out of five, the decision is made by someone else, and in one out of three cases, it is the family.

Also, it is predominantly men who travel on the routes through Libya to Europe as they are particularly dangerous and difficult and are therefore commonly seen as unsuited to women.

Lamine said that there were few single women in Palermo and that it would be difficult for me to meet them because they were working. It's no exaggeration to say that half the street sex workers in Italy today are Nigerian. Many migrant women and under-age girls, mostly from Nigeria and a few from Eritrea – some as young as 14 or 15 – were working on the streets around Via Roma, some parts of Ballarò and the surrounding area, as well as at the port and in Palermo's suburbs. Many worked as prostitutes in the daytime and returned to their camps in the evening. They were spending a large part of their working lives slaving in the sex trade to pay off the debts they owed to the traffickers for transportation to Europe – up to €50,000 ($60,000) each. Many of those who arrived ten years ago have paid off their debt and have set up their own businesses in the same industry.

Sadly, in many cases, the families of the trafficked women and girls are fully aware and even complicit in their trafficking. Not only had some mothers sent their daughters on the trafficking route but, in some cases, elder sisters who had been trafficked to Sicily and were working in the sex trade had their younger sisters sent to join them from back home. These girls then arrived in Sicilian towns to find that their elder sisters were the brothel keepers who were controlling them.

In fact, Lamine said, it was no exaggeration to say that some of the villages where these women and girls had come from were thriving on their prostitution.

When they arrived in Sicilian cities, some of these girls were kept in houses managed by brothel keepers and controlled by a Nigerian Mafia renting territory from the Sicilian Mafia so that, instead of competing directly, they worked under the wing of existing Sicilian networks. Migrant women and girls working on Via Roma in Palermo, for instance, were working on territory owned by the local Mafia and outsourced to Nigerian traffickers. This applied to all criminal activities, without exception. Migrants involved in crime, especially if highly profitable, work under the local Mafia in order to survive. According to Lamine, the brother of the president of the Nigerian Association had been working with the Sicilian Mafia, was arrested and was still in prison. He was only a small part of the local Mafia chain. Lamine also hinted at the uncomfortable link between the Mafia, the church and the state: it appears that often they cannot work without each other.

I told him that I was planning a trip to Catania. He said that he always associated Catania with the sight of teenage migrant girls selling sex on the streets there. He recalled that, around the train station and in the back alleys of the city, migrant women and girls could be seen working on the streets. The majority of them lived in the camps and came out to work during the daytime, but after a while many ran away. Some of these young women and girls had been sent abroad by their own parents who knew what would happen to them. It took many years for them to pay off their debt, after which some chose freedom. However, a large number of them continued to sell sex willingly, in order to send cash home.

The backstreets of Catania

Along the way to Catania tiny raindrops fell steadily. The valleys outside our train window were lit up by a rainbow, its colours clear and strong across the sky. Twenty minutes into our journey, the electricity suddenly went and the whole train came to a halt. Silence. A mobile phone rang in the distance, somewhere down the carriage. People asked the conductor questions as he walked up and down the train. Fortunately, it didn't take more than an hour to get the train going again and his sense of relief was clear. We reached Catania at dusk.

This city, founded in the eighth century BCE, on the eastern coast of Sicily, is known for its historic earthquakes – it was destroyed by them in 1169 and 1693. It has also suffered from several volcanic eruptions from Mount Etna, brooding in the distance, the most violent of which was in 1669. The history of the violent natural disasters remains impressed in people's minds and many artists have reproduced the dramatic images in paintings. However, Catania is home to Sicily's first university, founded in the 15th century, and is still one of the island's most important cultural centres. The city's structure and character are very different from Palermo. Not only is it smaller, with a population of just over 300,000, but it is much less formal and stylish than the island's capital. There is much more of a sociable mood here: on a Friday or Saturday night people seemed just to stroll around the streets, meeting friends and chatting till the early hours. No one indulges in binge drinking and you can have your balcony door open at 3am and enjoy the sound of people simply talking.

As always, the central station is a focal point for many migrants, who come from everywhere and anywhere, and who could be passing through to and from nearby Sicilian towns or mainland Italy. Many were waiting to board buses at the terminus, just standing smoking or sitting on their suitcases. All around the station, many more migrants were standing on street corners or having a bite to eat in cheap cafés before embarking on long trips.

Along the road opposite the train station, a couple of private vehicles were parked, the drivers standing outside the cars, waiting for potential passengers. Before long, migrant men and women in their twenties approached one of the drivers, exchanged greetings, unloaded their bags into the back of the car, and got in. Within an hour, the car was filled with six people, practically sitting one on top of the other. Although it was well over the passenger capacity, the driver was still hanging around, as if waiting for more people. Finally, he was satisfied, got into his seat, and drove off, as the voices of the men and women chattering faded away into the distance.

I asked a man standing next to me on the pavement where these vehicles were going. 'Cara di Mineo,' he answered. This was exactly the camp I wanted to visit and which activists refer to as an 'ethnic prison'. Cara di Mineo[26] is a former US army camp and now an emergency reception camp for asylum-seekers. It is the largest asylum reception camp in Europe and receives some €112,000 ($135,000) per month from state funding.

'You can't go in those cars. They're for Africans,' the man standing next to me said, smiling, referring to the overcrowded vehicle that had just left. 'This is the African way. The cars won't move until they are over-full.'

He said his name was Victor, and he was only in Catania for the day. He was 22 years old, from Nigeria. He had lived in Cara di Mineo for a year and five months and went on to say that the majority of migrants who are sent there usually spend between one and two years stuck in the camp. He had finally received the long-awaited documents giving him the right to remain in Italy and was now waiting for a passport. In the meantime, he could leave the camp and was moving to Parma in northern Italy where he hoped to find work. If he could find a job, he'd like to stay in Italy.

Now that the Mineo camp was history for him, Victor was able to talk about it without too much emotion – for example, when I asked him about the living conditions there.

'Well, I understand that it's not easy for them [Italy],' he smiled, without the slightest bitterness. 'They didn't owe me anything.'

Victor had been talking to a young Nigerian woman, who currently lived in Cara di Mineo. She was standing alongside me on the pavement, all dressed up and her face heavily made-up. She was looking around, as if checking out punters. When I approached her, she didn't want to have a conversation at all and turned away.

On the way back into town from the area around the station, I walked past some grim-looking back streets with filthy old graffiti on the walls. Down the alleys were rows of dingy apartments with several African women standing or sitting outside. They all looked to be in their thirties and forties, and were soliciting male passers-by. They had been here for years. They would have started their lives here selling sex while living in the camps, and simply carried on in prostitution because that was the only trade they knew. Later, all over town, I saw the same scene of African women standing on street corners, in run-down estates: none of the women wanted to talk.

On this day, more than 200 migrants drowned in two shipwrecks off the coast of Libya. Survivors who were brought ashore to Lampedusa told the story. Twelve bodies were found. Up to this point, more than 4,200 migrants had died in the Mediterranean Sea in 2016, the deadliest year so far, according to the UN.

Behind the razor wire

The bus trip to Mineo took an hour and cost five euros. The village was perched on the top of the mountains some 40 kilometres inland from Catania. With a population of just over 5,000, and peacefully isolated above the valleys, it felt secluded – even detached from the rest of the world, Indeed, so detached that there was no frequent bus or taxi service. A local man in a bar offered to help, and drove us all the way down to the camp, situated at the foot of the mountains. 'Mineo is a good place,' the local man said. 'Except for the camp.' I gathered that he was trying to tell me that the presence of migrants was a negative thing for the village. Later I realized that his viewpoint reflected that of many in the local community.

Cara di Mineo was an army-guarded, razor-wire-fenced compound that housed 4,000 migrants who were located in 403 terracotta-coloured buildings. As you approached the camp, you could see the entire blocks of housing from a distance as they were built on flat land in the middle of the fields. The area around the gate was surrounded by armoured vehicles and soldiers stood by bearing rifles. Dave took out his camera and took a shot of the scene from the gate, but he was immediately stopped by several soldiers who walked over and asked him to show them the camera. 'Please delete the picture,' one of them said. A senior officer heard the disturbance and approached us. 'What happened?' he asked. 'No problem, the picture's deleted,' I reassured him immediately, to avoid any trouble.

Outside the gate area, dozens of migrants were walking around in groups, to take in the last bit of sunshine at dusk. I came across several groups of young men in their twenties, from Bangladesh. One group stopped to talk for a while. They had all been at the camp for two to three months now and, like most migrants, they had followed the same route via Libya. One of them made gunfire noises every time Libya was mentioned. They had worked as construction labourers there and not been paid the full wages. After the hardship and misery they had experienced during their time in Libya, it was difficult to imagine what they must have felt like arriving in this centre after being rescued at sea: a military-controlled camp in the plains between hills. No communities around. No farms or livestock. Just miles and miles of wild grassland. This was their first sight of Italy and this was all they knew of the country.

The young men had been fingerprinted and interviewed and, at the time of our meeting in early November 2016, were waiting for a substantive asylum interview with the Commission.[27] Legally, the Commission should have made the decision within three working days after the interview. In reality, however, the procedure usually takes months. On 13 November, Monsur, one of the men from Bangladesh whom I met in the Mineo camp asked me to pray for him because he was attending his Commission interview the next day. He was told he would have to wait two months for a decision but then, for unknown reasons, he was given a second Commission interview on 16 December, and was faced with waiting all through winter for the result. He and his friends at the camp all wanted to stay in Italy and, ideally, to go to live in Rome. Waiting had been painful. They spent a lot of their time every day taking long walks in the fields.

At the time of our visit, 200 of the migrants at Mineo were from Bangladesh, while the other residents were from Eritrea and other African countries. Adults and children were housed together. Inside the camp, one room could be shared by up to 15 people, and they were given only mattresses to sleep on. Food provision was very poor: a tiny meal of pasta in the evenings, which was so awful it made them all laugh bitterly; they were only given two pieces of chicken once a week, for which people rushed to queue. Breakfast, which consisted of only a few biscuits, was between 6am and 8am – if you turned up after 8am, you would have no food until lunchtime. The young men said they were always starving and Monsur saved biscuits from his breakfast to eat when he was hungry.

Inadequate clothing was also a problem and the migrants still had only short-sleeved tops and flip-flops despite the chill autumn wind. The camp staff had not distributed suitable or sufficient clothing and the young men were doubtful they would receive anything warmer for the winter.

'The camp doesn't give us enough food or clothing but, strangely, they give us cigarettes,' said Monsur. 'But none of us smoke!'

We chatted, watching several African migrants playing football in the distance. When the sun set, everyone walked back to the camp, following the rules. Monsur and his friends took several selfies with us, giggling and saying they had to return to their pasta dinner. I watched them as they dragged themselves in their noisy flip-flops back into the camp. 'Ciao!' they shouted out, waving goodbye.

In March 2017, following months of waiting, Monsur received

a rejection letter for his asylum claim. He told me he was now planning to appeal. At the same time, he was considering joining his Bangladeshi friends in Milan. He felt that he could no longer carry on waiting and wasting his life inside this camp. 'Please pray for me,' he said.

'The camp is an open prison for us'

The following day, I met a modestly dressed man who introduced himself as Adedayo, opposite the train station in Catania, where private cars parked to pick up migrants to go to the camp at Mineo. Adedayo was a 29-year-old Nigerian who had been living in the camp for over a year. He had never been told why he had had to stay there for such a long time. He gave his fingerprints at Mineo, but added that sometimes coercion had been used to get fingerprints from migrants.

Conditions were tough inside the camp at Mineo and, as a result, some migrants had run away. But Adedayo said he would never do that: he believed in following procedures and did not want to fall out of the system. At the same time, he understood why people ran away – quite simply it was difficult to survive in the conditions of the camp. Many migrants had taken to begging in the streets of Catania and Messina, to bring in some cash for their daily basic needs. Adedayo admitted that he himself begged sometimes when he came to Catania once a week. He sent some of the cash from the begging back to his brother and two sisters in Nigeria who needed his support. He was an orphan and he had always looked after his siblings – they were all he had. He used to run a cosmetics shop with his brother, but they did not make enough money to survive. He took on the responsibility of earning a living for his family, but had to leave the country to do so.

'The camp is run by bad people,' he said. 'They work with the police and the Mafia. They don't give us a cent. We have no cash at all... The camp doesn't spend the government money on us. We have only two hours' Italian lessons each week, not enough to learn the language.

'The only thing they give us every three days is a packet of cigarettes. But many of us don't smoke, so we save the cigarettes and give them to the Bangladeshi men in the camp who organize selling them to tobacco shops. We then get three euros each time they sell the cigarettes... Then I spend some of this money on travelling to Catania in the car, which costs five euros, and buying ingredients to cook some decent African food, because the food they give us at the camp is horrible, just the same old pasta every day.' Selling cigarettes and saving cash for the car ride to Catania had become a routine in his life.

At Cara di Mineo, migrants' movements were controlled: the gate opened at 8am and closed at 8pm, and you had to sign in and out each time you came and went. Adedayo and his room-mates sometimes climbed the fence to get out of the camp after 8pm. Even though all he could do was beg on the streets in Catania, he felt freer outside. 'The camp is an open prison for us,' he said.

'In many ways, the life in Cara di Mineo is similar to the hardship back in Nigeria. Why did I flee to have this?' he asked. There was a great sense of regret in his voice. He said he felt he had been deprived of the opportunity to make a life for himself and his family.

The driver of the private vehicle was still hustling around, trying to cram more people into his car for Mineo. Finally, he ushered Adedayo to get in, too. We said we would meet again the following week. I handed him a new packet of cigarettes to make it easier for him to get the next car ride.

On this day, ten bodies were picked up by the Italian coastguard off the coast of Libya. Over 2,000 migrants were rescued. The following day, on 6 November, 800 migrants arrived in Catania, after being rescued at sea, in 16 different operations.

Meanwhile, on TripAdvisor, US tourists were asking locals about the 'refugee crisis'. One of them wondered 'if refugees have an impact on local life' and 'if it will affect tourism'. A few Sicilians replied with anger. One said: 'Don't watch too much Fox News.'

'God was all I had'

I got talking to a 34-year-old Ghanaian man named Addae at the street corner opposite the station. He had come to Catania to visit a close friend whom he calls his brother. Addae had lived in Cara di Mineo for a year, three years before. It was a tough period, he said, spent just waiting for documents. As a devout Catholic, he had only one way to cope with the stress – by praying. 'I depend on God and God only. God was all I had,' he said with conviction.

That year, he could not send a single penny home to his parents. Abject poverty had left him with no choice and had compelled him to leave Ghana in the first place and travel to Italy via Libya. 'This is the destiny of Africans,' he said.

'And it's very tough for Africans to live in Italy... although I don't blame Italy for it. They have many of us here.' He said he was aware of the disparity in the number of asylum-seekers received among the EU states.[28] As Eurostat shows, the highest number of first-time asylum applicants in the third quarter of 2016 was registered in Germany (with over 237,400 first-time applicants, or 66 per cent of the total applicants to EU member states), followed by Italy (34,600, or 9.6 per cent), France (20,000, or 5.6 per cent), Greece (12,400, or 3.5 per cent) and the UK (9,200, or 2.6 per cent).

Addae's experience at Cara di Mineo three years ago was identical to that of the migrants currently living there. During his year at Mineo, he received no support from the camp; the money provided by the state was never distributed to him – the only thing he received was a packet of cigarettes every three days. 'I don't believe in selling the cigarettes on to others. Why do I have to pass on the unhealthy habit to other people? So I just leave them aside,' he said innocently.

One thing that struck me in Addae's account was that he had heard about young migrant women and girls selling sex in Catania, although he had no idea whether they were under someone's control.

'The one time I felt very sad was when a young African woman in her twenties approached me on the street in Catania and tried to sell her services to me. "I have to survive. If you're interested in helping me, please do this for me," she said. I was saddened that someone from Africa has to end up doing degrading work like this to survive... But how can you try to help them? You don't know where to start.'

Addae's days at the camp were over. He had known it would be difficult to find work in Catania, and had moved to Malta for better employment opportunities, although the wage level was lower there and he was working illegally. He now worked as a construction worker, earning five euros per hour. Addae felt frustrated that, even now, with his formal refugee status and a UN passport, which he called the 'immigrant passport', he was not legally permitted to work outside Italy. He believed that the rules needed to change.

Getting to know Adedayo

The following morning, only three cars were going from Cara di Mineo to Catania at 8am. If you want to have a full day in Catania, you have to be an early bird. So Adedayo had to get himself out of bed at 4am, swallow a plate of spaghetti that his friend prepared for him, and get in the car at 6am for Catania. The dawn had hardly broken. He arrived two hours later, and we met at the usual spot, the street corner opposite the train station.

Adedayo accompanied me to a Tunisian café where many migrants spend their time. I was desperate for a cup of coffee, and ordered one for him too, although he called it 'the white people's drink.' He drinks only water.

As he sipped his water, he told me how tough it had been in the camp. The food provided was so inadequate that many migrants tried to cook their own – on the heaters. The camp management tried to stop that as it consumed too much electricity. But what could you do when the food was so poor and inedible? The ban on cooking simply meant that the practice became an important activity among the migrants. A group would gather in one room and, while some kept a lookout for the staff, others would do the cooking on the quiet. The sharing of food from home was common – when someone cooked, the amounts were always large enough to feed a group. They all found great comfort in sharing and Adedayo particularly enjoyed these meals with his fellow Nigerians.

I followed him into the Asian food shop where he usually purchased ingredients for Nigerian dishes. He needed some rice and the Bangladeshi shopkeeper showed him the huge variety of rice he had to choose from. Adedayo looked carefully at each type and then pointed to one, saying 'This is what we eat in Nigeria.' I also went to a Senegalese shop with him where he bought daily necessities such as shampoo and soap, which weren't provided inside the camp.

We were a few yards away from the back streets where African women did sex work. When he talked about fellow Nigerian migrants, he shook his head and said many of them, including under-age girls, worked in the sex trade. 'Their parents or mothers joined the traffickers in deceiving the girls into going to Europe,' he said. In many cases, mothers consent to the deception practised by traffickers and are completely aware of what will happen to their daughters when they arrive in Italy. He added: 'The other girls willingly choose to do sex work, to make an income for their families back home. Many of them were raped in Libya, on their way to Europe.'

Adedayo said it was a common perception among Nigerians that Nigerian women and girls who travelled to Europe have, in one way or another, become involved in prostitution. 'That's why I'm not allowed to marry a Nigerian girl here,' he said, smiling, 'My mother wouldn't approve. Like everyone else, she thinks Nigerian women are no good to be wives.'

Adedayo pointed ahead, to the street corner where he and other migrants gathered to go out begging in a group. His closest friend in the group was living in a shelter in Catania that housed up to 12 migrants. It was run by a Mafia member who also owned several other apartments that were used as shelters for migrants. Adedayo described how truly appalling the conditions were in this place, which lacked even water and electricity. His friend had to buy water from outside and boil it when he needed a shower. The Mafia owner clearly wanted to squeeze as much profit as possible from the migrants and was saving costs on all the basic facilities. How could a place like this qualify for state funding to operate as a shelter?

Yet Adedayo and his friends often experienced great humanity when they were begging on the streets. 'Some people are good-hearted and give me money. One time, a woman offered me a roast chicken that would cost three euros to buy. "It is very kind of you," I said to her. "But, to be honest, I'd prefer if you gave me just one euro, so I can go to buy what I like." She laughed.'

At other times, Adedayo and fellow migrants came across aggressive local youths who told them to stop begging in their town and to get out of the country. On one occasion, an Italian man propositioned Adedayo's friend and asked for sex.

Some people were scared of being approached by their group. 'They fear black people,' he said with a bitter smile.

All in all, Adedayo was earning €20 to €30 a day from begging.

We went to sit down on a bench in a small park and Adedayo told me that he had slept here many nights in Catania. Returning to Mineo cut the day short and, as they could not afford even the cheapest hostels, they would go to this park and spend the night sleeping on the benches.

Sometimes Adedayo and his friends would go to Messina by bus and beg there instead. They would sleep at the train station and sometimes at night police officers would bring them blankets. Some local residents would also bring them food. Adedayo spoke with gratitude about the people he'd met in Messina. They're nice, he said. 'People are of all backgrounds there. It's very mixed.'

Life on the street as a beggar was a necessity for Adedayo. There was no room for sadness or self-pity; he knew that all he could do was to carry on. After all, what was this compared with his working time in Libya? Those two years were the harshest that anyone could bear: in the background was a collapsed society where gun crimes were common day in, day out. Catania was gentle and kind by comparison. If he had not been lucky enough to find a good family that helped him out in Libya, he might not have survived. He could hardly believe now that he had even managed to send some cash home while working there, when many others were simply in slave labour. 'Must be luck,' he said.

Eventually, in 2014, the hardship in Libya pushed him onto a boat heading for Italy. The smuggler charged him €1,500 ($1,750) for the journey. After three days at sea, he landed in Lampedusa, where he was kept for two days before being moved on to Catania. The bleak sight of the camp at Mineo shocked him – as did the way of life he experienced there. What had scared him the most in the first few days after his arrival was when he talked to a migrant who had been in the camp for well over a year. 'How can anyone live there for so long?' he asked.

He was given an interview soon after his arrival. He didn't understand what the questions implied, and answered 'I left home for family issues' and 'I'd like to work in Italy'. He was subsequently refused asylum. After that, he appealed against the decision and had now been waiting for a year. It didn't look hopeful.

Over the years, Adedayo had learned simply to try to make the best out of the toughest circumstances. 'Libya was bad, but there was no return. Just like it is bad in Italy and there's no return.'

Given his circumstances, Adedayo seemed incredibly well adjusted. 'This journey to Italy is like going to university. I've learned a lot. You meet all sorts of people and experience everything.' Sadly, though, since he had been in Cara di Mineo, his mother had died in an accident. 'I never imagined not seeing her again when I left home,' he said quietly.

When we parted that day, Adedayo reminded me that he would be begging in Catania again the following Saturday.

Mafia Capitale

While I was still standing at the street corner, the bus-service information officer, Luciano, approached me and warmly introduced me to his friend and colleague, who drove the bus to Mineo daily. Then he invited me for a coffee.

I was interested in getting some local perspective. Luciano said the majority of Sicilian people have no problem with migrants and refugees. 'The people who have problems with refugees are in Mineo. I would say that about half the population there are concerned about the perceived problems brought by migrants...'

When chatting about Cara di Mineo, the use of the word 'Mafia' made him cringe. He said it was true that criminal networks were profiteering from the camp, but was unsure how bad it was. He was anxious to divert me from the subject, which seemed to make many local residents uncomfortable. It seemed that, although no one wanted to refer to it, the reality remains that Cosa Nostra still holds its grip on many of the city's businesses. Most of the 10,000 businesses there were still paying protection money, known as the *pizzo*, to the Mafia.

The business of asylum reception management was so profitable that – inevitably – Cosa Nostra would have to have a hand in that, too. The organization Borderline Sicilia has reported on some of the criminal activity suspected at Cara di Mineo. In June 2016 it said:

> The investigations into the CARA di Mineo, within the remit of 'Mafia Capitale',[29] is producing new subpoenas for fraudulent misrepresentation and serious fraud, including the falsification of the number of migrants at the centre. The number has continued to rise in recent weeks, with new transfers following on from the disembarkings, not only at the ports of Catania and Augusta, but also Pozzallo, Trapani and Reggio Calabria... The building houses around 3,500 people and explicitly carries out all the identification and selection procedures pertaining to the hotspot approach, and seems also to be used as a Hub [a mass reception centre for asylum-seekers], given recent mass transferrals of Eritreans who have agreed to relocation. It is thus simultaneously a location under investigation and also entrusted with a range of new functions, occurrences not only with no clear juridical regulation but, above all, even without pertaining to the duty of protecting migrants' rights. It is a ghetto in the middle of nowhere, outside of which, week after week, the army and police forces multiply.
>
> Registering their [migrants'] presence and taking their fingerprints means to receive the correlating payment: these are the only practices undertaken scrupulously within the camp. If the majority of the new arrivals then leave, the only important thing is that they are replaced immediately... In recent years, those who arrive almost always end up in psychological collapse deriving from, on average, 18 months of a state of abandonment.

Frustrated love

Addae, the Ghanaian I had met some days earlier, had just returned from his trip to visit friends in Rome and his sister in Palermo and we agreed to meet at the bus station. His sister and her husband had left their child in a boarding school in Ghana while they were both working in Palermo to make ends meet for the family. Addae said it was quite common for Ghanaian parents to work abroad and leave their children behind in good schooling for which they pay. But when I asked Addae what line of work his sister was in, he looked embarrassed and said that he did not know because she was reluctant to tell him.

He went on to say that if he ever met a Ghanaian woman and wanted to date her, the first thing he would have to find out is how she had come to Europe, and whether she owed money to smugglers – because as a boyfriend or partner he would be inheriting the woman's debts. In some cases, Ghanaian women are working to pay off their debts to the smugglers who brought them to Italy. He even knew of a hairdresser who recruited people from Ghana to come to work for him by smuggling them into Italy.

Addae looked sorrowful when he recalled a relationship that he had left behind during his time at Cara di Mineo. One of the canteen staff in her late twenties fell for him; she was very concerned about his situation and conditions in the camp, so often invited him to stay at her home in Mineo, up in the hills. Addae was unsure whether their relationship would be frowned upon, and therefore kept it to himself, revealing it only to a close friend in the camp.

One day, she invited Addae to her family home to meet her parents. This was an important event for him and he was very nervous. However, during the meal with the family, everyone seemed in good spirits and it looked like all was going well until all of a sudden, words were exchanged in Italian and everyone went quiet – clearly her father and sister were unhappy about something. Later, she revealed to Addae that, at the dinner table, she had broken the news to the family that she and Addae were in a relationship. Her mother and brother seemed to accept this, but her father and sister disapproved.

Addae was very hurt by this: he could not bear not being accepted by her family and gradually began to distance himself from her. As her family only spoke Italian in front of him, he could not work out what they were thinking, and he grew tired of the situation. He stopped visiting her and her family and eventually broke off the relationship.

When his documents arrived two months later, Addae decided to leave and move to Malta to work, although she wanted him to stay. He said that the only way they could marry and be together was if they moved to live outside Italy, but she felt she could not leave her family and the life she knew behind. On the day they parted, she cried. They cried together.

During the entire time Addae was at Cara di Mineo, he never received any money from the government – not a cent for the whole year. And he was not sure that his name was removed when he left the camp: he was aware that many migrants' departures were not reported because the camp management intended to pocket the money from the state.

Addae said he was all right now and that he had an active social circle in Malta where he had befriended both African and British residents. 'There are no racists like her father in England, are there?' he asked me. He then asked if he could join me on the trip to London and I began to realize that he didn't really have much he would regret leaving behind in Malta.

During his time in Catania, Addae used to buy and collect cheap shoes and clothes for orphans in Ghana and send donations to them. He felt fortunate enough to be in a position to help someone, and continued to do so, even building up relationships with some of the orphans, whom he was going to visit when he returned to Ghana at Christmas.

That evening, I received a message from Banta in Palermo: 'My room-mate is ill, with a terrible skin condition... He's had this problem since 2014. He can't sleep at night. It's contagious. The camp is not willing to help him because the medicine is expensive. Yesterday I was just like a mad lion with them... Eventually, they called the committee around 5pm – they bought medicine and today they took my room-mate to the doctor.'

The following morning began with the news from the US that Donald Trump had won the presidential election. We could foresee a rapid escalation of anti-refugee, anti-Muslim, anti-immigrant policies in the very near future. We were at the top of Mount Etna; it was three degrees below zero, too cold to be outside. So we went into a café, where we sipped coffee and ate pasta, while the news on the TV above our head was showing Trump loud and clear, dubbed into Italian.

Meanwhile in France and Britain...

In early November 2016, around 2,500 migrants from Sudan, Somalia, Eritrea and other countries were living on the streets of northern Paris. Many of them were waiting for their asylum claims to be processed and, although they were entitled to emergency housing, the city couldn't cope. Other migrants were simply trapped in the underground world of the *sans-papiers*, not knowing where to turn. Many were camping outside the Stalingrad or Jaurès metro stations – others were along the banks of the Canal Saint-Martin. The temperature was falling by the day, yet their number had not decreased. Instead, more seemed to be arriving, especially since late October when the Calais camp had been demolished.

The migrants not only had to worry about the arrival of winter, but also about the riot police who would arrive to pull down their tents, moving them on at regular intervals. And the eviction did come: armed police aimed to remove the sight of homeless migrants from the streets of Paris, and they did just this. Their police vehicles, parked between metro stations, were a presence intimidating enough to deter migrants from returning to their former locations.

In mid-November, the UK Home Office published highly restrictive eligibility criteria for under-age asylum-seekers hoping to be transferred from France to Britain, contrary to the original principles of the Dubs Amendment. Under the new guidelines, to be eligible for transfer under Dubs, children from the Calais camp had to be 12 years old or younger; at high risk of sexual exploitation; or aged 15 or under and of Sudanese or Syrian nationality. Minors who had relatives already in Britain were still eligible under European family reunification rules. Since the demolition of the Calais camp, only 318 minors had been brought to Britain thus far, 200 of them under the EU family reunification programme. Alf Dubs, the Labour peer who made the Dubs Amendment possible, said the new criteria were rolling back on the commitment. A group of Kindertransport survivors also wrote to the Home Secretary, Amber Rudd, calling on the government to accept 1,000 children from the Calais camp by Christmas. Despite Dubs and EU rules that the UK must take in unaccompanied children who had family ties in the country under the Dublin Regulation, these pleas fell on deaf ears.

In late November 2016, Safe Passage, a charity that offers legal support to asylum-seeking children applying to join relatives in the UK, expressed their concern about the wellbeing of the under-age migrants in the reception centres in France. Among the 33 minors they interviewed that month, some said they had not been provided with clean clothes since their arrival, the food provision was inadequate, and there were no facilities suitable for children. Others said they were being made to live with adults. The charity had also reported cases of forced labour: some children were found to have been sent to work in agriculture.

Chasing the dream

Banta said he wanted to go to Germany as soon as possible. He had a view of Germany and the Scandinavian countries that seemed quite optimistic. He admired the law and order there, and was convinced that Germans and Scandinavians all believed in multiculturalism. He looked to Germany, in particular, for the long term and hoped he could settle there eventually. 'Gambians have a place in their society; they're well integrated there,' he said.

Gambians make up the third-largest group – around 14,500 people – of African asylum seekers in Germany. Many of them aren't granted refugee status and are living on the edge of society, working in the lowest-paid, menial jobs with neither rights nor protection.

'I'd like to give my son a good education,' Banta added.

'Your son?' I wasn't aware that he had a son. Now he told me that, yes, he had a 10-year-old son in Gambia and I was curious to know why he had never mentioned this before. He replied: 'I didn't want to go around telling my misery to everyone.' He went on to explain that he had been in a relationship with a Muslim woman and they had had a son. But the woman's family had wanted her to marry a man of her own religion and arranged for her to wed a Muslim entrepreneur, ending the relationship with Banta. The child could not be accepted by the new husband and is now looked after by Banta's mother.

It was a painful past and I understood why he did not want to share it at the beginning. Leaving his son behind had been extremely hard; Banta had had to tell him the lie that he would be home soon. 'He's my best friend; there was not one day he went to school without talking to me first.'

Banta was cheerful today – a rare occurrence. His housemate Austin and his wife were holding a birthday party for their two-year-old son. He enjoyed spending time with the family and playing with the child; he was very loving to children and now, in retrospect, I knew that his mind was always on his son.

The next day, Banta was furious: he and his housemates were making a complaint to their camp management about the food provided at the Moltimotiv café. On more than one occasion, it was stale, left over from the previous evening. It smelt. Their complaint could have resulted in the café losing its contract with the camp.

Banta had also stopped going to his favourite bar, Kalacutta. Apparently the Nigerian owner had got into trouble with the police due to the increase in the selling of drugs there – and this time it was hard drugs. 'I thought I'd better stop going there,' he said. 'This is not my country and I don't want to have a bad name with the Italian authorities.'

Dire straits

It was not an uplifting arrival in Messina, the third-largest city in Sicily. In the rain, Dave and I crossed the tramway and tried to find our lodging. I believe you can decide whether you will like a town or not at first sight, and Messina depressed me instantly. Antonio Mazzeo, an activist who wrote for Borderline Sicilia, described Messina as a 'city of bad welcoming'.

'Hundreds of refugees are half-hidden in the tent city of Pala Nebiolo, the former baseball pitch at Conca d'Oro-Annunziata, owned by Messina University. Forty degrees in the shade in summer, the cold touches zero in winter. When it rains, however, it's still worse: without any drainage, the ground is covered in water and the reception centre is submerged in puddles. In the former barracks of "Gasparro" in Bisconte, in the building generously declared to be habitable, more than 200 people are packed tightly, within 550 square metres of space, the bunk beds touching each other and with an endless queue for meals and showers. A shameful building, truly disgusting, a shame and disgrace for the state institutions and local administration, which does not seem able to look or listen, and which chooses, as always, not to speak.'

Migrants arrived and left the city from the bus terminus next to the railway station. Groups of migrants gathered, talking. I approached a group of six teenagers. They were from Gambia and Nigeria, and were seeing off a friend who was leaving for Turin. They all lived in the same camp, Gasparro, 30 minutes' walk from there. One of the more outspoken boys introduced himself as Modou, a 17-year-old, the only one in this group who could speak English. He told me they were all aged under 18.

According to them, Gasparro was accommodating more than 200 migrant minors at that time. They wouldn't have lived like this back in Gambia: the 200 minors shared three large rooms, sleeping on mattresses and bunk beds; each received 15 credits per month for their phones, one euro per credit, instead of cash from the camp. They had pooled their credits and bought a phone to share among them. 'But we are entitled to more than this amount,' said Modou. 'Should we tell the *carabinieri*?'

It was no surprise to hear that Gasparro provided insufficient clothing and that the teenagers spent most of their credits on buying clothes for themselves, apart from calling their parents. Modou showed me the second-hand jumper he had bought for himself in the market.

All of them were waiting, and had no information from the camp as to where and when they might be transferred. This was an emergency camp which was not supposed to hold migrants for longer than 72 hours, but most of the minors had been kept there for months. Modou had already been there for a month. Given the poor conditions and long wait, it was no wonder many children had run away. 'If I have cash, I will leave too, and go north,' he said.

These teenagers had nothing to do all day. They wandered around town purposelessly. Apart from the language classes that they attended, there was nothing to focus their attention on or to

Migrants rescued from the sea arriving in Messina.

look forward to. Often, they walked to the station area, just to hang out and meet Gambians from other camps. Later that day, I met a 16-year-old Gambian boy wandering the streets on his own. He stood out because he was so tall and thin. He was eating from a packet of crisps, looking around as if he were lost. He told me he had arrived here only a week ago. 'I'm trying to get to know the town,' he said.

His first camp in Sicily was called Pala Nebiolo, an emergency camp. Following that, he was transferred to Gasparro. He was really clued up for his age and told me he had tried to find out about the reception system and what camps there were for minors. He believed that the best place he could be transferred to was a camp in Calabria where he had been informed he would be able to go to school and would receive €20 every eight days. But he had no idea whether he would be sent there.

Antonio Mazzeo said of the reception system: 'In Messina – as at the Cara in Mineo, the CIE[30] in Trapani and the camps for migrants and asylum-seekers throughout Italy – the rights and duties of the reception system are ignored, denied and violated. In some situations it is also an opportunity for profiteering by those usual suspects, the pseudo co-operatives, businesses, fronts and non-profits, out to make a profit, who exercise a smug monopoly over the management of emergency disembarkings, artificial creations of Fortress Europe, of the military-industrial complex, translational securitization and xenophobic, racist opinion leaders.

'After the publication by the Prefecture of Messina of its expenses data for 2013-14, it is now a proven fact that the "unwelcoming" in the city of the Straits has been billed for millions by a handful of privileged businessmen engaged in "solidarity". From the first arrivals in the safe port of Messina in October 2013 down to 31 December 2014, the prefecture has handed over more than €3.2 million ($3.7 million) for refugee management.'[31] It is entirely evident that it is not the asylum-seekers who have benefited from the funding.

A few days later Modou, who was still housed in the Gasparro camp, told me that he received credits worth four euros, which he spent on food shopping in a supermarket. There is not much you can buy with four euros: a packet of biscuits and a loaf of bread. He also talked to his mother on the phone. Being the only son, he was very close to her and often said 'I miss my mother very much.' His father had died in 2014 and every now and then he dreamed about him, waking up every time. There was so much sadness in his face and eyes when he talked about his parents.

He said he'd like to see London one day. 'What is it like?'

'It's quite a multicultural place,' I answered.

'What does that mean?' he asked. When I explained, he said: 'I like that.'

Modou also told me he liked the idea of living in Sicily. He was eager to be part of society. 'I want to be in the Italian football team some day.'

One day, Modou and his housemates decided to report the poor standard of food in the camp to the *carabinieri*. They were given pasta without any sauce, for lunch and dinner every day. It made him angry to be treated in this way. The next day, the camp made immediate improvements: the quality of the food was much better now.

'That's brilliant,' I said. 'Your collective effort worked!'

'Yes! And the camp manager came to ask us to forgive him. Because he didn't want us to be transferred to another camp and lose him the business.'

Inside the Gasparro camp, several teenagers had already requested a transfer as they were so angry with the intolerable conditions and treatment – particularly with the below-standard diet and the lack of pocket money each minor was entitled to, as allocated by the state. Some refused to eat breakfast, demanding to be transferred as soon as possible.

The following day, we were at the harbour when a rescue boat arrived. It was carrying 260 migrants, mostly men, from Gambia, Nigeria and other countries. They had just been picked up by the Malta-based charity Migrant Offshore Aid Station (MOAS), which deployed two rescue boats in the area. The men were barefooted, looking overwhelmed and confused. Several Red Cross staff were giving out red blankets and slippers to them. They were standing in long queues, waiting to go into the Red Cross tents to be processed by the staff.

Two of the rescued men came over to us at the fence; they looked cold, despite the blankets wrapped around them, but they smiled shyly at us and one of them asked for a cigarette. He introduced himself as Abdoulaye, and asked for my name and phone number. 'We don't know anyone here, we don't know anyone,' he repeated. 'Can we call you?'

We must have been the first people they had seen in Italy, apart from the officials inside the fence. The Red Cross staff asked them to return to the queue and they waved goodbye, saying they would call.

The migrants were split into two queues – those who had been processed were directed towards the large coaches which would take them to various camps in Messina. I saw Abdoulaye and his friend waving at us enthusiastically from inside the coach. Across the fence I wished them all the best, wondering where they would end up. What would their lives turn out like?

More than 340 migrants drowned that week in the Mediterranean Sea, according to Médecins Sans Frontières (MSF). A survivor from one of the boats said that around 130 people had been packed into a rubber dinghy and set sail from near Tripoli. A few hours later, the armed smugglers who were on another boat took away their engine and lifejackets. After two-and-a-half days at sea the boat sank and around 100 people were drowned. Only six bodies were found.

In the past, smugglers had generally used repurposed commercial vessels fitted with satellite phones and GPS, or large fishing boats, to transport migrants across the sea to Europe. But to evade detection by the European Union's Operation Sophia, smugglers have resorted to using smaller boats unfit for the journey. It seemed clear that Europe's anti-smuggling missions have not only been unable to stop the crossings, but in effect have also made it much more dangerous for migrants who try to cross the Mediterranean.

A plaintive letter

I was about to leave Sicily behind me and take the ferry to the Italian mainland. I couldn't help thinking about the people I'd met and said farewell to, and what might be happening to them.

Banta told me that he had got a job for five days, picking vegetables on a farm. Every day, he worked from 8am to 7pm, with one hour for lunch. He wanted to make some money because he would be leaving the camp at the end of November, as new people were moving in, and he would at last continue his journey. He believed that his departure would mark the end of the problems he had suffered over the past three years.

I received a message from Amat Jawneh, the Gambian man I had met in Corleone. He said he was very unhappy, so I gave him a call. He told me that they had not been given any water, including drinking water, for two days. There was no heating and no adequate clothing had been provided by the camp. Amat had to spend the €25 that he received every ten days on buying cheap clothing from a shop in town. It sounded like he was near breaking point.

Amat didn't want to run away, like many others do, because he was expecting to receive his documents in February. Then he would be free. He was planning to travel to Finland where there are well-established Gambian communities. He knew little about Finland, but seemed certain that things would work out well for him there. I advised him to start making inquiries about living in Finland, if that's where he wanted to go, and to prepare for his new life after February.

Amat said he had worked for a day on a farm planting trees, for €20. There was very little work available in the winter and he felt the pressure as his parents kept asking him when he would get his documents and be able to start working. They needed his support.

Alaji, the 17-year-old Gambian boy housed at the Casa Marconi in Palermo, told me that conditions there were just the same. 'No jacket, no shoes. The food is very bad here. They're eating our tiny amount of money. They don't want to help us.'

'Have you reported it to the *carabinieri*?' I asked, based on the experience of those migrants we had met who had successfully changed their conditions by reporting them.

'The police will not take any measures. They came to our camp and didn't do anything.'

He wished for a transfer, but as he had heard that camps in Palermo were better than some others, he feared getting transferred to a village.

Alaji was communicating and exchanging experiences with other migrants in a variety of camps in the region. He sent me a letter written jointly by migrants from all backgrounds, in Palermo, titled 'Isolated, Cold and Waiting: Letter from Invisible Migrants' ('Isolati, al freddo e in attesa: lettera dei migranti invisibili').

> To the Prefecture, the Questore and all Italian citizens. We are migrants living in some of the CAS (Extraordinary Reception Centres) in the Province of Palermo. We come from many countries – Gambia, Mali, Nigeria, Côte d'Ivoire, Senegal, Guinea Conakry, Sierra Leone, Bangladesh – but today we speak with one voice. We thank Italy for having taken us in after the long journey we had to make, but today we are writing this letter together so as to tell you about our difficult situation. We left our countries fleeing from suffering, but in this country we have found it yet again, even if it is another kind of suffering: there is some kind of perverse reasoning beneath all of this. We live in these CAS, frequently in totally isolated places, faced with many, too many problems. Many of us have been in these centres for more than seven months, while we know that in truth we are not meant to remain in 'extraordinary' reception centres for so long. We ask to be listened to.
>
> The time we have waited for our documents is seemingly endless. In this period, we do not know what awaits us, and we are perplexed about our situation. Frequently not even the date for the first appointment in the Questura,[32] so as to give our fingerprints and request asylum, has been set.

Indeed, many people have not even been told what asylum is: that you may have been persecuted for political or religious reasons, or for being gay, and that each case will be treated with appropriate attention. The incredibly slow pace of receiving documents leaves us extremely worried and unclear about our future. We simply want to know the truth, and for someone to tell us what's going on, instead of avoiding us and always telling us to wait till tomorrow.

What can you do, waiting in a centre for a year and three months, without documents nor information, if you don't have work, and if, when you are sick, there's no appropriate care? If, when you ask for something you really need, you are simply told to get out of here, if you do not like where you are? We are asylum-seekers: where are we meant to go? A reception centre should welcome and help people. What's the point in it otherwise? In some cases we have even been threatened that if we complain, we will not receive any documents. If you ask for information, they ignore you and drive you out, even physically. You come here to find freedom, and instead your head is filled with stress through frankly impossible living conditions. In our countries we had many problems, but at least we knew how to confront them. Here, it's the not knowing which is so terrible.

During the waiting period, the living conditions are degrading for a human being. In one of the CAS the water is switched on only twice a day, for one hour each time, and it is always cold. If we need water at other times of day, we have to take it from the cistern, where the water is putrid and stinks, and is not good enough even for animals... and we are human beings. Another problem is food: we only ask that we are given the possibility of cooking for ourselves. In another centre, they do not give us appropriate clothes, and many of us arrived here directly from the port of Palermo, with literally nothing. The clothes we have were given to us by other brothers who were in the camp before us. But it is almost November now, and it is cold up here in the mountains, and many of us are still in flip-flops. In another centre still, when the police came to check the building, we told them how cold it is, that we sleep with all our clothes on, that there's no heating. The response was that we don't have heating in Africa. Who can you turn to, to flag up this kind of injustice?

From May till now, there was no Italian school in the camps; lessons have begun only in the last few days. The very few of us who speak Italian learnt it in camps for minors – but there, however, the first appointment with the Questura was never made. Whoever is brought to the CAS from the centres for minors does not understand why the assistance which was given to them before, when they were considered under age, turns into total abandonment as soon as they turn 18. Whoever is brought here directly from the port thinks that Sicily is made up only of forests – that's how isolated these centres are. And the only Italians they will have seen are the camp's workers. We are invisible. We want to do so many things, we are young and want to continue to live our lives, not waste our lives away waiting here.

Therefore today, all together, we ask: for our documents, and that the procedure for requesting asylum be speeded up – we cannot wait 11 months for the first appointment in the Questura; we ask that our human rights are respected – we do not ask much, only to be treated as human beings in the camps, to be listened to, and to be ensured the services to which we are entitled; we ask for the most isolated to be transferred to camps which can guarantee the above, including better living conditions.

Migrants in the CAS in the Province of Palermo

Naples

After three hours on the ferry, Dave and I arrived at Naples, a vibrant and at times chaotic metropolis with a population of three million. It is a place where the reality of urban living is fiercely present the entire time. The first sign of this vibrancy welcomed us right outside the train station, where drivers and hustlers of all types approached us, soliciting and demanding our attention. The hotel was situated in the middle of Via Domenico Capitelli, a tiny street lined with ice-cream parlours, popular *baba* stores (*baba* is a yeast cake saturated in syrup made with hard liquor, usually rum, and sometimes filled with whipped cream or pastry cream), and shops of all kinds. Across the balcony, a dentist waved at me from the apartment opposite, asking if we wanted any dental work. The street led straight to the Piazza Del Jesu Nuovo of the old town where fights break out at times and police vans are constantly parked nearby.

Italy was in the run-up to a referendum to change the electoral system and I took the opportunity to talk to our hotel staff worker, Giuseppe, about it. He was a university student in political science, and had to work in the hotel trade while studying. He believed that many of those intending to vote 'No' in the referendum (and thus oppose the reforms proposed by the then prime minister, Matteo Renzi) were discontented youth and workers. He said the problem of youth unemployment was very serious in Naples and worse than in the rest of the country (currently, unemployment in Italy is 11-12 per cent nationally; youth unemployment is 37 per cent nationally). Many young people here, including university graduates, have moved or are moving to the north of the country or migrating to Germany and other countries to work. Net migration from the south to the north of Italy between 2001 and 2013 was more than 700,000 people, 70 per cent of whom were aged between 15 and 34; more than a quarter were graduates.

Giuseppe himself knew many young people who had migrated abroad from Naples. This became much more of a trend after 2009 when the Eurozone debt crisis hit, affecting southern European economies particularly hard and pushing a generation of young southern Europeans, including Italians, to move to wealthier northern Europe seeking work. Around 400,000 tax-paying migrants from Greece, Italy, Spain and Portugal are currently working in Germany, often prepared to take up the lower-paid jobs that few Germans want to do. This recent migration has helped change the face of society in Germany: one in ten, or around 8.2 million people, are non-German. Many of these young Italians do not return to work in Italy, according to Giuseppe. This is the case particularly in the south, where poverty is visible.

'The south sees itself as separate from Italy,' he said, 'People from Naples see themselves as Neapolitans first. They don't see themselves as benefiting from the EU and EU money.'

The regional divide between north and south is chronic in Italy.

As *The Economist* commented, the country is in effect made up of two economies. CityMetric reported that the GDP per person is over 40 per cent lower in the Mezzogiorno region – the eight southern regions, including Sicily and Sardinia – than it is in the northern and central regions of Italy. Milan, for instance, is twice as wealthy as Naples. CityMetric compares this disparity between regions to the economies of Britain and South Korea.

The Mezzogiorno has suffered sustained contraction for years. Of the 943,000 Italians who became jobless between 2007 and 2014, 70 per cent were from the south. While the workforce nationally contracted by four per cent during that period, the rate in the south was 10.7 per cent. The situation is worsened by the lower birth rate in the south and the northward migration to both northern Italy and other European countries. According to Istat, the National Institute for Statistics in Italy, over the next 50 years, the south could lose 4.2 million of its residents, in other words, a fifth of its population, to the north or abroad. As a result, businesses here are finding it more difficult to find young people with the skills to do jobs – for instance, there's now a shortage of engineers.

The lack of investment in infrastructure here is part of the problem. It contributes to the stagnation and poverty that feed the existence of criminal networks.

African migrants in the market-lined streets of Naples.

We moved to accommodation near the train station at the weekend. It was a world away from the old town area: streets were littered with refuse, and commercial rubbish bins were a major sight in this part of town (collection of the city's refuse was a major business, outsourced to the local Mafia by the local authorities). From our balcony, I could see middle-aged women soliciting and selling sex right outside our door. Drug sales were such a part of the scene that walking through some parks it was hard to avoid stepping on syringes left on the ground the previous night.

The poorest area around the station has attracted migrants for decades due to the low cost of rent. The migrants live and work alongside local residents. Italy, due to its emigration, an ageing population and a shrinking workforce, began to draw migration from around the world during the 1980s. Since the fall of the Berlin Wall in 1989 in particular, and with the EU enlargements in the 2000s, an increasing number of people migrated from Eastern and Southeastern Europe, including Romania, Albania, Ukraine and Poland. The other direction of migration has come from North Africa, including Morocco, Egypt and Tunisia, and numbers have increased since the Arab Spring. Asylum-seeking migrants from Italy's former colonies – Eritrea, Libya, Somalia – have recently added to the growing diversity of the population. Today, there are around five million foreign-born residents in the country, about nine per cent of Italy's population.[33]

In Naples, the foreign-born population is not as high as in northern cities. The distribution of immigrant communities is as uneven as the distribution of the country's wealth by regions – and very much a reflection of that unevenness. Nearly 85 per cent of immigrants live in the northern and central parts of Italy, while only just over 15 per cent live in the southern half of the country. In Naples, there were only about 20,000 foreign-born residents in the late 2000s, most of them from Ukraine, Poland and the Balkans. There is a small but visible Chinese community there, with Chinese-language billboards outside small trading firms and family businesses along the streets. Alongside them are the Tunisian and Moroccan communities with cheap diners and canteens serving tagine and couscous.

A migrant at work selling merchandise on the street in Naples.

Leading to the station is a long street nicknamed 'African Street' by migrants. It is filled with African stores selling mobile phones, clothes, handbags and all sorts. African men and women, some just passing through the city while others are living in asylum shelters, were standing on street corners chatting. Naples seemed to calm down and relax a little here.

A young man was sitting on a railing, looking up and down the street. He was wearing headphones and was talking on his mobile phone. His dark hair was spiky, he was wearing a T-shirt and a pair of distressed jeans, which made him look like the Italian stereotype of a 'black guy' – the image of an Afro-American rapper.

His name was Abdul, 21 years old and from Nigeria. I invited him for a cold drink and a chat. We sat in a café next to the street corner where he always hung out and, as we talked, he pointed above the café, and told me that the area upstairs was an asylum shelter where his friend lived. It used to be a hotel building, a typical gloomy budget hotel next to a station, and as it was not making money, the owner turned it into a camp for asylum-seekers. Downstairs, a café; upstairs, a camp for migrants. The latter was probably much more profitable for the owner. Abdul said the shelter was notorious for its poor conditions, which made it pretty standard for Italy's asylum reception system.

For the past two months Abdul had been living in a camp

that used to be the Mango Hotel. This had been his first shelter in Italy, located in a district called Qualiano, half an hour from central Naples. At the time of our meeting, it housed more than 100 migrants from Nigeria, Gambia, Bangladesh and other countries. The facilities were not sufficient and there was little to do in the camp, except learn Italian for one hour per day. Living so far from the urban centre, Abdul often felt isolated and lonely. He came to central Naples once a week, just to be amongst people. He would come and sit around on this street corner, next to the shelter where his only friend was. He would simply watch pedestrians walking past, and let the sun shine on his face. 'The African Street is my favourite place in the centre of Naples. It feels like Africa,' he said.

But Abdul never got into a conversation with anyone there, even though he had been coming to that street every week. He told me he was an orphan. He was a loner who had not got out of the habit of thinking alone. His past had failed him and his future remained uncertain. He remembered what his father used to tell him: don't trust anyone. And he took those words to heart. He became a Christian; even in the camp, he continued to go to church service regularly. 'God is my only real friend,' he said, 'I only depend on God.' But, as he spoke of his loyalty to God, his belief in his destiny and his solitude, his voice revealed a lot of sorrow, which hardened into anger. It seemed as if the toughness of living in Naples had hardened many of the newcomers to the metropolis: they had to learn to cope with the difficulties particular to this place or it would break them.

Messages from Sicily

Modou, the 17-year-old Gambian boy, wrote to me from Messina: 'I want a transfer more than anyone.' In addition to the lack of pocket money at Gasparro, he was also unhappy with the lack of facilities there. No activities were organized for the teenagers. He loved football, but the camp staff did not allow sports. 'This is another reason why I need to go,' he said. Despite everything, though, he had not joined the others in their breakfast 'hunger strike' to push for the transfer. It seemed a step too far for him.

In the morning, in central Naples, we walked into a large student demonstration that argued for a 'No' vote in the referendum on 4 December. The majority of the demonstrators were from the trades unions, colleges and universities in the south. There was a clear sense of frustration and resentment against the north-south divide. Italy was bearing a debt burden of similar levels to that of Greece in 2009; the south bears the brunt of the country's slow economic growth. These young demonstrators were concerned about their job opportunities, their livelihood and future. They were determined that the austerity policies of the EU should not continue to restrict their lives; a 'Yes' vote would confirm the existing centre-left government, which would mean the continuation of austerity policies.

However, a large section of the 'No' voters came from the political right. For instance, the Northern League held demonstrations across the country, such as in Florence in early November 2016, in which their beliefs and demands – their opposition to immigration, a demand for lower taxes, a suspicion of supra-national bodies such as the EU – were expressed by highlighting the electoral victory of Trump and claiming alliance with his policies.

From Palermo, Banta told me that he was getting ready to leave the camp and Sicily behind. His three years of living on the island had not paved the way for a future there. His isolation and experience of entrapment in the asylum reception system had compelled him to think beyond this country and move on somewhere else. But exactly where? And what future was he moving towards? At this point he still did not have a clear idea. Perhaps the transient nature of his life as a refugee in Italy would continue as he crossed borders to other EU countries to seek betterment. In any case, he was looking forward to the change. He told me he had that day bought new winter clothes for the journey.

4

Northbound

Never did I expect to witness the limbo of migrants' lives at and around the Colosseum, the large ancient amphitheatre, situated in the centre of Rome and a magnet for tourism. This is an extreme image of parallel societies: tourists, mostly from Europe and the developed world who can afford travel, alongside impoverished migrants seeking a living on the edge of society. These parallel societies can be witnessed all over Europe today.

Groups of migrants from Africa can be seen in tourist areas like this all over Rome, trying somehow to make a living; the majority are in the asylum-seeking process, awaiting interviews or documents. Some have run away from the hardship inside the camps and fallen completely outside the system.

In the midday heat, a young man was standing at the side of the footpath leading up to the Roman Forum, holding wooden bowls in his hand. Sweat was running down his forehead. He paced up and down, approaching most tourists, trying to sell the handicrafts for €35 ($41) each. He introduced himself as Ousman, a 29-year-old from Senegal. He said the bowls came all the way from his home country, via one of his contacts in Rome. The Senegalese migrants at the Colosseum all seemed to be selling the same handicrafts. Although it was a nice piece of carved woodwork, it was probably too much for an ordinary tourist to commit to, and few people even stopped to take a look. His daily sale was usually only about two of those wooden bowls.

Ousman told me he left Senegal in 2013 and travelled through Mali, Burkina Faso and Niger, to reach Libya. There, he stayed for eight months, earning next to nothing. The hardship finally pushed him to get on a boat, along with 65 other Senegalese and Gambian migrants, heading for Italy. It was a small boat, he said, with a maximum capacity of 60 people. They were provided with only 20 litres of water to survive on. Fortunately, they were rescued by

Italian coastguards, and in the following three days on the rescue boat, they were given food, water and medical care until they reached Taranto, a coastal city and a main naval base in the south of mainland Italy. They had reached land on 16 June 2013, a date he would never forget. He was kept in Taranto for seven months, and was transferred to Rome afterwards.

Ousman had been living in Rome for over a year now. When he first arrived, he was placed in an overcrowded shelter that accommodated many from Senegal, Nigeria, Mali and other countries. He shared a room with four others. The only good thing for him, he said, was that he was given Italian lessons from the second day after his arrival.

His first few days in the capital city were daunting. He felt alone, and consciously looked out for another African face on the streets so he could talk to someone familiar. From the very beginning, he was looking for work opportunities. He gave his phone number to strangers on the streets, asking for any kind of work, because the allocated €45 per month simply wasn't sufficient for living in this city. However, he was not permitted to work without documents and these entailed a long wait. Without any means of supporting himself, he decided to work on the quiet, selling wooden bowls to tourists.

Then he met someone from his home country who had formal immigration status here. The man had a spare bed in a room shared by two in his apartment on the outskirts in the southern part of the city. Ousman decided to move in and, since then, he had been living independently with fellow migrants. The only downside was the 30-minute commute to and from the apartment to work on the streets in the centre of Rome.

Despite the little English he spoke, I understood that he was very grateful for having been rescued by Italian coastguards, and to Italy which had changed his life. A year on, he had become accustomed to the 'Italian way' and grown to like it in Rome. Unlike many other migrants, he had no intention of moving on from Italy, feeling no need to seek higher earnings or the perceived higher standard of living in the wealthier Scandinavian countries or Germany, nor did he consider going to Switzerland or France, as many other

Senegalese did. He just wanted to be here in Italy; it was clear how much he wished to be part of society, to interact freely with local Italians, and not merely through selling handicrafts on the street. Above all, he wished to make a living with pride and dignity.

Meeting Abraham

The area around the central station was where many migrants found a place to sleep when they arrived or when they were just passing through from Sicily on their way north. At the square in front of Termini, Rome's central station, dozens of migrants spent the night sleeping on newspapers. Several Tunisians in their twenties told me they had been sleeping there for over two months. They looked utterly exhausted. In the daytime they would walk around the city, hoping to be lucky enough to find some casual work.

About an hour's walk from the central station, on Via Cupa, was a temporary voluntary emergency shelter. It was run by Baobab, a community group that worked to provide services for migrants. This shelter was raided by the police in the winter of 2015 and was closed down until summer 2016. It was located in a reasonably affluent neighbourhood where there were many trendy bars, theme pubs and bistro restaurants. Around a corner, I walked all the way to the end of a residential street where I saw many tents set up to provide somewhere safe for the migrants to sleep. Several community workers were at a shop, giving advice to people.

The majority of migrants there were Eritrean, most of whom did not speak much English. One of them said he had been in this shelter for three months, which surprised me, as I thought this was a temporary place of transit. A young Tunisian man interrupted and said he could help with interpreting but I realized he was not really able to understand my conversation with others, although he remained keen. Finally, an Eritrean man approached to offer help. He spoke good English and had literally just arrived in the shelter. He was 21 years old, and his name was Abraham.

Abraham was a student in Eritrea. His father had put money together for him to travel out of the country, which was becoming increasingly unsafe. 'There's no democracy and no future there,' he said.

In Eritrea, human rights violations and oppression under the authoritarian regime of Isaias Afwerki had become everyday experiences, to such an extent that the country began to be described as Africa's North Korea. There had been no elections since 1993; the 1997 constitution was never implemented; the national assembly had not met since 2002. Citizens were being deprived of their basic civil right to assemble or organize. There was no independent judiciary system, and persecution of all forms, including torture, forced labour and disappearances, was common. The situation had been reported by the UN commission of inquiry as crimes against humanity; the report concluded that Eritreans endured 'systematic widespread and gross human rights violations' and 'a total lack of the rule of law'. This was why 5,000 Eritreans were attempting to flee across the Sahel every month. This was the background to the exodus of Eritreans seeking refuge across borders to Europe. The UN commission also urged countries in Europe to offer protection to Eritrean asylum-seekers.

In the past few years, the number of people fleeing from the tyranny in Eritrea has grown steadily. In 2014, it was reported that almost as many people were fleeing from Eritrea as were from the war in Syria.

Abraham's sister lived in England; he had a brother in Switzerland. No one wanted to stay in Eritrea. On 20 August 2015, his father paid €1,500 ($1,750) to get him from Eritrea to Ethiopia, and another €1,500 for him to travel from Ethiopia to Sudan. Another €1,500 was spent on transporting him from Sudan to Libya. Like everyone else, Abraham had gone through hell on earth in Libya. During his five months there, one month was spent in prison, though this was simply the random punishment of a private company meted out to employees who dared to ask for wages. Abraham's father had to pay a further €2,000 to a smuggler to get him out of Libya: this time, onto a boat for Sicily.

Abraham surprised me with his good memory – no one remembered all their dates of departure and arrivals as well as he did. 'I arrived in Trapani, in Sicily, on 31 August 2016, where I was finger-printed,' he said. The camp there was overcrowded and had poor facilities. 'I ran away, to Catania, and then Milan. And then Como.'

I looked at this exhausted, fragile boy, and couldn't believe he had been on the move constantly.

'And then I crossed the border from Como to Switzerland, and then to France. Finally, I arrived in Nice. I felt relieved to have arrived in France. But it was there in Nice that I got caught. They sent me straight back to Italy, to Taranto.'

Abraham didn't give up. He ran away again and took a bus to Rome. When I met him, he had not yet secured a place in a tent and still had to talk to the volunteers on site.

Abraham's plan was to reach France and, ideally, to get to Britain. Alternatively, he wanted to get to Germany, where he said the housing is much better and the state support much more generous. All the migrants arriving at this shelter in Via Cupa had already been fingerprinted, but few seemed to want to stay in Italy.

While we were talking, I saw more and more people forming a queue for dinner. It was 7pm. I decided to come back another time.

When I returned a day later, the area was surrounded and cordoned off by the police. No one was allowed in. When I asked why, a police officer said: 'There's a demonstration taking place inside.' It turned out to be a lie. A councillor, Gianluca Bogino, who was present when the police surrounded the shelter, told me that it was raided and closed down by the police for reasons of 'security' and 'public order'. All the migrants, over 200 of them, were taken to the police station for ID checks and various procedures. What would happen to them next was unknown, he said. I immediately thought of Abraham and wondered whether he was being detained by the police. The councillor told me that some migrants had fled from the shelter when the police raided. Maybe Abraham had been among them?

A few hours later in the evening, Abraham called. He was in Milan! I couldn't believe it. He told me that he had left Via Cupa on Friday morning, just before the police raided at 8am. It almost seemed as if he had had a tip-off but, of course, it was pure luck.

Abraham had gone to Milan as part of his plan to try to get to France again. This was his second attempt and his final aim was still to reach Britain. When he called, he was staying in a shelter with friends in Milan and they were planning the next part of this endless journey.

Many like him have ended up in Ventimiglia, attempting to cross the 5.6 kilometres of mountain passes and tunnels between this border town in Italy to Menton in southern France. This frontier is known as the 'Mini Calais' where migrants gather to wait for the opportunity to cross the border. There is a heavy police presence on both sides of the border; arrest is a constant threat. Over 90 per cent of those arrested are returned to Italy, according to the local police department in the Alpes-Maritimes region of France. Meanwhile life has been made harder for the migrants as the local authorities in Ventimiglia have stepped up measures to prevent informal migrant settlements near the border. In 2015, the mayor, Enrico Ioculano, issued an order forbidding the distribution of food and drinks to migrants, an offence punishable by a fine of around €200 and a three-month prison sentence.

A few weeks later, Abraham reached France and was staying with his friends on the outskirts of Paris. After that, I was not able to reach him on the phone, but in March 2017 he called me from a French mobile phone. He told me he had given up on his plan to go to Britain and had claimed asylum in France. He had been living in a camp in Vierzon, south of Paris, for two months, and was still waiting for his documents.

In Italy, there were no housing options, except through charities, for migrants attempting to transit through the country towards northern European countries. Via Cupa had housed an estimated 60,000 migrants between 2015 and 2016 and the Baobab centre had strongly criticized the city council for failing to provide any form of housing for migrants travelling through Rome. Since the raid, volunteers were once again searching for alternative spaces where dispersed and displaced people could be housed. The reliance on non-state actors for accommodating refugees and asylum-seekers is nothing more than a stopgap and is clearly unsustainable as a solution. A Médecins Sans Frontières (MSF) research report, *Out of Sight,*[34] in March 2016 found that more than 10,000 refugees and asylum-seekers were living in abandoned spaces, handmade shacks or camping tents throughout the country. That number was an improvement on 2015, during which nearly 154,000 people arrived in Italy, while fewer than 97,000 beds were provided. The report also stated that just a third of documented refugees living in such places have regular access to services they are entitled to, such as healthcare.

Not far from the central station area, on Via Curtatone, was a block of 1970s-style buildings that used to be government offices and now housed more than 1,000 migrants. The majority were Eritreans, followed by Ethiopians and other nationalities. The sign hanging outside the buildings said, 'We are refugees, not terrorists', which revealed something about the local hostility and migrants' response to it. Clearly the centre had attracted a lot of unwanted attention from the authorities and the media. This was why the manager refused to talk to me. He simply said: 'It's an independent structure; we cannot talk to anyone.'

When I saw a man leaving the building, I approached him and tried to talk. His name was Abubaker, from Sudan. He told me confidently: 'Government housing is very poor, overcrowded; we have to share a room with three to four people. And the €45 allocated to us per month is not enough to live on. That's why we choose to squat here... I have my own room here. They tried to evict us a few times, but we insist on staying.'

The sign outside the migrant shelter in Rome translates as: 'We are refugees not terrorists'.

Abubaker had been living in Italy for five years, but he had never had a job.[35] It was not permitted. He had relied on support from friends but, to survive, he would have to ignore the rules and try to find illegal work.

In response to a parliamentary inquiry on the occupied building in Via Curtatone, the Interior Minister declared on 3 December 2015 that there were 103 ongoing 'illegal' occupations in Rome. Of these, at least three – in the buildings in Via Cavaglieri ('Palazzo Selam'), Via Collatina and Via Curtatone – host mainly Eritrean refugees, numbering over 2,500 people in total, including women and minors. Palazzo Selam, a block of three glass towers situated in the suburbs of Rome, is the largest, and has housed over 1,000 East Africans for more than ten years.

MSF is asking national and local authorities to guarantee migrants, asylum-seekers and refugees who live in these informal settlements dignified living conditions and basic rights, in particular the right to healthcare.

Meanwhile in Britain and France...

In June 2016, it was discovered that hundreds of asylum applications from Eritreans were being incorrectly refused by the British government owing to its mistaken policy on accepting refugees from the country. In March 2015, when Theresa May was Home Secretary, Eritrea's country advice was changed to 'citizens who left Eritrea without permission would not face persecution if they returned.' This resulted in a sharp decrease in the number of Eritreans granted asylum in the UK, from an approval rate of 73 per cent in the first quarter of 2015 to 34 per cent in the second quarter.[36] However, the majority of these rejections were being overturned on appeal. In the first quarter of 2016, 86 per cent of all appeals from Eritrean nationals were granted. This clearly meant the asylum decisions were based on a falsehood in the first place. Britain's home affairs select committee called on the Home Office to explain why it had still not updated its guidance on asylum-seekers from Eritrea, even though it has acknowledged the guidance to be wrong.

In October 2016, a legal ruling found that the majority of

Eritreans fleeing the country risked persecution or serious harm on returning.

Refugee Youth Service reported at the end of November 2016 that, since the Calais camp had closed down, nearly a third of the 179 asylum-seeking children being tracked by the charity had gone missing from reception centres and camps. The Refugee Youth Service was a project that offered support to those aged 12 to 18 living in the Grande Synthe camp in Dunkirk (and minors who were living in the Calais camp before the closure). These teenagers had arrived unaccompanied, and were living amongst adults in the camp, where they were unable to access safe services and facilities as such infrastructure was not the concern of the camp's management AFEJI,[37] which had done nothing to identify the unaccompanied minors, let alone ensure their protection inside the camp. Refugee Youth Service was therefore providing an open space where the child migrants were able to connect with others of the same age and were given shelter, clothing and protection.

According to the charity, the lack of information and knowledge about their destiny led to the minors' disappearances. They called on the British and French governments to provide them with clear information. They also asked the authorities to report children as missing when they disappeared from reception centres.

'Emergency camp' in Bologna

Bologna was a complete change of scene from Naples. The contrast between the two is the embodiment of the north-south divide. Bologna is the largest city of the Emilia-Romagna Region in northern Italy, an important transport hub, and one of the country's wealthiest cities: in 2011, it ranked first out of 107 Italian cities for 'quality of life'. It's a city of trendy cafés, sushi bars, porcelain shops and designer garment stores. Besides its wealth, it is also known for the massacre of 2 August 1980, a brutal terrorist bombing of the central station. This was the work of the neo-fascist organization Nuclei Armati Rivoluzionari in defiance of the city's affluence and liberal culture; 85 people were killed.

What had brought me here was a message on WhatsApp from Abdoulaye, the Gambian man I had met at the port of Messina when he had just got off the rescue boat. He told me he had been sent to an emergency camp in Bologna and had not been able contact me until now, when he met an 18-year-old boy called Mustafa from his hometown and borrowed his mobile phone. Abdoulaye asked if we could meet again.

His camp was on Via Enrico Mattei, about five kilometres (or half an hour's bus trip) from central Bologna. It was a cold, windy day at the end of November when we visited this isolated location on the main road, where there is little trace of Bologna. There were already 1,000 migrants living in the camp, although the management was still trying to house more; two busloads of people arrived that day and Abdoulaye and his friend Mustafa were moved to a tent, with no shower anywhere near them. The newly arrived people were put in Abdoulaye's previous accommodation – 12 to a room, with only one bathroom. Hardly anyone was able to sleep.

When the front gate opened to let in a car, Dave and I walked in, expecting to be stopped. It looked like a busy day for the camp, with dozens of new people queuing in the front yard waiting to be fingerprinted. No staff noticed our presence. When we found Abdoulaye I could see how distressed he was. He had no smile on his face and looked anxious, but he couldn't find the English words to describe how he felt. He brought with him his friend Mustafa, who could speak English and was willing to help with interpreting. Mustafa looked a lot younger than 18 years of age, and had a childlike smile all the time – he could easily have been taken for a 15-year-old.

We decided to find a place where we could have a proper talk and, looking excited about our meeting, Mustafa put on his white woollen hat and a jacket. Out on the main road we found a local café a good ten-minute walk away. I could see Abdoulaye was keen to tell me all about the camp and his new life here and as soon as we all sat down with a warm cup of coffee he poured out the frustration and anger of the past few weeks. It had been a terrible shock to arrive in this well-fenced, prison-like compound in the middle of nowhere, far from the local community. 'I don't like Italy,' he said, with complete certainty. But the camp was the only Italy he had ever seen; he had never had an opportunity to experience the country or to get to know its people.

I took out the camera and showed him photos of the two medieval leaning towers, a symbol of the city, as well as the cathedral and simple street scenes in the centre of Bologna. He was pleasantly surprised and looked at the pictures for a few minutes.

But the realization that there was normality beyond the camp highlighted the injustice of the misery he had been living through. He spoke urgently: 'The camp is very, very bad. The place is overcrowded and dirty. No lounge, no TV, no facilities for sports or anything else. And the food's bad.'

I led them to the canteen inside the café and asked them to choose any lunch they liked. They both ordered the simple dish, chicken breast and potatoes. Mustafa didn't want any vegetables, just like a kid. 'Spinach is like medicine,' he said to me, frowning. But he loved the white bread – something that he had never seen in the camps.

Abdoulaye buried his head in his hands when talking about the past. 'Ah, I suffered a lot in my life... A lot.' He was a soldier in Gambia and, with Mustafa interpreting for us, he continued: 'I witnessed a lot of horrific crimes done by our leaders... People disappeared and got murdered. It was real hell.' Yahya Jammeh was a young army officer who rose to power in 1994 following a military coup. Eventually elected president, and subsequently re-elected three times, he created a brutal regime that lasted 22 years. Jammeh could tolerate no opposition. He suppressed basic civil rights, and ordered the killing of 12 students and a journalist on a demonstration in April 2000. Disappearances and indefinite detention of citizens without trial was commonplace. He banned homosexuality in 2008, saying that he would 'cut the head off' any gay or lesbian person discovered in Gambia, and warned them to leave the country.

Repression in Gambia continued into 2016, until the presidential election. In April 2016, more than 50 people were arrested during a demonstration. That July, an opposition leader and another 18 people were sentenced to three years in prison for taking part in the April demonstration. The opposition politician Solo Sandeng died alongside two others during their detention.

'People were being persecuted all around me and I was fearful that it might happen to me one day. I lived in fear,' said Abdoulaye. 'One day, I was told to go to my superior's office. I didn't know why. But I got a tip-off that my life was in danger. I immediately knew that I had to flee. I went to Senegal, and then Algeria, where I stayed without papers. There, someone advised me to move on to Libya, but the person who transported me made me work really hard in Libya.

'Then I went from employer to employer without pay. Eventually, I worked for someone for three months, and got two months' pay, which I spent on fixing the boat ride to Italy. When I left Libya, I had no idea where I would end up or what I wanted. All I wanted was to run away from Libya.'

Abdoulaye was rescued after only one hour at sea, though his journey from Gambia to Italy took seven months altogether. 'It's too much, too much,' he said, not able to describe the anguish, but simply looking straight at me, with so much pain in his eyes. The past was like a heavy piece of luggage that weighed him down. He had not yet been able to come to terms with it.

Mustafa butted in, wanting to tell his story. His eagerness was undisguised. He had an optimistic outlook on life and always tried to lighten up a conversation, however depressing the subject-matter. His giggle was contagious. Despite the age difference, he and Abdoulaye had become inseparable since they met in the camp. They seemed to complement each other, although Abdoulaye would say that Mustafa was far too young to be a real companion for him.

Mustafa told me he had stayed in a camp for minors in Agrigento, and that he had recently been transferred to Bologna because he was now 18. He left Gambia because his family abandoned him after his father died. His mother remarried but his stepfather did not want him around, so he left the country to try to build a life elsewhere. Like so many others, he ended up in Libya, where he too was jailed and beaten by an employer. A local couple saved him, and got him onto a boat to Italy. He was a minor when he arrived.

As Abdoulaye had never seen an Italian city before, I suggested that we took a walk around Bologna together. They were pleased.

Mustafa ran back to the camp to pick up the thick jacket that staff had recently given to him.

In the centre of the town, the sight of the two crooked 12th-century towers brought a genuine smile to Abdoulaye's face. These were the leaning towers he had seen in the pictures an hour ago and it amused him now to see them right in front of his eyes, located at the intersection of the roads that lead to the five gates in the old circle of defensive walls. Bologna has one of the best preserved and largest historical centres in Italy. Mustafa was delighted to be here; he had not seen these sights before when he had visited Bologna on a bus one day. We walked around posing for the camera and taking snapshots in turns. Abdoulaye noticed that Mustafa was still wearing the tag on his new jacket. 'That's how new it is!' said Mustafa, giggling.

We strolled through the busy shopping streets and laughed bitterly at the unaffordable clothing in the shop windows. Then we went to have coffee and croissants in a café with the cathedral right in front of us. 'Is this really 600 years old?' Mustafa asked. He was amazed to discover that Bologna was such an ancient city. Its first settlement dates back to around 1000 BCE and it was an urban centre under the Etruscans and the Celts, and then the Romans. At one time in the Middle Ages, it was the fifth-largest European city. Founded in 1088, its university is the oldest in the world.

We joked, and it was heartwarming to see that Abdoulaye and Mustafa both laughed a lot – although behind the laughter, there was always the awareness that the fun was only temporary. Abdoulaye fell silent for a moment.

'Are you all right?' I asked.

'I'm just thinking. Just thinking,' he said, squeezing out a smile.

Then, his tone heavy, he told me that he would hate returning to the camp. He became angry when he thought of the treatment there and the absurdity of the system; although he tried to understand it from all points of view and in context, he could only explain it to himself in terms of structural prejudice. 'It's just miserable. The staff ignore what we say most of the time. I think it's because they don't like black people.'

An African man and woman walked past and Mustafa started

talking to them. The man was from Senegal and the woman from Gambia. They had both run away from the camp and, now without documents, were living on the streets. Homelessness and utter poverty, without any means or support networks, are the obvious risks of running away from the asylum reception system. Abdoulaye shook his head, feeling deeply sorry for the couple and saying he would never resort to that.

We walked past several beggars sitting or standing at the corners of streets in the affluent shopping area. Abdoulaye always stopped to greet and talk to them. They were from Gambia and had run away from the camps. He was greatly affected emotionally by their predicament.

By the end of the day, they both marked Bologna ten out of ten. Abdoulaye said it was his happiest day since he had left Gambia. Mustafa said the same. We returned to the camp with them in the evening but the security immediately stopped us and questioned us as we tried to walk through the gate. Sadly, we had to rush our goodbyes to Abdoulaye and Mustafa.

The next day, Mustafa told me that, without any notice, Abdoulaye had been transferred to Cesena, a historic town and quite scenic town 15 kilometres from the Adriatic Sea. The hope was that conditions in the new shelter would be better and Abdoulaye would be happier there. Mustafa remained in the camp in Bologna – and was still there six months after we met, waiting for an asylum interview with the Commission.

Milan and its migrants

Hundreds of migrants took to the streets of Milan on 24 November 2016 to protest against conditions in the camp at Bresso. Ri-Make, one of the groups involved in organizing the protest, said:

> Today for the first time in the history of this city, more than 500 refugees have crossed the centre clamouring for rights and dignity... If there's a reason that enables us to carry on, it is solidarity.
>
> Refugees and activists together, with one voice, say that another way to organize society is possible. Never before

has an event like this taken place in Milan. Never before has a Prefect met with a delegation of asylum-seekers. And if we were able to get to this point, it is certainly time to carry on and gather more strength along the way.

On 17 December 2016, migrants and activists came together again on the International Day of the Rights of Migrants. Ri-Make said of the event:

> The refugees of the 'home centre' in Bresso are again coming out from their camp surrounded by barbed wire to denounce the conditions in which they're forced to live... For months, with one voice, they have asked for their documents in order to stay in Italy, in order to rebuild a life. Just a decent life in this country... The delegation of refugees from Centro di Bresso and the solidarity network People Before Borders was received by the Prefect of Milan, Alessandro Marangoni... We asked the Prefecture to send us a reply by Christmas: with the arrival of winter, life in the camp will be even harder to bear. If there is no response, we will no doubt return to demonstrate in front of the Prefecture until we get concrete solutions! We have one great strength on our side: solidarity. We know that, only if we are united, can we regain our rights, and not leave behind those who are worse off than us.

Our arrival in Milan, just an hour from Bologna, was met with depressing rain. The central station of Milan is a magnificent construction. Designed by French architect Louis-Jules Bouchot and built originally in the 19th century, it was restructured and officially reopened as a new station in 1931, under Mussolini, with little trace of the original style left. The huge steel canopies, soaring marble pillars, gigantic hallways, all reflect the era when a fascist regime wanted to demonstrate its power.

Today, the central station is the city's major gathering point for migrants, mostly from Eritrea, Somalia, Ethiopia and Gambia.

In the daytime, many migrants came from hostels and centres in Milan and the surrounding areas: they were here to meet up and pass the time. One afternoon I met three Gambian boys sitting in the square in front of the station, watching passers-by. The most communicative was called Sirif, a 21-year-old. They were living in a camp in Alessandria, a historical town two hours away by train from Milan (and 90 kilometres from Turin). They travelled to Milan to 'get some fresh air'. Sirif said he went once or twice a week.

Sirif left his home in Gambia because there was no future there. Unemployment was extremely high, averaging 29 per cent in the past few years; the economic instability caused by the political repression had created a lot of fear and insecurity, which compelled many to leave the country. Like most other Gambians who took the same route, Sirif had experienced the violence and toughness of Libya. Had they ever been warned of the risks involved in going to Libya? If so, why had the hardship there not deterred people? Sirif said that most Gambians who ended up in Libya did know of some of the risks – although they might not have been told about the extent of the misery. However, when they weighed up the gains and losses in their minds, many of them decided to take the risk because their circumstances in Gambia were so desperate. 'It couldn't be worse than staying in Gambia'; 'What have you got to lose, as life's so bad in Gambia?' ran the thinking.

Sirif and his friends told me that the first place they had arrived in was a town in Sicily, though they did not even know its name – no one had ever told them. They were then put in a hostel for two days before being shipped to Serravalle Scrivia, a small town with around 6,000 people, where they stayed for five months. After that, they were transferred to a SPRAR shelter in Alessandria and had been there ever since – for a year and a half.

They had no idea or information on why they were waiting and how long it would continue, although Sirif believed that their next destination would be somewhere in the same region. In late November 2016, they were all waiting for their commission interview. In the event of being granted refugee status, they all wanted to stay in Italy and work in Milan. Sirif said he didn't yet know what type of work he wanted to do, but his wish was to continue living there. He was keen on learning Italian.

While they were eager to be granted formal status and lead

a normal life, their isolation in this society was evident and undeniable. When they came to Milan, they would just sit in the station square all day. They did not know anyone, so they would just chat among themselves, or simply watch the world going by. Just being here, even among strangers, made them feel less on their own.

Many migrants came to gather at the station square after 5pm, to pick their place to sleep for the night. They were not allowed to sleep inside the station and I saw many carrying their bedding and clothes with them to occupy any space they could in the square. Some of them looked worn out, having travelled great distances and slept rough along the way. Many of them came to the station square to sleep because they were trapped in Milan on their way north to their final destinations – usually Germany, Switzerland, Sweden or Norway. They had no cash to undertake the next phase of their journey, and yet could not find any work to maintain themselves in Milan; some had run away from the camps and had no official papers.

A young boy aged 18 from Gambia came to talk to me, introducing himself politely as Omar. He said that over the past three months he had occasionally come to sleep the night there because his camp, just ten minutes from the station, was so overcrowded. 'I have to share the space with 80 people... People sleep on bunk beds and mattresses all over the floor. There's no treatment for sick people. They leave me in the same room with people who have a contagious skin disease,' he said. 'I prefer to sleep outside.' Having lived in Italy for four months now (he had been housed on Lampedusa for a while), he saw overcrowding as the biggest problem with asylum housing in Italy.

As a regular at the square, Omar had become acquainted with many migrants there. 'People are sleeping here because they all want to go to Como and they're all waiting for an opportunity to smuggle themselves to Switzerland or Germany, by bus or by train... If they get on a train, they'll hide in the toilet.'

During the summer and autumn of 2016, up to 500 migrants were camping outside the train station in Como and in the parks there, waiting to cross the border to Switzerland. Wealthy tourists, many of whom were on their way to a skiing holiday, were asking questions on TripAdvisor about the 'refugees taking over'. They associated Como with George Clooney and his stunning 19th-century lakeside villa – not with migrants sleeping rough on their way north to seek refuge or betterment of their lives.

The migrants keep trying to move north: every time the border controls become tougher, they find new routes to reach their destinations. When France and Austria imposed stricter border controls with Italy, more and more migrants began coming this way, via Como, always northbound.

As Omar noted, Switzerland too had got much tougher with its borders and had strengthened the patrols around its frontier town of Chiasso. Thousands of migrants had been caught; many who had smuggled themselves across the borders had been sent back to Milan – and back to this square. Some of them had been sent back four or five times now, but they don't give up. They just carry on trying to cross the border.

On this evening, after visiting the homeless migrants at the central station, it was particularly surreal to see the shopping streets of Milan lit with decorations, ready for Christmas. Lanterns of different shapes hung above the well-dressed Christmas shoppers, walking their expensively groomed dogs and looking into glittering windows filled with glamorous objects. Shops for pet dogs were filled with pretty, warm jumpers and elegant little caps of all colours to dress up your beloved poodle or chihuahua. The sight was nauseating.

The super-glamorous 19th-century Galleria Vittorio Emanuele II, one of the world's oldest shopping malls, is a four-storey arcade, covered by an arched glass and cast-iron roof, next to the cathedral in central Milan. Inside, the grand glass dome soars above you, while on two sides the rows of shops arrogantly display objects that only oligarchs can afford. Handbags that cost €2,000 each, pairs of high-heeled leather designer shoes worth more than two months of a labourer's wages. A homeless migrant camping out at Milan's central station would be stunned if they witnessed the callous wealth of the ruthless rich.

Another evening in Milan, Dave and I walked past a centre where a conference was taking place organized by the Northern League, a separatist, far-right movement founded in the early 1990s. It campaigned for the independence of a northern Italian region called Padania, meaning the valley of the river Po. Its founder Umberto Bossi promised to 'free hard-working northerners from subsidizing lazy southerners'. Adopting similar language and style to that of Marine Le Pen's Front National in France, the Northern League is among Europe's ultra-nationalist and neo-fascist groupings. In late January 2017, Matteo Salvini, leader of the Northern League, attended the meeting of Europe's far-right parties in Koblenz, Germany, where Marine Le Pen called on Europe's voters to 'wake up' and follow the example of US and British voters. '2016 was the year the Anglo-Saxon world woke up. I am certain 2017 will be the year when the people of continental Europe wake up,' Marine Le Pen said. Also present were Frauke Petry, leader of Alternative for Germany (AfD), and Geert Wilders, leader of the Freedom Party (PVV) of the Netherlands. Le Pen, once again, condemned German Chancellor Angela Merkel's refugee policy as a catastrophe.

Over the past few years the Northern League has seemed to be reviving, as a result of what the political scientist Ilvo Diamanti calls 'LePenism' – in other words, 'the leverage on nationalism that responds to the fears generated by economic crisis and global insecurity'.[38] The League has strongly argued against immigration, calling former Prime Minister Matteo Renzi an 'accomplice' in aiding 'illegal immigration'. I approached the only female member, Laura Piccardi, outside the Milan conference, and tried to talk about the position of her party on migration to Italy. She explained her party's position supporting a 'No' vote in the referendum, but, as to migration, she gave only a brief statement: 'We are against clandestine migration. We're against economic migration,' she said. 'We have to put Italians first.'

The racist politics of the Northern League have often been paraded out on the streets. Its supporters, along with those of another far-right group, Casa Pound, joined an anti-migrant protest on 1 November 2016, in Milan. Hundreds of far-right protesters marched to the city's Montello barracks, to protest against its conversion into an asylum shelter. The protesters chanted anti-refugee slogans, marching with numerous Italian and Casa Pound flags and banners saying 'Italians first' and 'Defend Milan'.

Moving on north

Banta was due to leave the camp in Palermo the next day. He told me he was heading to Stuttgart in Germany, to join his friend, who had organized accommodation for him. Banta was going to be living with a number of Gambians in the same house and would start looking for work as soon as he got there – any kind of work.

Banta was to pass through Milan, and we agreed to meet for a proper farewell before he set off to Germany. He told me he would arrive some time after 8pm and Dave and I went to meet him at the central station. I knew that he had no friends in this city but had no idea what his plans were for the rest of the evening. To ensure that he had a place to sleep on this freezing cold December night, we decided to book a hotel room for him. Many migrants were still sleeping rough in all corners of the central square. Was he thinking of doing the same?

At 10.40pm, Banta finally arrived. Walking down the stairs into the main hall inside the station, he smiled, waving at us. He was smartly dressed in a white jumper and a black leather jacket, with a nice white woollen hat. His hair was short and well-combed. He had only a small red suitcase with him. 'You look good!' I said. He embraced us warmly. He told us what a long day it had been, getting up at dawn and travelling all the way from Palermo.

As he did not own a smartphone and was not able to access information online, Banta had not fully worked out his travel plans. Now he checked the train timetable in the hall: the first train for Stuttgart would be in the morning. He decided to travel by bus, in order to save money, but the bus station was on the outskirts of the city in a place named Lampugnano. Banta therefore decided he would stay the night in Milan and fortunately the hotel room we had booked was not far from the station. By the time he settled in the hotel, it was midnight. At least he would have a good night's sleep.

The next day, we went to say farewell to Banta at Lampugnano, and found it far out in the suburbs, with no trace of Milan. The metro station looked like a deserted building and Banta said he had received some hostile stares from passers-by. 'Have they not seen a black man before?' he said.

A friend of his, a young man in his twenties, had travelled from Palermo to join him, so that they could continue to Stuttgart together. I had met him a couple of times before: he shared a room with Banta in the camp in Palermo and had a serious skin condition that kept him awake through the night. He was carrying a small rucksack and a pile of papers in his hand. That was the only luggage he had after all his years in Italy. He told me he was going to Stuttgart to seek medical treatment because there was nothing they could do about his illness in the hospitals in Sicily. The papers he carried in his hand were to show the shelter and hospital in Stuttgart his status and his medical situation. He was going to be living in a shelter there.

As he did not know how to describe the disease he had, he lifted up his shirt, to show me. It was a heartbreaking sight. It looked like burned skin all over his chest and back, and a little on the side of his cheeks. It looked as if he had been in a fire. I asked if it was painful and he said it was often itchy. He could not tell me the name of the disease, but said it was not uncommon in Africa. He held on to his papers tightly and did not want to put them away in his rucksack – they proved his identity and he dreaded the thought of losing them.

We waited with them for the bus to Stuttgart. People gathered at the station with their luggage, many leaving for different towns and cities in Germany. Banta looked uneasy. Was he apprehensive about what he would find in Stuttgart when he got there? I knew he was not sad to leave Italy behind: his life here, spent in the asylum reception system, had been filled with endless battles with those in charge of the reception businesses. He had not been given the opportunity to experience life as an equal in this society. When he waved us farewell, he was also leaving the memories of hardship and misery behind – he was moving on.

The following day, I received a message from Banta on WhatsApp that he and his friend had safely arrived in Stuttgart. And he had been welcomed not only by his friend there, but also by the exciting news that a new president had just been elected in Gambia. His name was Adama Barrow and he had been born in 1965, the year of Gambia's independence from British colonial rule. Aged 51 on his election, he was a successful property developer and had been nominated as the candidate for a coalition of seven opposition parties, promising greater respect for human rights and support for an independent judiciary and press freedom. Barrow has a strong British connection: he lived in Britain for several years in the early 2000s studying for his real-estate qualifications, working as an Argos security guard and supporting Arsenal. He returned to Gambia in 2006 to set up his property business.

Alaji, the 17-year-old Gambian teenager we had met in Palermo, also wrote to me to say how happy he and his family were with the election results. His father had once been persecuted by the dictator Yahya Jammeh and had fled the country. He had sought and was granted asylum in Britain and now lived in London.

Meanwhile, Abdoulaye, the Gambian we had visited in Bologna, had managed to get himself a mobile phone – I could only imagine how desperately he must have saved all his cash for it – and sent me the first message since he had arrived in Cesena. 'How are you? I'm fine here. This is my phone,' he wrote. When we talked, he too told me he was very happy with the election result. He had suffered under the previous regime and, like every other Gambian I talked to, he was now feeling joyful about the future of his country – and for his family and their wellbeing.

Getting to know Sirif

We moved to a more multi-ethnic part of town near the central station. The streets were filled with Chinese and Indian shops and restaurants, lower-cost dining places that suited me better, and from here I was able to visit the station square at any time.

Sirif was coming to Milan today, and asked to meet me at the square. He wore a huge yellow jacket given to him by the camp and stood out in the crowd. We went to warm up in a café. The waiter looked East Asian and watched us with suspicion, refusing to smile the whole time he was serving us. I tried to ignore it and was not sure if Sirif noticed his unfriendliness, or whether he was simply used to it.

Sirif had an accepting attitude towards his life in Italy. He didn't complain about conditions in the camp in Alessandria, but instead had come to terms with his circumstances and wanted to make the best of it. When asked, he simply said, shrugging his shoulders: 'You are getting what is given, and that's all you take.'

Sirif is the son of a teacher of English in Gambia. He regretted not having listened to his father about going to school: he had always tried to skip classes whenever he saw the chance, he told me, laughing. He took out his phone and showed me a picture of a beautiful young woman. 'It's my sister,' he said, one of the people he was closest to. He also missed his mother, who was always upset and worried about his journey. When he was working in Libya, selling bottles of water on the street, she cried every time she heard from him and became so anxious and worried about his situation there that she couldn't eat. Sirif was lucky enough that he had never been locked up in Libya, but he understood the suffering of many Africans there. He showed me a video of many African and Asian men crying out for food from the windows of tiny prison cells. Some of them were trying to climb out of the windows: their cries were desperate. The video had been sent to him by a friend who had witnessed this horrific scene.

Sirif was a Muslim; he was content that he'd been provided with halal food in the camp. This was the only camp I came across in Italy that made an effort to cater for the culinary needs of people of different religions. Sirif and other Muslim asylum seekers were also given a prayer room, which was highly unusual in this country's reception system. At this SPRAR in Alessandria, Sirif was particularly pleased with the integration programme, where local youth would come in to take part in all kinds of activities with the migrants. Sirif enjoyed playing football with the local boys of a similar age. They often talked with one another. 'They ask me questions about my past and what happened to me, and I ask questions about them and their life,' Sirif said. Their interaction was not just limited to the activities organized by the camp. 'We often meet outside and play football in the playground nearby.'

According to the MSF report *Out of Sight*, such integration programmes are not an integral part of the reception system. Of the

154,000 people who migrated to Italy in 2015, 84,000 applied for asylum, but fewer than 20,000 were placed in state-run integration programmes where they learn basic Italian language skills and get assistance with job placement. Sirif is among the fortunate ones.

Sirif was looking forward to Christmas, because the local youth would be joining the migrants and Italian as well as African food was going to be shared. 'In Gambia, I never celebrated Christmas, but I enjoy Christmas time here.' He was keen to interact more with local people and get to know the local communities.

He and other migrants were allowed to cook their own food in this SPRAR shelter. Every weekend, he enjoyed planning meals, shopping for ingredients and rice locally (they spent a small amount of the €70 per month allocated by the state), and cooking home dishes with his housemates in the kitchen. From Monday to Friday they ate the food provided by the camp, usually pasta and sometimes chicken and rice. Weekend meals, cooked by themselves, were the treats.

Sirif believed that he would be granted formal status, even though the waiting had been testing. 'I believe it will be OK. I've never done anything wrong in this country; I've always behaved. I help out as much as I can in the camp, even doing the cleaning for them.'

It seemed that Sirif had reached the stage of getting ready for a future life in Italy, which is the ideal aim of the SPRAR. He was feeling relatively at ease with his situation.

On 2 December, Sirif too was particularly pleased with the election results in Gambia. He was thrilled that his parents were so happy.

As we took a walk around the station area later in the afternoon, we saw more migrants coming in and gathering in the cold. 'They might have just arrived, or might have been here for some time,' said Sirif sorrowfully, 'Some have been sent back here from the border, and have no money to move on.' A migrant approached, begging for some coins. I could see Sirif was saddened by the man's desperation. 'When you're in this situation, you lose all sense...' I think he was referring to losing the sense of pride and dignity.

Finally, one day in late January 2017, a couple of months after we met, to his great relief Sirif received his leave-to-remain documents which confirmed his refugee status: the waiting had not been in vain. This would be the beginning of a new life! He was so looking forward to it. He was now waiting for a transfer to Tortona, a town with a population of just under 30,000, in the province of Alessandria. Tortona: he thought about this place every day – what would it be like?

In early February, in the depths of an icy winter, Sirif continued to see homeless migrants sleeping rough at the station square in Milan, every time he went there on outings with his friends. He empathized with them, seeing them wrapped in their bedding in the open air – he knew that their situation could be that of any migrant. No migrant's destiny is in their own hands.

On 5 December 2016, Prime Minister Matteo Renzi resigned after defeat in the referendum to change the constitution, with 59.1 per cent of Italians voting against the proposed reforms. It was a victory for the populist and rightwing parties: the 20-point margin was a major win for the Five Star Movement, which led opposition to the reform, and the Northern League. Only a few weeks earlier, Trump had won the US presidential elections, encouraging Beppe Grillo, co-founder of the Five Star Movement, and Matteo Salvini, head of the Northern League, to talk of victory.

In and around Milano Centrale, Omar was living by what he described as 'hustling' – trying to help older people buy their train tickets from the machines and asking for some cash in return. But as the temperature was dropping quickly, at times below zero, he was finding it more difficult to stay outdoors for a long time. 'I get very tired by the cold,' he said.

Over the next two months, Omar started to sound incoherent and seemed to be suffering from huge mood swings. Sometimes he said he was fine, other times he was feeling suicidal. Rage would take over at times and it would be impossible to communicate with him. His mental health appeared to be deteriorating.

Europe pays Libya to 'deal with' migrants

A couple of days later, Abdoulaye told me on WhatsApp that heating was not provided in his camp in Cesena. He was getting worried as this was just the beginning of winter and it was already freezing cold. Modou, the 17-year-old Gambian boy in Messina, had even more problems: he told me that his camp never provided heating or winter clothing. Nor did they provide proper medical care. 'The doctor only stays for 30 minutes each day. There was little help when I had stomach pain,' he said. He was only young, but already felt disrespected and undervalued. This systematic substandard treatment evoked sentiments with historical roots: 'We're kept like slaves in the camp,' he said.

Two days later, Modou was almost in tears. Some locals had painted racist graffiti outside their camp. 'Refugees not welcome' was written in English on the wall of the building. 'I want to know why people are so hateful,' he said. It was hard to imagine how he felt: not only was he living in dreadful conditions inside the shelter, but outside he was also confronted with such ugly levels of hostility. It was useless to tell him that perhaps some people needed to find reasons for their own sad lives and therefore had to find someone else to blame; useless to tell him that these ignorant few must not get him down. He had learned about racism in Europe in the most blatant and nasty way.

There was little that Modou could do about racist graffiti, but he could do something about the ill-treatment inside camp. He and his housemates got together again and made a complaint to the management about the lack of winter clothes. And their collective complaint worked once again – they were promised some clothes the following week.

The following morning, at 8am, I received a call from Adedayo, the Nigerian man at the camp in Mineo. He sounded anxious. He said things had gone from bad to worse, and the camp management was restricting migrants from going in and out of the camp even more than before, for fear that people would run away as a result of the poor conditions there. Adedayo was planning to do exactly that, something he had never considered before. But now the situation inside the camp had become utterly unbearable. In late June 2017, he called and told me that he had finally run away from the camp and was staying with a friend in Catania. He was free at last. Two weeks later, he moved to Venezia Mestre, the Venetian mainland, to join his other friends. 'I will be able to find work here,' he said. 'I will try my very best.'

Just over a month after the protest in Milan over living conditions in a reception centre, migrants took action again on 3 January 2017, barricading staff inside a camp in Cona, near Venice, following the death of a 25-year-old woman from Côte d'Ivoire. The camp, opened in 2015, housed around 1,500 migrants, far exceeding the capacity. The protest was against living conditions and the lack of medical care. Protesting migrants were furious, cutting off the electricity supply to the centre and setting fire to it. The official cause of the woman's death remained unclear, although it appeared that she was taken ill and the delay in calling an ambulance was suspected to have caused her to die of a blood clot in a bathroom.

Instead of looking into the appalling conditions and the lack of care inside the asylum reception system, the response of the Italian authorities was to announce that they would accelerate deportations of migrants whose asylum claims had been rejected. It was announced that at least one Centre for Identification and Expulsion (CIE) would be opened in every region in the coming weeks, where failed asylum seekers would be held for deportation.

As Lucia Borghi of Borderline Sicilia said:

> The reception system in Italy is about to be replaced by still stricter means of control, selection and repression, destined to create nothing but suffering, rage and violence. Policies directed along these lines, besides being in contravention of international agreements and laws, are clearly incapable of guaranteeing basic human rights. Behind the numbers of deportations, expulsions and detentions there are people who have been judged only on the basis of the country they have come from, and not their individual stories...

The authorities also vowed to push for an agreement with Niger and for a renewed repatriation deal with Tunisia that would facilitate returns and reduce the numbers of arrivals in Italy.

Italy had signed a bilateral agreement with Libya in 2004 that allowed it to deport failed asylum seekers and undocumented migrants to there. Italy also paid for the construction of several detention centres in Libya, with the aim of preventing sub-Saharan African migrants from entering Italy. Recent news reports have provided a glimpse of the appalling conditions and severe violation of human rights inside those detention centres.

However, the new Italian government – led by Prime Minister Paolo Gentiloni, who took office in mid-December 2016 – set out further measures to deter migrants. Marco Minniti, the Minister of the Interior, went to Tripoli to sign a bilateral agreement on combating irregular migration with Fayez al-Sarraj, head of the UN-backed Government of National Accord (GNA), one of the three 'governments' vying for power in Libya. Italy also reopened its embassy in Tripoli, the first European country to do so after two years of ongoing conflicts between different factions.

By January 2017, discussions were beginning among the EU states over another agreement which they believed would reduce migration via the central Mediterranean route from Libya to Italy. Joseph Muscat, the Prime Minister of Malta, proposed a system by which European and Libyan vessels would intercept migrant boats in Libyan waters and return them to Libya. The migrants would then be processed by UNHCR and International Organization for Migration (IOM) officials funded by the EU. Those migrants who qualified for asylum would be allowed to enter Europe while others would be resettled in Libya or repatriated to their countries of origin. In February 2017, the EU deal providing Libya's UN-backed government with €200 million ($230 million) was agreed, totally disregarding the fact that Libya was in the middle of a factional war, and would not be able to implement EU plans. The country was a lawless state where the horrific treatment of African migrants had been well documented. Recent testimony from the IOM reveals that West African migrants are being bought and sold openly in modern-day slave markets in Libya. It would seem that the trade in human beings has become so normalized that people are actually being traded in public.[39] The predictable outcome of this agreement would be that migrants who failed in their asylum application would be abandoned in Libya's horrendous detention centres, where they would suffer all kinds of abuse and torture and where they would be quite likely to die.[40]

Lucia Borghi, of Borderline Sicilia, summed up the hell created by external as well as internal controls of the border regime.

The journeys of death, violence and disappearance unfold before our eyes every day... The invisibility of those who remain tormented by months of torture and under the threat of death in Libyan prisons, of those who disappear at sea and in the desert is equal to that of those who manage to arrive in Italy, where the discussion regarding migrants is reserved to the subject of implementing means of controlling and repressing them... In the last few weeks the news about the next immigration deals has picked up an alarming pace in newspapers and TV, with announcements about getting a grip on rejections, the opening of new detention centres (CIE) under military control, fast-track expulsions for those refused international protection, agreements with North African countries just as unlikely as they are crazy, and obviously the usual hypocritical fight against trafficking.

Meanwhile in Italy, two weeks after the Venice protest, many Somalian asylum-seekers clashed with the riot police in Florence outside the office of the regional authorities. They were protesting about the tragic death of Ali Muse, a 44-year-old Somali asylum-seeker, who was killed in an overnight fire that occurred in the poorly maintained shelter at Sesto Fiorentino where he lived. Around 80 Somali migrants were housed in the centre, which was converted from an empty factory. Ali had returned to the burning building to get his ID documents, and been caught in the blaze.

'The state is responsible for Ali's death,' the protesters chanted. The police had to form a human barricade to stop protesters from forcing their way into the Prefecture.

By the end of 2016, 181,000 people had made the journey via Libya to Europe. More than 5,000 migrants lost their lives that year crossing the Mediterranean and Aegean seas – they were drowned, suffocated or crushed during the crossing. It is believed that many deaths were actually unrecorded, the bodies either disappearing or washing up on the shores of Libya.

5

Ghettoes of Europe

Banta had arrived in Germany and was glad to be in Stuttgart. He had settled in and was sharing the house with several Gambian migrants. Finding himself at last in a pleasant and friendly social environment, he was looking forward to Christmas.

Soon after the presidential elections in Gambia, the dictator Yahya Jammeh, who had ruled the country for over two decades, had rejected the outcome and his defeat by the opposition leader, Adama Barrow. Jammeh called for a fresh vote. Banta said the worrying thing was that some of the army still supported him. Given the situation, he was very concerned about the possibility of a civil war.

Two weeks after settling in Stuttgart, Banta started to enquire about work. 'It's a nice city for work,' he said. Unfortunately, his Italian papers did not grant him the right to work outside Italy and he knew he would have to find work in the informal economy. It would be menial work, low-paid.

However, a few days before Christmas, it seemed that Banta was going out very little, rarely leaving the flat. He had stopped telling me about what life was like in Germany and his impressions; he lacked enthusiasm. Then he revealed that, since the terrorist attack on a Berlin Christmas market on 20 December 2016, he had been feeling very low. His friends feared going out. The attacker Anis Amri had not been arrested at that time, and there was the concern that he might be anywhere in the country. Besides, migrants were being targeted for blame. As a response, the German government proposed policy changes that would speed up deportations and increase the monitoring of migrants. There was a lot of suspicion and distrust in the air – it felt unsafe to be out on the street.

Germany had been seen as the ideal destination for tens of thousands of migrants who entered Europe either through Greece or the Mediterranean route to Italy. It was seen as a country that respects human rights. To be precise, 202,834 migrants sought refuge in Germany in 2014. The following year, as wars and destruction continued in Syria, around 1.1 million migrants arrived in the country, with 476,649 of them claiming asylum by the end of the year. The number of asylum-seekers arriving in Germany then decreased to around 280,000 people in 2016,[41] as a result of the EU-Turkey deal and closure of the Balkan route, as well as further tightening of the EU's external borders.

While the authorities were talking about stretched resources, and part of society remained convinced of the negative impact of the newcomers, what is the reality of the asylum reception system and how has it impacted on the lives of refugees and migrants in Germany?

Segregation in Berlin

Berlin, with a population of 3.6 million, was temporarily housing around 70,000 asylum-seekers and refugees as of early 2017. In the capital of the wealthiest European country, however, most migrants had been offered second-class accommodation. Since 2012-13, the federal state and municipalities had been commissioning an increasing number of non-state actors – such as charity organizations and private companies – to provide asylum housing. In Berlin, 85 per cent of asylum-seekers were being housed in mass shelters, structured like camps, and only 15 per cent in private apartments, according to the Refugee Council. The mass shelters were located in former hotels, gyms, sports halls, schools and airports.

Anyone visiting Berlin would no longer find long queues of asylum-seekers right in the centre of the city. There were no longer endless queues outside the LaGeSo (the State Office for Health and Social Affairs), which had been moved to the suburb of Wilmersdorf, so wealthy North American and European tourists did not have to suffer the sight of newly arrived migrants. Once you went a little further out of the town, you found their shelters tucked away deep in an industrial estate, or a business area on the outskirts of the city, or in the three hangars of the former Tempelhof airport in the middle of nowhere.

The Tempelhof camp, where thousands were being housed, was

most notorious for its overcrowding. Not only was it overflowing, with roofless, partitioned rooms where residents lived without any privacy, it also lacked basic facilities. The poor conditions, in addition to the isolated location, led to cases of depression and attempted suicide among the migrant residents. However, the authorities not only never attempted to improve conditions, but even intended to maximize the capacity of the camp and accommodate even more people.

Those who benefited most from this kind of segregated housing arrangement, which was the norm in Berlin, were the operators of the mass shelters and camps. As refugee housing was state-funded, any individual or organization could apply for funding, and bid for their application to be accepted, simply on the grounds of lower cost. The state had established no criteria for the funding applicants – any business could apply, even a security firm that had no experience in working with migrants. This created a situation where the businesses running the shelters had neither the expertise nor the slightest knowledge of the people to whom they were supposed to provide services. How could they be in charge of shelters? It seemed the state was only interested in the cheapest bidder. Shelters then received a certain amount of funds per person housed there, with the state having absolutely no control over how funds were spent and allocated. The result of such a business-oriented system is a shelter for 1,000 people with only four bathrooms, and the placement of culturally or politically conflicting groups in the same room. Billions have been made out of asylum shelters, while the standard of housing is often far below average. The general consensus is that there are only 'less bad' shelters, not good ones.

Some politicians think that containers offer a solution to the shortage of housing in Berlin, which had in fact been created by the mass privatization of social housing under the previous administration, though the policy has been continued by the current city government. In December 2016, immediately after taking office, the 'red-red-green' (SPD-Left Party-Green Party) administration in Berlin reneged on its promise to provide asylum-seekers with housing in apartments. It decided to continue the rightwing refugee policy of the previous Social Democrat-Christian

Democrat administration, and to move asylum-seekers from mass shelters to container settlements.

Both the containers and the mass shelters are mostly located in industrial areas on the outskirts of Berlin, far away from the transport system and urban infrastructure. And both are managed by independent operators contracted by the state, which pays them a daily rate for each person housed for a period of three years.

These mass shelters and container villages are, to all extents and purposes, ghettoes, created to isolate migrants and keep them away from society. The system identifies migrants as different, separates them from society, and stigmatizes them as a 'problem' for the city and the country. They are therefore segregated. The solution of 'mass containment' of migrants has all the appearance of a race-based policy.

Consequently, only five per cent of Germans have ever been acquainted with a refugee and, according to the Friedrich Ebert Foundation, one in two Germans distrusts refugees. Yet most Germans are unaware of the reality of the lives of these 'outsiders' – and know even less of their destinies.

The majority of asylum-seeking migrants who end up in Berlin are, in fact, being trapped in the asylum system without the chance to move on and live a normal life where they can explore the opportunities for employment and education. Due to the increasingly strict asylum law introduced by the Christian Democratic Union (CDU), only a minority, usually those with skills and a profession in demand within the country's labour market are to be granted asylum. Those who do not fit the requirements are unwanted and will be sent out of the country straight away. In October 2016, interior minister Thomas de Maizière proposed that refugees should be separated into two categories, those who come from a 'safe' country and those who do not; the former would be fast-tracked for immediate deportation. This arbitrary categorization puts many at risk of human rights abuses when they are returned to the countries from which they fled. Even those granted asylum would face a lengthy wait to be reunited with their families: earlier in 2016, the German parliament passed laws establishing that asylum-seekers who are victims of the Syrian war but not 'personally persecuted' have to wait two years before they can apply to bring their families to Europe.

Isolated from the rest of the city, residents in shelters and containers have no-one to turn to but the staff, who may not always be helpful. The consequences of the inadequate reception system are serious. Many migrants had fled from conflicts, wars, persecution and abject poverty before reaching Germany. Assistance such as therapy is not available and the lack of care and degrading treatment they had already suffered and tried to escape from was repeated in the receiving country. This often deals a severe blow to an individual's mental health. Between 40 and 50 per cent of the asylum-seekers who arrived in Germany during 2015 are now psychologically ill and suffer from various conditions including post-traumatic stress disorder (PTSD). Around one in five asylum-seeking children suffers from PTSD. But in autumn 2015 the federal chamber of psychotherapists revealed that few have received psycho-therapeutic treatment.

To protect the wellbeing of migrants, the Refugee Council in Berlin has pushed for an immediate end to policies that require asylum-seekers to live in shelters while their applications are being processed. It argues that much of the city's social housing is standing empty and that there are around 7,000 unoccupied flats in Berlin – a fact ignored by the politicians. The Council believes that private housing in the community is the best way for migrants to integrate.

Frustration and anger with conditions in the mass shelters have led to several protests. In Berlin, dozens of young Iraqi and Syrian migrants protested in front of the Jahn sports hall on the Columbiadamm in July 2016. There have also been several hunger strikes in Berlin's shelters.

Two asylum shelters

Shortly after arriving in Berlin I went to visit a mass shelter in Spandau, AWO Wohnheim Spandau, which was notorious for being overcrowded. It was situated on a long avenue in the west of Berlin, half an hour away from the Spandau Prison where Hitler's deputy Rudolf Hess served his life sentence from 1947 until he committed suicide. (The prison was demolished to prevent it from becoming a Nazi shrine and there is now a shopping centre on the site.) In the middle of nowhere, behind fences, trees and bushes, the shelter itself looked like a prison. The severe atmosphere surrounding the place was a forewarning that I would not be permitted to enter.

From outside the metal fence I saw several migrants standing around their block of flats. A man was looking out of a window below which the word 'Welcome' was written. His building was marked 'House One'. Further along, I saw several teenagers and children playing in the yard. On seeing me looking in, three of them came over and looked at me with curiosity. Two were 14 years old, one was 13, and they had all come from Syria. One of the 14-year-olds was holding a baby in his arms. He told me that his parents were still in Syria. There were 70 unaccompanied children in this camp and they had all travelled to Germany via Greece.

When asked if they were all right, their responses expressed a sense of acute anxiety. They had been in this camp for a year now and still had no idea about their future. Nine of them shared a tiny room. Facilities were lacking; the only social space they had was the front yard where they had been playing. When asked, 'Is this a good shelter?' they unanimously answered, 'It's bad', one of them signalling with a thumbs-down.

As we talked, a guard approached and snapped at them in German, probably telling them not to speak to me. I doubt he would have been so aggressive speaking to German children. Frightened, the young Syrians ran away and the guard came up to ask me to leave. 'I'm actually outside your site,' I pointed out, speaking over the fence. It was clear to me that the camp was under intensive control. But with what justification?

Thirty minutes away was Spandau old town, a different world from the one inhabited by asylum-seekers and light years from the 'problem' of 'the other'. It was almost the equivalent of a UKIP fantasy English village: not a trace of non-white people. Here, I was served the world's blandest and most expensive sandwich by a reluctant waitress. It was in smug towns like this that I was constantly reminded how very different I was from the local residents – and I was only visiting.

Pankow is the second-largest borough in Berlin and another asylum shelter is located there, on Storkower Strasse. This shelter was set up in April 2015 in a former office building, once a job centre. The exterior of this orange-coloured square-box construction stood out in the neighbourhood. I had written to the staff here previously with no reply, so decided to call in directly and ask if I could speak with one of the organizers. The receptionist took me to see the co-ordinator, Anahita Izahi, an artist who worked here part-time. She then introduced me to their manager, Jan Schebaum.

Mr Schebaum greeted me and briefed me about the shelter while finishing his sandwich. He used to run a gym two years ago, he told me. Now he was running seven asylum shelters in Berlin. Why the career change, apart from the obvious profits involved in receiving state funding? 'I find it fulfilling,' he said. 'When you end a day, you feel that you've done something useful. I didn't make anyone richer or sell something to anyone, but I helped some people. This is a great feeling.'

Storkower Strasse shelter in Berlin.

He took me on a tour around the five-storey building. There were, at the time of my visit, 255 beds there and it was clearly overcrowded. There were 70 children. The majority of migrants housed there were from Syria (100 altogether), Afghanistan, Chechnya and Central Asia. There were two to four beds in each room; there were common sanitary facilities, and only two self-catering kitchens shared among so many residents, although they were kept clean and tidy by the residents themselves. There was just one dining room on each floor.

Mr Schebaum greeted several migrants as we passed in the hallway. They said 'Hello' and 'Welcome' to me. Most migrants had been there for six to eight months and were awaiting asylum decisions. Some had been there since the shelter had opened in April 2015 – for more than a year. So far, only 20 people housed here had been granted refugee status.

'Residents from Syria don't have to worry about getting asylum, but those from Afghanistan may have problems,' Mr Schebaum said. 'Then it becomes stressful as they're waiting longer and longer. Then we're here to give advice to them... We have developed a trusting relationship with our clients. We want them to feel they're being treated with care and that we care about them. They are not just numbers for us... It is working, because I can see they come to us with problems and ask us to resolve them.

'Some people say these kinds of shelters are not good and we have to find them flats immediately because that's real integration. I don't agree with that. I think it's useful for them to be here first. This is also integration... Here you have an opportunity to meet with people from your own country and get information about Germany. Here, you learn to accept living with each other. I think that's a major step to integration. If you need help here, you can always ask. We work 24 hours. Three years ago [in Berlin], it was about one social worker for every 100 refugees. Now it's one for 50-55... I think it's not a bad place as a first step.'

Mr Schebaum said that, as soon as places became available, he would move people into flats. 'There was an Iraqi man with two sons here. He was suffering from a lot of stress and couldn't even tolerate the noise from the children playing outside. We had to move him to a flat. Usually it takes six to eight months to find a flat... They're all on a waiting list.'

As the migrants weren't permitted to work, Mr Schebaum said 'community work' could be offered by charity organizations – and only charity organizations. However, the wage was 80 cents per hour, lower than the normal rate. In this shelter, he could also offer the residents 'community work', such as cleaning and keeping the garden tidy.

In order to complement the state benefits they were receiving, some migrants went out to look for work on the black market. For those migrants who were categorized as from the 'safe countries', the situation was much more desperate, as they were not even allowed to do the 'community work' for 80 cents per hour. Mr Schebaum pointed out that this was discriminatory. 'The people from the Balkan region will do any work. The work that Syrian guys don't want to do... The system is not fair to them [those from "safe countries"]. As long as they're here, they should be given the opportunity to work... Our laws have to be updated.

'We have to understand the fact that we are a country of immigrants. Give work visas, let people learn the language. But our law hasn't caught up with that fact. It would have solved many problems... Maybe the asylum department wouldn't be so busy...'

He said it was fortunate that not many migrants in this shelter had been deported. He didn't like the way people were dealt with by immigration and police officers in the case of deportation. 'For one person, there are six police officers. You can imagine how many officers would be here for a family of five. It's not good for people to have armed police here... Besides, they have only 20 minutes to pack their belongings.'

Mr Schebaum wanted to have a cigarette break, so we went outside. He showed me the exterior of the building where people could do some gardening, which he believed could be therapeutic. I asked him about the location of the shelter, which was clearly isolated and without any community facilities nearby. I suggested that this was not at all good for the residents. 'Yes, this is a business area. We have laws that forbid building refugee homes in a business area,' he said, 'That's because, in a business area, there's not much around but shopping centres. No cinema, no theatre, no culture... It's cut off, and therefore it's unsuited for refugee shelters, as it's the opposite of integration.

'But when I talked with some guy in the department, they said they would make a special allowance because we're in a crisis situation [needing more shelters]... And they said they would change the law, to take circumstances into consideration.' (At the end of 2014, a special derogation in planning law was introduced allowing accommodation for asylum-seekers and refugees to be built in places that are not suitable for residential purposes.)

As he acknowledged, the location was far from ideal, but had been accepted in his funding application for a shelter simply because of the lack of places for the incoming migrants.

So how had the local community responded to the new residents in this business area? Mr Schebaum said the locals were comfortable with their new neighbours because this community had always created space for refugees and homeless people. Then he added: 'As for those people who might feel hostile to refugees, I wonder why they never come to ask people like me, who know refugees.'

After the cigarette break, we returned inside and he proudly showed me a room he said he had built. It was an exercise room. 'It's a useful way to relieve stress and tension. When they're stressed, they may have problems with sleep, and in that case sports can be useful... There are also bicycles for hire. And a children's playroom. We built this with donations.'

Meeting an Afghan filmmaker

I returned to the shelter at Storkower Strasse another day and talked with a resident living on the second floor, called Noor Khashman, a 25-year-old woman from Damascus, in Syria. She was a business graduate and had worked in sales in Damascus. Noor had divorced her husband after a five-year relationship. When her family was leaving Syria, she had asked him to come with her but he said he had to stay to find the funds. He said he would join her later, but the promise was never fulfilled. He met someone else in Damascus. Noor was devastated, and suffered so much that she had to seek counselling. Eventually she had to divorce him. She said she still needed time to recover emotionally.

Noor shared the room with her mother and younger brother. Her older brother was staying in another room. They had been in Germany for ten months, including one month in Dresden, which was the worst time they had had in this country. 'People are strange there. They don't like Arabic people,' she said. 'They made facial gestures to me...'

At that time, Noor and her family were staying temporarily with her cousin in Dresden. Her cousin's family had lived there ever since arriving in Germany. 'They have big problems with local people,' she said, shaking her head.

'Berlin's different – it's wonderful.' She changed her tone and looked content. This was where she had claimed asylum eight months before. 'People here are good. I feel like I'm in Damascus. I feel at home here. I have many friends here, from Syria and Palestine. Two of my uncles are here. I go to the gym and know people there... I'm now learning German, although it's a harsh language and will take more time to learn... So when I'm at school, I use both German and English to make myself understood. But I'm doing my best to learn.' Some time in the near future, Noor would like to work.

Overall, the shelter at Storkower Strasse was overcrowded, some of the basic facilities were insufficient for the large number of people housed there, and the location was unsuitable for asylum-seekers, especially families with children. It was, however, better than many of the other shelters. Many migrants in Berlin were living in places that were much worse and were quite simply unsuited for human habitation. One of these was in Notunterkunft Winsstrasse, hidden away in an alleyway that could easily be missed by passers-by. It used to be a gym until an NGO called People's Solidarity took over and started running it as an asylum shelter. The organization managed at least four such shelters in Berlin.

When I arrived, it looked derelict, with old graffiti scrawled on the wall outside. I looked in at the windows; it appeared empty inside. The co-ordinator, a woman called Natalija Miletic, answered the door. Inside, it looked as if some building work was going on, but she agreed to show me the gym where 200 migrants lived. It was the size of a basketball court and it was hard to imagine that 200 people could actually fit in there. Mostly from Syria, Iraq, Iran, Afghanistan and Eritrea, the residents had moved in on 4 December 2015 and had now been living in this space for nine long months. The gym was partitioned into roofless rooms, and was divided into two sections, one for the 30-40 families (there were 30 children), the other for single men, three to five in a 'room'. There were only curtains, no doors to the 'rooms'. There was no privacy to speak of. There were only four toilets shared between 200 people. And there was no kitchen – migrants received packed boxes of processed food. It was a sad, distressing scene. Could we imagine Europeans and their children living in this state? How did the organization possibly think these conditions would be suitable for the asylum-seekers? And how did the NGO's application get accepted by the state?

There was a great deal of anger among the migrants. They were all desperate to move out. 'The conditions here are simply not humane,' even the co-ordinator Ms Miletic acknowledged. Eventually, the migrants were moved to several other shelters.

Before I left, Ms Miletic pointed to a big pile of toys in a corner of her office. 'These are donations from the neighbourhood.'

As I carried on talking with Ms Miletic outside the building, a young man approached and greeted her. He introduced himself as Masih Tajzai, from Kabul, in Afghanistan. He had lived in this 'gym camp' (as we referred to it) but only the week before had moved to a recently built camp on Treskow Street run by Unionhilfswerk. I asked to meet him again.

That afternoon, I visited Masih in his new accommodation. It was a brand-new building, the glass exterior shining in the sun. This didn't look like the usual kind of shelter. Unusually, migrants were allowed to have visitors inside the building, as long as they signed in and out. The staff held my ID during the visit. Masih came down to fetch me and, as we walked along the corridor, I saw a poster on the noticeboard advertising en event with Masih named as DJ.

This structure had capacity for 500 people. Currently, 100 asylum-seekers were housed there. Masih led me up to the sixth floor where his room was – there was no lift and I was out of breath by the time I reached it. He introduced me to about a dozen men

Masih pictured inside the shelter in Berlin.

from his home country who all greeted me warmly. Many of them were separated from their families. Masih shared a bright room with one other person and together they kept it clean and tidy. From the open window he showed me the view of the city. This was certainly a change from the standard mass shelters in Berlin.

Masih spoke fluent English, with a German accent. He said he had been learning German every day. Aged just 29, Masih came from a family of artists in Afghanistan; his father worked in theatre, but in 1996, with the Taliban in power, the social environment began to deteriorate and he decided to leave with his family for Pakistan. In 1999, Masih took part as a child actor at the age of nine in a BBC radio drama about Pakistan called 'New Home, New Life'. His work helped with the family income. In 2001, he returned to Afghanistan with the family, and started joining theatre workshops in 2004; soon after he set up and ran his own. His career blossomed.

By 2006, Masih had started filmmaking and worked as a producer for a French company. In 2008, he and his father joined forces, started their own production company and worked with various documentary filmmakers from Europe and America. One of the films he worked on, with director Sam French, *Buzkashi Boys* (2012), was nominated for an Academy Award. Beautifully shot, this short film is set in war-torn Afghanistan and recounts the story of two young boys in Kabul who dream of playing *buzkashi*, the Afghan national sport (in which horseback riders compete for possession of a headless goat). But, constantly restricted by their extreme poverty, the boys are unable to participate in the sport.

The film was produced with a joint international and Afghan crew, of which Masih was the local director. *Buzkashi Boys* is a rarity for international audiences because it shows the everyday life of Afghan people. For the nascent Afghan film industry, which was practically destroyed during the previous three decades, especially during the rule of the Taliban when it was outlawed, *Buzkashi Boys* was a huge boost.

Masih got married in 2011 and had two sons, now aged four and six. In early 2015 he was filming for an NGO, International Medical Corp, in Kunar province in east Afghanistan documenting their activities, when real trouble started. He became aware that something was wrong when he noticed they were being watched and photographed. When it happened a second time, he began to feel that something ominous was about to happen: two hours later, during filming, they were hit by shells from the Taliban.

When he returned home, he saw the same people who had been sneaking around the village during filming watching near his house. He knew instantly that he was being targeted. He informed his father and they decided it was time for him to leave. 'It wasn't easy to leave, as I'd built up my career there. But I had to,' he said. He went from Iran to Turkey, then to Greece. He spent a total of $7,000 to cross the borders. Because of his income in Afghanistan, he was fortunate enough not to have to borrow cash to make the trip and, in fact, lent money to several people who also wanted to leave the country. At this time, over 2.6 million Afghans were already living in exile as refugees, according to UNHCR. Masih told me about his traumatic journey.

I captured every second of the journey in my mind. Iran and the sea were the most challenging... When crossing the border from Iran to Turkey, the problem was that we had to climb mountains for 25 or 26 hours. People [in the same group] weren't used to climbing mountains. Many of them died on the way. I saw them falling around me. There was nothing I could do. I wasn't able to help them. There was a family, the father was too old and he died. The rest of the family was unsure whether they should stay with the father, or continue with the journey — but the behaviour of the Iranian soldiers was known to be very bad and they often torture Afghans... So the family decided not to stay with the father's body. They moved on. And there were these two young boys... They were running and fell down the mountain. No one was able to help them. I don't know what happened to them. The Iranian police came and started shooting up the mountains... They wanted to stop refugees... They didn't care that it was humans up there. One bullet came so close to me. I stayed low, and waited, and then continued walking again.

The Turkish army took us and put us in a shelter for 15 days. Conditions were really bad there. I was so exhausted that I felt like returning to Afghanistan... When they released us, we went to Istanbul, where they were selling refugees from one smuggler to another; eventually the last one would push you onto a boat to cross the sea... It was $1,500 for each person. At sea, the waves were so high. We saw two boats sink. We heard the news every day, about how many people were dying. The waves were so rough that we had to stay in the jungle [woods] and wait. There was nothing to eat there, and it was cold...

I saw smugglers taking some families who couldn't afford to cross the sea. They took them to the jungle. The smugglers were raping three girls, a mother and a child from those families each night. No one could help them. They were told they would be sent on a boat the next day, to Greece. But it didn't happen. The smugglers were just using them every night. It happened around me. The smugglers had guns with them. There was nothing we could do. These things happen to people on this kind of journey.

Finally we made it to cross the sea. The capacity of the boat was 12 persons, but they crammed 35 to 37 people in there. When we reached Greece at last, there were other problems... There were a lot of people waiting to be fingerprinted... Then we travelled through Macedonia and Austria, and finally reached Germany.

It took him two months in total to travel from Iran to Germany. It was an incredible feeling for Masih to arrive in Leipzig, the largest city in Saxony and the first place he saw in Germany. But the trauma had been tremendous. He simply felt lost. 'I was asking, "where am I?" "Leipzig," I was told. Five minutes later, I forgot the name of the city and asked again. My mind couldn't focus on things.'

Masih went to Hamburg where his uncle and aunt lived. The city also has a well-established Afghan migrant community. There he stayed in a camp which housed up to 2,000 people. 'There were a lot of fights between people in there,' he said. 'It's hard to get to sleep because kids were running about at 3am, and there was a lot of noise around.' Then he received a letter instructing him to move to Berlin within 24 hours. There are many creative industries in Berlin, and he has found this to be excellent for his future career. He doesn't need to be near his relatives and firmly believes in standing on his own feet. 'It's much nicer to be independent.'

However, unfortunately, Masih was placed in the 'gym shelter' at Notunterkunft Winsstrasse. As asylum-seekers could not apply to live in the community for the first six months, he had to put up with the appalling conditions there. 'The government doesn't easily give permission for us to live in the community. There's a long waiting list if – or when – we're allowed to apply to live outside,' he said. 'And, even if we do live in the community, we still have to deal with deep distrust and fear from local people.'

He said that there was no real interaction with the local community. 'Some people look at me with great suspicion.'

There appeared to be no real mechanism to facilitate genuine interaction between new arrivals and local communities. 'Integration' is a word that constantly permeates the political discourse. However, the general approach is top-down and is not generated from within communities. For instance, in April 2016, the German coalition government announced new legal measures requiring migrants to integrate into society. Under these measures, asylum-seekers faced cuts to their direct state support if they did not follow mandatory integration measures such as language classes, lessons in German laws and basic cultural knowledge. Chancellor Angela Merkel said that the aim of these unprecedented integration laws was to make it easier for migrants to gain access to the German labour market, with the government promising

100,000 new 'work opportunities', including low-paid workfare jobs. However, the market-orientated, top-down approach is more likely to create resentment rather than 'integration'.

Thinking about his own hardship in retrospect, Masih seemed able to smile it away. 'I have friends in France who are complaining a lot about the system and the way people behave. I have friends in Finland, and even though they have lived there for many years, they don't have many opportunities as refugees... If you compare situations in these European countries, then you understand that in Germany they're not treating refugees too badly.' He believed that the underlying fear of 'outsiders' should not exist, but he also said he understands that it takes time. 'Let people get over their fear in their own way.'

Masih very much wanted to be part of society and did not want to be seen as a refugee. He wanted to be freed from the label and the stigma. He wanted to be able to live independently and freely. He had applied for a flat outside the shelter and, if permitted, he would be able to move out in early October 2016.

But before that could become a reality, Masih had to live in the shelter, like everyone else. He lived on the state benefit of €350 ($400) per month. He was working on several projects, free of charge, because he was not yet permitted to work. Some of his housemates would try to find illegal work in restaurants and construction to have a bit more cash in their pockets. As the government does not permit asylum-seekers to work in the first nine months of their stay, they inevitably end up doing jobs without rights or protection, often exploited and working more than 13 hours per day, for minimal wages.

In October, Masih received permission to move into a private apartment with his room-mate from the shelter in Berlin. At last he had a taste of the independent living that he had craved. Now he could do the things that everyone else does: go to the cinema, to the gym, go to a club, or stay home and have dinner with friends. He could finally live like a normal human being. The only thing that he still was not permitted to do was work. Although he was still waiting for his asylum decision when we talked again in February 2017, he was already planning his future work. He wanted to make a documentary about Afghan migrants who were refused asylum and were to be deported. He continued to visit Afghan friends and acquaintances who found themselves in this desperate situation and tried to give them advice. Sometimes he also acted as a DJ in a club where Afghan asylum-seekers and refugees spent time. It was a rare venue where Afghans could sometimes meet and interact with local people. These days, Masih's schedule was also filled with events, film screenings, talks and seminars where people came to listen to him talking about filmmaking: it all helped take his mind off the asylum decision while he was waiting.

In March 2017, Masih was granted permission to live in Germany for three years. He was finally able to apply for his wife and two sons to join him in Berlin.

Far-right attacks on the rise

Among the worst aspects of the life of an asylum-seeker or refugee in Germany is local racism and far-right activity. The economic insecurity and austerity of the past decade, together with the rise of far-right movements across Europe and the absence of effective political alternatives, have created an environment that facilitates the steady growth of racism. Refugees became the new public enemy who could be blamed for all social ills. In what was once East Berlin, where four of the five container shelters were built (Marzahn, Pankow, Köpenick and Lichtenberg), anti-refugee racism has expressed itself in the most aggressive way.

I met with Tahera Ameer, activist and project manager at the Amadeu Antonio Foundation in Berlin, and talked to her about the rising level of racism and racist attacks on refugees and asylum-seekers. The Foundation is named after Amadeu Antonio, a black Angolan who came to live in the former East Germany as a contract worker in 1987. On the evening of 24 November 1990, a group of local white youths wielding baseball bats went searching for non-white people to attack. They found Amadeu Antonio and beat him unconscious. He fell into a coma and never regained consciousness. He died on 6 December – just a few weeks before his son, Amadeu Antonio Jr, was born.

Amadeu Antonio was the first person known to have been

killed in racist violence in Germany after the Berlin Wall came down. But he wasn't the last. Another 183 people have lost their lives as victims of far-right violence since Germany's reunification. Hundreds of other deaths have not yet been confirmed as hate crime. The Amadeu Antonio Foundation was established in 1998 as a non-governmental organization aimed to bring neo-fascism and rightwing extremism to an end. It was a response to the neo-Nazi subculture that permeates former East Germany and has crept into the rest of Germany. The Foundation focuses its work on monitoring and combating antisemitic activity, neo-Nazism and hate crimes against minorities and migrants. It does so by operating projects that promote alternative youth cultures and community networks, thus creating spaces in civil society where racism can be challenged more effectively.

I met Tahera Ameer in her office, located near the Berlin Wall exhibition. She was managing the project Protective Shield, set up in 2013 to work with communities and local initiatives and respond to the rising number of attacks and assaults on refugees and refugee shelters. 'In 2015, there were five assaults per day in Germany. In 2016, there were four per day. This is clearly a very serious situation,' she said. Amnesty International reported that, in 2015, 1,031 criminal offences were perpetrated against asylum shelters in Germany, a five-fold increase on the previous year. In just the first quarter of 2016, authorities registered 347 crimes against asylum shelters.[42] Ministry of the Interior data revealed that a total of 3,533 attacks had been made on migrants and asylum hostels in Germany in 2016. In Berlin, according to data in the Amnesty International report, attacks on asylum shelters almost doubled in 2015 (40 cases), and increased again to 72 cases in 2016.[43] The situation has been so severe that shelters sometimes feel the need to involve the police force when migrants move in. When the new shelter opened in Pankow in April 2015, for instance, the first group of migrant residents had to move in under heavy police security (an employee of the State Security Services was attacked only days before by the far-right NPD party).[44]

German police say there have been more than 550 attacks on refugee residences in 2016, including arson, gunfire and a grenade. But Ms Ameer pointed out: 'The police only recorded assaults around the shelter. It happens a lot more.' The Amadeu Antonio Foundation records every assault on refugees, not only those around shelters but in all public spaces, such as buses and on the streets. For 2016, Ms Ameer revealed that the Amadeu Antonio Foundation had recorded 46 per cent more assaults than the police did – some of the reasons being structural, institutional racism and the lack of cultural diversity within the police force. She said that these issues have long been ignored by many campaign organizations because they have no way of dealing with them.

The violence was committed by either far-right groups[45] or racist individuals who might not be connected with organizations but are much influenced by extreme-right movements. Ms Ameer said that the most frightening aspect is that these individuals are growing in confidence, as a result of the increasing number and activity of far-right groups.

In Rostock, a northern German city, a shelter for unaccompanied asylum-seeking children between the ages of 7 and 17 was evacuated due to far-right protests in July 2016. The continual local protests against refugees and asylum-seekers and the authorities' fear of encouraging further far-right and racist activity finally led Rostock council to halt construction plans for a new shelter for asylum-seeking families in early August.

The worst incidents of assaults and attacks, in terms of the level of brutality, are concentrated in the eastern part of Germany. Cities like Dresden are particularly notorious for racial violence. '[Refugees and asylum-seekers] are frightened...,' said Ms Ameer. 'They probably wouldn't know that their situation in Dresden is not normal unless they had talked to their friends or contacts in Cologne and other cities. In any case, there's no way they could just get out of the region. They have to stay where they're assigned to be.'

In Berlin, Ms Ameer knew of ten attacks on asylum shelters in 2016. 'Rightwing extremism is a very serious problem here... The situation in the eastern part of Berlin, like Marzahn, Pankow, and Lichtenberg, is as bad as in rural areas of eastern Germany, although the difference is that there is no opposition to racist attacks in the rural areas,' she said.

Every time information about the opening of a shelter was made public, it was followed by anti-refugee protests, which were then followed by attacks on the shelters. In October 2014, when the building of a second asylum shelter in Marzahn Hellersdorf became public, far-right groups started to mobilize the local community against it. Their demonstrations continued into the next year. In early September 2015, the authorities made public that a former school on Glambecker Ring was to be converted into a new asylum shelter. This triggered another wave of protests and then attacks against the building and some of the volunteers who were on site to support refugees. In the first months of 2016, several asylum seekers who lived there were attacked.[46]

On 16 August 2016, in the Marzahn area, racist thugs brought pig heads to an asylum shelter and wrote on the door: 'The whole of Marzahn hates you, you parasites.' As it turned out, the hostel was managed by a former candidate of the neo-Nazi German People's Union.

The Amnesty International report clearly documents the great increase in arson attacks on refugee shelters in 2015. The Amadeu Antonio Foundation recorded over 196 acts of arson directed at refugee housing across Germany during 2015. On 16 April 2015, 100 far-right thugs marched through Nauen, a small town just west of Berlin, carrying German flags and posters saying 'No to the Hostel!' and 'Nauen will stay white!' A week before this march, the planned asylum shelter, converted from a school gym, was set on fire, just before the migrants were due to move in. This arson attack was reported as the fifth within a single week. The racists were imitating events not long before that in Tröglitz, in the eastern state of Saxony, where an arson attack took place on a shelter. The warning, 'Asylum-seekers look out, Tröglitz is here too', was sent to a local youth centre in Nauen and marches in which the NPD was involved continued to take place there.

Racists in other areas followed suit, and in the days following the arson in Nauen, a shelter scheduled to house asylum-seekers was burned down in the Baden-Württemberg town of Weissach im Tal. Fires were also reported near shelters in Leipzig, Döbeln, Salzhemmendorf and Berlin. It appeared these were all organized far-right attacks.

On 8 August 2016, in the early hours of the morning in Berlin, a fire bomb was thrown into a container shelter that housed 185 migrants in Refugium Buch on Karower Chaussee Street in Pankow. It caused a fire in which six migrants suffered injuries as a result of smoke inhalation. (Luckily, the shelter wasn't fully occupied at the time, although the capacity was for 480 people. More people could have been injured had it been full.) According to Ms Ameer, the following day members of the NPD, which has considerable support in Berlin, came to hang their anti-migrant posters outside the burned-down shelter.

The role of the police with regard to the increase in racist attacks on asylum shelters has been questioned by campaign groups such as Amnesty International. In the most troubled district, Marzahn-Hellersdorf, for instance, Amnesty stated: 'The Berlin police acknowledged that the opening of refugee shelters in Marzahn-Hellersdorf, as well as in other Berlin districts, sparked protests because of the presence of strong far-right structures in those areas. They [the Berlin police] stressed that the police constantly monitored the far-right scene and took action in specific instances... However, the Berlin police have not adopted any overall plan or strategy to prevent attacks in Marzahn-Hellersdorf, despite the available data regarding the rise in hate crime in the district... The police did not have a comprehensive risk-assessment plan aimed at identifying the asylum shelters or the districts particularly vulnerable to hate crime.'[47]

For asylum-seekers, although Berlin in general is a better and safer place than other cities in eastern Germany, some shelters in the capital have suffered so much from racist harassment and attacks that many migrants prefer to sleep on the streets, which is obviously unsafe in such a situation. Some, however, are prepared to consider this option when they know that they will have to wait a long time in shelters that are often the target of racist activity before they can apply to live in the community, which is relatively safer.

Apart from the growing physical racial violence against migrants, there has also been an increase in far-right propaganda online over the past two years. Not only does their online material aim to incite racial hatred among those who believe migrants are a threat to their way of life, but some websites have also been set up to appeal to the middle class, as detected by the Antonio Amadeu Foundation.[48] Their 2016 report found 300 'No to refugee homes' Facebook profiles, which were designed to appeal to 'concerned citizens'. The report said this was generating support for the Alternative for Germany (AfD), the anti-Muslim, anti-migrant far-right party whose popular support has been growing, as demonstrated by a poll in January 2017 that suggested it would take 15 per cent of the vote if a general election took place the next day. Indeed, in the election that autumn, AfD gained nearly 13 per cent of the vote and 94 seats in parliament.

Ms Ameer shared with me the personal history that had politicized her. She grew up in a small village near Hamburg in northern Germany. Her father is a Muslim Indian who moved from India to Pakistan, where he lived for two years but did not settle down, and eventually migrated to Europe in the late 1970s. He worked as an engineer.

'My father didn't speak much German, and was never really accepted. I understood that only in retrospect,' she said.

She said that from the age of 12, she began to focus on the history of the Holocaust and read all about it. I was surprised how young she had been when she became interested. 'Well, maybe because I was always the only child who was asked "Where are you really from?"' she said, smiling.

'At the time, I didn't understand it; I was totally naïve. My father always told me I was German. I couldn't even speak Urdu and had no idea about Pakistan or India. I thought we were just Germans... It took me years and years, till I was in my thirties, before I realized for the first time that I'm not a white German.'

I was truly surprised. 'How did you find out that you're not a white German?'

'Someone told me that,' she said. 'The focus of my study at the time was the literature of the Holocaust and its survivors and I ran workshops after which I often broke down... A friend of mine said to me: "You're always talking about yourself as amongst the white Germans, as part of the perpetrator society where people should take responsibility [for racism]... But, let me tell you, you're not one of them. And maybe this is your problem and why you're suffering emotionally. You're one of the victims [of racism] but you don't realize it. You think you're part of the perpetrator society."' Ms Ameer then suddenly realized that she wasn't who she thought she was. This dramatic personal history has been part of what led her to develop her work and get involved in anti-racist campaigning; she now feels she needs to move from challenging structural racism within mainstream society to lobbying to bring minorities from the sidelines to the centre.

As it turned out, the far-right party Alternative for Germany (AfD) made huge electoral gains and entered the state parliament for the first time, with 14 per cent of the vote in Berlin's state elections in mid-September 2016. Angela Merkel's CDU won just 17.6 per cent of the vote, its worst-ever result in the city, and was pushed into third place by AfD in Mecklenburg-Western Pomerania. AfD is now represented in 10 out of 16 state parliaments.

Dresden, the capital city of Saxony, is just two hours away from Berlin, but I was reluctant to go there. It is notorious amongst migrants for its undisguised hostility towards ethnic minorities and new migrants. PEGIDA – a German far-right group that translates as Patriotic Europeans Against the Islamization of the West – has held rallies in the city. There have been attacks and assaults on asylum-seekers and refugees in the city for years.

On 15 January 2015, a 20-year-old asylum-seeker from Eritrea was stabbed to death near the shelter where he lived in Dresden. He died from wounds to the neck and chest. His brutal murder happened at a time when PEGIDA's rallies were attracting tens of thousands, when anti-migrant sentiment was heightened and racism was commonplace.

A group of anti-racist activists attempted to provide some balanced information and education for the public in Dresden. During my stay, a series of films around the central theme of migration was shown in the square in front of the cathedral. One of the short films was called *Winter in Lampedusa* and Dave and I went along to watch.

Dozens of residents showed up on this very windy and cold night and we had to move into a tent to avoid the bad weather. The film was a documentary that these concerned activists had made about the life of Lampedusans in the middle of winter, alongside the ongoing arrival of migrants there by sea and their entrapment in the asylum system. Although it was dubbed in German and I did not understand the text, it was reminiscent at times of the Italian documentary film *Fire At Sea* (2016), directed by Gianfranco Rosi.

However, small groups of artists have not been able to change the general atmosphere in Dresden. In February 2017, rightwing protesters took to the streets against an anti-war sculpture in the centre of town. The artwork was three upturned buses, meant to resemble a sniper barricade used by rebels in the Syrian town of Aleppo. They were being put in place ahead of the annual memorial of the bombing of Dresden in World War Two. Not only was there an angry protest, but death threats were even made against supporters of the sculpture.

I also visited Heidenau, a dull little dead-end village, 16 kilometres south of Dresden. Heidenau, with a population of 16,000, is set amidst sandstone mountains and is known as the Swiss Saxony. It has also been notorious for racial violence against refugees and migrants. It is a solid electoral base for the NPD. Here, in August 2015, following an NPD demonstration, there was a violent racist protest against a new asylum shelter that housed 600 migrants in a former warehouse. For two nights, 250 protesters brandished bottles and waved flags associated with far-right groups. Some chanted *Wir sind das Volk* ('We are the people'), a slogan frequently used by far-right groups. Skinheads from a far-right group known as *Freie Kameradschaften* were also present. There has been no local police investigation of these groups – nor about their connection to the NPD. Notably, however, political activities organized by far-right parties have often been followed by violent attacks on their perceived enemies. As the Amnesty International report points out: 'The rise of anti-refugee demonstrations, albeit often nonviolent, has been accompanied by a rise in violence against refugees in the same area.'[49]

The scenario of a large, well-coordinated extreme-right network is not only realistic but highly probable. One aspect of racist crimes and how the police deal with them is well illustrated by the murders perpetrated by the National Socialist Underground (NSU). Three members of the NSU – Uwe Mundlos, Uwe Böhnhardt and Beate Zschäpe – murdered ten people, eight of them of Turkish descent and one of Greek descent, between 2000 and 2007. The group also carried out two bomb attacks in Cologne in 2001 and 2004 as well as several robberies.

On 4 November 2011, after robbing a bank in Eisenach, Uwe Mundlos and Uwe Böhnhardt set the mobile home in which they were hiding alight and killed themselves shortly before police found them. The same day, Beate Zschäpe set fire to the flat in Zwickau in Saxony where the three had lived together – it was there that the police found the firearm used in nine of the murders as well as a list of about 10,000 potential targets for violent attack across Germany. They included asylum shelters, ethnic-minority-owned businesses, Turkish cultural and community organizations and leftwing organizations. Zschäpe also sent a propaganda video to several policymakers and the media, before turning herself in to the police. The video started with a cartoon pink panther looking at TV news of the murders and wondering when the world would find out who committed them. At the end of the video, she directly named the group as responsible for the murders and other crimes. Since 6 May 2013, Zschäpe has been on trial in Munich.

However, the case of the NSU murders and how they were dealt with has revealed a deeply rooted disease in German society: institutional racism within the police and intelligence services at all levels. It is this that accounts for the failure, over the course of an entire decade, to identify and investigate the racist motivation for these murders, and therefore to overlook aspects of the crimes that clearly pointed to the involvement of a far-right group. As the Amnesty International report points out, the failure of the German authorities to investigate, prosecute and sentence racist crimes effectively is a long-standing concern that predates the arrival of asylum-seekers. Institutional racism also led to the harassment of the victims' families by the police. They were repeatedly questioned about any involvement in criminal activities.

'In all these years, they've never treated us as victims,' said Yvonne Boulgarides, wife of the locksmith Theodorus Boulgarides, murdered in his Munich shop on 15 June 2005.[50] 'We were always treated as suspects by the police or politicians, as if we were hiding something. Nobody asked us about our opinions or listened to us,' she said. Even after the involvement of the NSU became clear, the victims' families first heard of it from media reports rather than the police authorities.

In January 2012, in response to these massive failings, the German Federal Parliament established a Committee of Inquiry into the authorities' failure to effectively investigate the NSU murders and to bring those responsible to justice. On 22 August 2013, the Committee published its final report. This acknowledged the authorities' failures to take all reasonable steps to investigate the racist motive behind the murders. However, the inquiry report avoided stating that institutional racism had played a part in the failings.[51]

Nevertheless, given this context, the authorities have now become more inclined to consider far-right organizational connections with racist violence. Consequently, after the violence in Heidenau, 250 investigators raided homes in Bavaria, Saxony, North Rhine-Westphalia, Rhineland-Palatinate and Mecklenburg-Western Pomerania, in an effort to destroy the far-right terrorist group Old School Society (OSS), which public prosecutors believed was seeking to acquire explosive material for terror attacks against asylum shelters.

Finally, in January 2017, German prosecutors charged three men and one woman with forming the OSS two years earlier, and planning to bomb an asylum shelter. They had been using social media to recruit and mobilize violence. They trained members to manufacture nail bombs, and had a concrete plan to carry out an explosives attack – two of them went to the Czech Republic in May 2015 to purchase firearms – on an asylum shelter near Borna, a town southeast of Leipzig in Saxony. Fortunately, they were arrested in May 2016 before the planned attack could take place, as part of the national raids to eliminate the group.

In the same month, prosecutors in Rhineland-Palatinate were investigating whether two men, aged 18 and 24, arrested in December 2016 for storing large amounts of explosives, were members of the OSS. The younger man had admitted attending an OSS meeting the year before. Following their arrest, almost 90 residents had to be evacuated from an area of Lauterecken over safety concerns, as police removed a large amount of homemade explosives from the home of one of the suspects. One bomb found there had a swastika on it, according to the police.

Back in Heidenau, asylum seekers had been moved to another location following the violent protests. Local residents seemed to be unwilling to talk about where they had now been housed, and replied vaguely when asked. Eventually, I found out they had been accommodated in the town hall. When I visited, the 1,200 migrants had again been moved to different shelters – this time outside Heidenau. It is most likely that this was the result of continuous local protests.

Another asylum shelter had also suffered from numerous local protests and attacks: the former Lindhof Hotel, which was converted into a shelter in summer 2015, in Dresden Stetzsch, a 20-minute train ride northwest of Dresden.

Dresden Stetzsch is a quiet, almost lifeless, village along a main road, where it is almost impossible to find a cab or to hitch-hike as vehicles will never stop. You can walk for miles without seeing another person. How could this have been considered a suitable location for an asylum shelter, when migrants do not speak the language and are unable to communicate with locals? Their isolation becomes entrenched in a situation like this.

It took a while to find the street where the shelter was located, mainly because all the residential streets look similar around there. I finally found the former Lindhof Hotel, a three-storey building that had a prominent balcony on the first floor. As I entered the building, several migrants walked past and greeted me. They came from Afghanistan. They took me around the building and showed me one of their rooms – they were sleeping in bunk beds, several people to a room. Hung on their doors were signs written in English, saying 'Locals Only', clearly in humorous mockery of the local hostility to them.

The manager of the shelter arrived and introduced himself

as Michael Hoffmann. It was a hot midday and he rolled up his sleeves, revealing a pattern of tattoos on his left arm. He told me he had been the manager there for ten months. He was in his thirties. His mother had been a social worker involved with refugees since the 1990s, and perhaps her influence had led to Michael running an asylum shelter. It was opened in July 2015, providing housing to asylum-seekers from Syria, Afghanistan and Pakistan.

That year there were many problems with the local community. However, he said he had expected that and had not been surprised by the local hostility. 'They are suspicious of Syrian refugees, suspicious that they might be terrorists... They read a lot of things in the newspapers and they end up believing them. They don't understand that refugees are just normal people.

'Some of the hostile people are just from the local area, but others are in rightwing groups. Between 10 and 20 young men came and yelled at our residents... They came every week. It was very stressful for our residents and we had to close the windows. But the migrants have far more problems back in their own countries than dealing with racists here. Bombs, deaths and destruction. So this is nothing for them, by comparison. On Christmas Day 2015, the racists came to cause trouble. On New Year's Day, they came again and threw firebombs at the house. The Syrians tried to make light of it, saying, "Wow, they [the racists] are bringing us fireworks!" They are scared, though, of attacks on the streets if they're alone, so they tend to go out in each other's company.'

Mr Hoffmann said there had not been any problems recently. Time had passed and the locals had become accustomed to the migrants' presence. They had also seen that nothing negative had happened since the migrants moved into their community. Therefore, many locals had 'come to terms' with the new members of this village. 'Some local people, young and old, now come in and have lunch with the refugees here,' he said. 'They are interested. They want to have a look and speak with the migrants. They're getting a better understanding about the refugees, their background and what they're like. Some have accepted them.'

The asylum-seekers here had been waiting for documents, most of them for a year. 'Some want to return home, because Germany isn't easy, with all the bureaucracy,' Mr Hoffmann said. 'When they do get their documents, many want to move to cities like Berlin or Cologne instead of staying here.' It's difficult for them to find work in this area. There is very little industry; menial work in the restaurants is all they could hope for. Language is an obvious barrier and a two-tier system exists for asylum-seekers learning German: the Syrians can attend language classes paid for by the government, but the Afghan and Pakistani migrants have to pay for themselves. This prevents many from even trying to learn the language, and in turn their opportunities for work and a future life in this country diminish too.

The anti-migrant hub

Bautzen also has a reputation for violently rejecting refugees and I wanted to see what the town was like. It lies in Saxony, an under-populated state that has been assigned only five per cent of the total number of asylum-seekers in the 16 states of Germany. Yet the arrival and presence of 'outsiders' had sparked the most violent response seen in the country. Most of the aggression had been directed at asylum shelters.

In February 2016, in Bautzen, an asylum shelter converted from the former Hotel Husarenhof, which was to accommodate 300 people, was burned down just before the migrants were due to move in. It was a frightening sight, with walls and roof charred by flames. While the shelter was burning a crowd of around 30 Germans gathered, cheering the flames and chanting anti-migrant slogans.

While Dave and I were still in Dresden, a waiter cringed when I mentioned we were going to Bautzen. He told us there had been a far-right protest the previous week which had ended with 80 neo-Nazis fighting 19 migrants in the town centre, and the same had happened just a few weeks earlier. Shaking his head, he described the pecking order of racism, and said that top of the hated list came refugees and migrants in Bautzen. 'Bautzen doesn't represent us,' he said. However, this waiter had travelled widely and worked abroad for years. He was used to living amongst multi-ethnic communities. Perhaps he didn't really represent rural eastern Germany.

People associate Bautzen with its two Nazi prisons, built with yellow bricks. One of them, built in 1904, is nicknamed 'Yellow Misery'. In the fascist period from 1933 to 1945, both were used to detain political prisoners, with a capacity of 1,600 people. This dark past seems to connect with its more recent image as a far-right bastion.

We arrived in Bautzen in bleak twilight. On a hilltop, the streets paved with pebble stones, you can stroll about the town and enjoy the peaceful affluence. There was not a 'foreign-looking' soul to be seen in the centre of town, except for myself, and it appeared to be even more of a traditional white stronghold than Torquay in southwest England. As we did not understand much German and everywhere else was shut, we found ourselves in a restaurant where almost every dish had a mustard theme. There, I experienced the first bit of local hostility to 'outsiders'. Every time I spoke, the staff waiting at table avoided any eye contact with me, as if I were somehow invisible or my presence was damaging. I also received a lot of unfriendly stares from local diners during the meal.

The Spree Hotel shelter, the first privately run asylum shelter in Bautzen, eight kilometres outside the town centre, was where I intended to visit. It was literally in the middle of nowhere, although there was plenty of green space around. In front of the main entrance was a large front yard where many migrant children were playing. It was midday, and the staff all looked busy. I got talking to several Somali and Syrian men who were sitting chatting to each other on the benches outside the front door. One of the Somalis told me that he had been there, waiting for his papers, for ten months. The other one said he was worried that Bautzen was not a safe place to live in. No-one leaves the site after 7pm.

Several migrants were walking up a path to the lakeside park 15 minutes away. It was safer out there in the fields – much more so than in town where the local people were. Some were also riding bikes that could be borrowed from the shelter. It was a tranquil area where they could stretch their legs and breathe some fresh air. In the distance, by the lake, sat a man in his twenties who had just walked there from the shelter. He was staring into the water in front of him, while butterflies flew around over the grass close to his feet. This must have been a precious moment for him, where he could clear his head away from the permanent company and daily routines at the shelter. Five minutes further along the lakeside was a beach with lots of boats pulled up onto the sand. Next to it was a 'pretend beach café', as we called it, with a wooden porch, beach chairs and umbrellas outside. Tourists – they couldn't have come from very far – sunbathed on the pretend beach, facing the lake. The migrants from the shelter never came to this café; they would not have been able to afford the drinks.

At dusk I finally managed to talk to the shelter manager, Peter Rausch. He had been working hard all day, he said, and it had been quite hectic. He peered at me over his glasses across the table. He told me he had been running the shelter for two and a half years.

'It's out of economic necessity that I decided to run this shelter. I had run the place as a four-star hotel for 15 years but it just didn't work out the way I wanted.' Mr Rausch said that he had once worked for the Hilton, Continental and Sheraton chains in the UK, France, Jordan and Syria. To get away from the hierarchy of the hotel business, he had acquired this property in 2000 and set up his own business. He sold it to an investor in 2007, but continued to manage it.

'This place was never love at first sight: the building, the location, and I'm not from here. I come from the Black Forest in the western part of Germany,' he said. When he heard local authorities were looking for a shelter for refugees, he saw the business opportunity. 'There was a place in town but everyone was against it. I approached the town of Bautzen in October 2013 and said I could house the shelter here. They were happy about it. When the news became public in March 2014, there was a tremendous storm over it; people were asking, how can you transform a four-star hotel into a refugee home?'

At the beginning, in July 2014, the shelter received only 16 young men, aged between 19 and 25, from Tunisia. By the time of my visit there were migrants from 19 different countries, though mainly from Syria, Afghanistan, Pakistan and Chechnya. Since the summer of 2015, the shelter's capacity has had to increase to accommodate more people arriving in Germany. In autumn 2016, nearly 300 people were living there. There were 30 families living six or seven to a large room. There were 39 children. Single men were living three or four to a room.

'It's been very stressful for them. Some of them have been waiting for an asylum decision for a long time,' Mr Rausch said. 'Ten men have been in this shelter since it began and have waited for two and a half years. No idea whether they'll ever get an answer. Some people would disappear after a while, for instance, the Moroccans, who know their chance of getting accepted is practically zero. They might even get a new name in another city. Around 50 to 60 people have disappeared from this shelter.

'But even when migrants get their refugee status in the end, they must stay in the same region for three years, unless they have a job somewhere else. This is to reduce pressure on the cities. However, rural areas like Bautzen aren't prepared for the housing demands. There are not enough one-bedroom flats,' he said. And where might they seek work? He told me that some of the Pakistani residents were working in a baking factory in town. But apart from small businesses like that, there was little work to be had.

While showing concern for the migrants as his clients, Mr Rausch admitted that he wanted to keep the shelter as full as possible because he needs to earn money. 'I can say that, after two and a half years, my financial problems have been solved.' He lit a cigarette. 'This is a financially solid company. My revenue is about €1.2 million [$1.4 million] a year. I get €13 per person per day [from the state]. That's a five-year contract. As long as I've got 200 people in here, it's all right. It's the normal rate.'

At the height of demand, as the number of migrants arriving increased in summer 2015, the rate businesses were asking was as high as €22 or €23 per person per day, a ludicrous amount. 'That was in the emergency situation though,' he said.

Mr Rausch had made enough money to be able to expand his workforce, and now had five staff in the shelter, including two social workers, translators, and a driver to collect donations from charities. 'The other shelter in Bautzen, with 350 people, doesn't have enough staff,' he said competitively. He also said he was 'doing something on integration'.

'What I didn't expect when starting this shelter is that I would regret being in the hotel business for 35 years... I should have done this from the beginning. I like what I'm doing. This is much more stressful, but much more rewarding. Earning money and having fun at the same time – this is completely new to me. I'll do it for as long as I can.'

During our meeting, I could see from his office windows that police cars were patrolling the road outside and officers were guarding the shelter. He said that a police patrol was there every day, several times a day, as a response to the far-right activity against this shelter. He said he felt reassured by the police presence.

Business profits aside, how did he deal with all the aggression from the local community? He said with a sigh: 'It was a disaster at first. Every week there were protests. You have Nazis in this area, a situation I didn't really predict, so I had to build a fence outside and set up video surveillance.

'It lasted for the first eight months... and then it died down. When the second shelter was opened, it was in the town centre, so the trouble went there, because it was easier for the protesters to get to. There was no fence there.'

With all the trouble that has taken place here, Mr Rausch said local people were trying to change their image. 'But in the 2015 election, 25 per cent voted to the right of the CDU... You have got some hard-core Nazis living in Bautzen; there are Nazis all over Saxony, all over Germany. If they organize a protest, they can mobilize within a week, with social media... Most of the Nazis are from outside; only 15-20 per cent [of protesters] are local to Bautzen. It reflects badly on Bautzen. The NPD is the main part of this. Maybe they will be banned soon, because it's against the German constitution.'

The ban on the far-right NPD party, which has 5,000 members and links with some violent Nazis, was applied for in 2013, and was the second attempt to outlaw it. The case of the NSU murders in 2011 prompted politicians to explore a legal ban. However, in 2017, Germany's Supreme Court rejected the proposed ban. Despite support from all 16 of the country's states to outlaw the NPD, the Federal Constitutional Court rejected the attempt.

Mr Rausch didn't think the hostility from locals was only connected to unemployment, which was a serious problem 15-16 years ago. However, an unemployment rate of 8.3 per cent is high enough to cause concern. 'And you have many long-term unemployed people here, in their fifties, and it is hard to find another job,' he said. 'There are no big industries here... Young people go to the west of Germany because the wage level is 25-per-cent higher than in Bautzen. And there are plenty of work opportunities there.'

Mr Rausch believed that there are many misconceptions about refugees in Europe. 'I don't believe there is a refugee crisis. We are talking about 1 million people versus 80 million people. I don't think it's a crisis. A tremendous challenge, yes. But not a crisis. A crisis is if Russia wants to occupy Germany. That would be a crisis. If everyone cools down and thinks about it, they'll see that it presents a tremendous opportunity. When I came to Bautzen in 2000, the town population was 53,000; today we have 40,000. You don't have to be a prophet to see that our town population is decreasing. We don't have enough babies any more. In ten years, we have seven million fewer workers. Bautzen's becoming a pensioners' town. Young people are going away, to Dresden, to the west of Germany.'

Indeed, Germany is in need of 400,000 skilled workers every year, in order to maintain its economic strength. Its shortage is so severe that the law requiring employers to give preference to German or EU job applicants over asylum-seekers has been suspended for three years.

Mr Rausch welcomed refugees and migrants on the basis of their economic value to the country. 'It's an opportunity that we have young migrants here, who are going to have children, who will stay here and will earn money... We need workforce,' he said. He then pointed to a big pile of documents on the side of the desk, saying, 'When I had a hotel, the pile of applications for apprenticeships was about this high... But in the last two years, there's not even been a single one! There are not enough young people. The refugees are an opportunity, for the labour market, for the town, and for society.'

But things don't change much in Bautzen. In early November

2016, a mob of up to 50 neo-Nazis went chasing migrants in town. Two of the migrants had to run for their lives, with racists shouting abuse behind them. One of them was hit by a bike thrown at him by one of his attackers.

Trapped in the system

In spring 2017, through the No Borders group in Leeds, I came across Shareef Masri, a 31-year-old Syrian asylum-seeker, who had been so demoralized by his experience in the asylum system in Germany that he was desperately asking activists for help and advice to obtain a transfer.

In Syria, Shareef was a graduate in Accounting and Economics, and he told me that he had only one exam left before becoming a Certified Management Accountant when the revolution started. He eventually left the country when it became a war zone. His father was not well enough to leave home – he had been in business dealing with medical supplies for hospitals before he became disabled after a stroke and the onset of Alzheimer's in 2005. Since then he had been looked after by his wife in their family house in Damascus. Shareef's mother was also taking care of his grandparents after their house was destroyed in the war. His married sister also lived in Damascus. The rest of his family had migrated out of Syria before the war: his sister was living in Qatar and his brother in Ireland.

In the first two years after leaving Syria, Shareef lived in Lebanon, and then moved to Egypt, where he spent another two years. As he did not have formal residency status in either country, and his passport was about to expire and could not be renewed, he left for Turkey. From there, he went on to Greece, then through Macedonia, Serbia, Croatia, Slovenia and Austria, and eventually reached Germany on 20 December 2015. Shareef's initial plan was not to go to Germany but Norway, but after arriving in Croatia he found that strict controls by the police and military forces prevented him from moving freely. Along with fellow migrants, he was taken from Croatia and handed over to the next military unit, in Slovenia; during the trip they were not allowed to buy food or even use the toilet. He was only freed when they reached Germany.

'When you hear the name Germany, the first thing that comes into your mind is civilized western Europe. Right?' Shareef said. 'Well, that's not what we found. The treatment by the German border police was even worse than the Macedonian and Serbian – they put us in a yard with high fences; we were in a cage, without access to water or a bathroom. If you needed to go to the bathroom, you would have to call for a police officer, who would sometimes respond and other times wouldn't.

'Following that, they forced us to strip naked, in the middle of cold December, Guantánamo style. They then searched us, and took our passports away by force. This was why I wasn't able to go anywhere else afterwards.' Shareef then spent two days in a camp in Deggendorf, near the Austrian border, being fed canned food, until they sorted out his papers. For the following year, Shareef was moved from one camp to another in the state of Bavaria.

His second camp, a sports hall, was in a town called Röhrenbach. There, he shared a crowded space with 150 people, mainly from Syria and a few from Iraq. He was there for nearly a month, after which half of the asylum-seekers there left Germany, with some going to other EU countries and others back to Turkey via Greece (after what they had experienced in Germany). The camp management then told the remaining asylum-seekers that they were closing the camp permanently because the town wanted the sports hall for special occasions. Shareef and other residents were moved to Munich.

The camp in Munich, which he described as looking like a concentration camp, was basically two plastic-covered tents – one for families, the other for single people – in a former garage, accommodating around 200 Syrian, Afghan, Somali and other African asylum-seekers. It was an isolated location away from any residential area. 'For almost a year, my camp in Munich did a great job in isolating refugees from the rest of the community, while it did a poor job in isolating refugees from extreme winter cold and summer heat,' he said. Shareef stayed there for 11 months, during which he suffered the most dreadful living conditions. People were crammed into roofless compartments, partitioned by wooden boards. Sanitary facilities were lacking and were poorly maintained. The place had no hygiene control. Processed food served in foil containers was of a very poor standard. He started filming the interior of the camp with his mobile-phone camera, and posted it on YouTube. He wanted the world to see life inside a camp in Germany.

He said: 'I have some questions for the viewers to ask and for the German authorities to answer: How can you isolate refugees and then demand them to integrate?'

Shareef was then transferred to another camp in the same area in Munich, where he was still living at the time he talked to me. It was a three-storey building for around 250 single people. He had no idea how long he'd be kept there. The camp management seemed to enjoy threatening the migrants with 'a transfer to a worse place' if any of them caused any trouble.

Shareef said that, for him, the one thing that was worse than poor living conditions was the degrading way asylum-seekers were treated. 'Even today, the camp management breaks into our rooms without any warning or cause, and they have the right to search our private belongings, look at our mail, close the laundry room and kitchen without any reason, shut down the heating system when it's cold, etc...

'The treatment we are getting is worse than criminals get. Yet I did not commit any crime. The only comments that we get from Germans are 'We have too many refugees'. These kinds of remark are an excuse for bureaucracy, hypocrisy and racism in Germany.' He found it difficult to sum up his experience of racism, but told me that he'd suffered all forms of racial prejudice. 'One time, a man tried to run me over with his car when I was on my way back to the camp. There have also been many bomb threats made to our camp...

'Here, nobody will rent you an apartment no matter how hard you try. A woman once said to me "I will rent my apartment to Germans only". I'm entitled to rent an apartment by law, but I've tried almost 400 landlords and apartments online, all with negative responses. When I consulted several migrants in the city about this, they said "it's almost impossible to rent an apartment in Munich if you don't have a German name". I refuse to change who I am just to fit in with this narrow-minded community.'

Shareef found it hard to cope with the level of racism around him. 'You have racism when people describe you as a "scheiss Ausländer" ["shitty foreigner"] on the street, and when you don't get allowed into most social places, such as clubs and bars, and when people avoid sitting next to you on a train or bus, which happens to me a lot. It's hard for me because there's nothing I hate more than racism. But all I can do is try to keep my communication with Germans to a minimum...'

In Germany, Shareef would never be able to be reunited with his family. 'The law in Germany doesn't consider them [parents and siblings] primary family members, but only secondary, so there is no family reunification opportunity in my case.

'Racism is what's truly stopping me from starting my life over again,' he said, 'I need to get out of Germany as soon as possible and as far away as possible... My needs are simple. I just want to live in a place where people respect me for the human being I am, regardless of my colour and religion... where I can work and continue my studies.'

Amat, Modou and Banta move on

Back in the camp in Corleone, Sicily, where Amat was still living in the winter of 2016, it was rare to hear him talking without anxiety. But when I next called him he was cheerful, having just talked with his mother on the phone. 'She's well,' he said, reassured.

Amat spent most of his time in solitude. He had his guitar with him, and would spend the whole evening playing it. He had learned to play in Gambia and now his housemates would sometimes knock on his door, asking to come in and spend time with him. They treated his room as a social space; he said it was because he kept it nice and clean and stored up much-needed drinking water. His housemates would come to ask for help if they had run out of their own water.

As it was near Christmas, I asked Amat if anything was being planned at the camp. 'The camp doesn't organize anything for Christmas,' he said, 'not even for the Christian migrants here.' It seemed like they would cut costs on everything.

I asked if he was going to do anything different on New Year's

Eve. 'No, nothing,' he replied quietly. No activity was due to be organized in the camp – and he didn't want to go out.

'Why not? Why don't you go out, for a bit of an adventure, on New Year's Eve?' I said.

'I don't feel too safe in town,' he replied. 'I don't want to appear like I'm mixing too much with the locals.'

'Why not?' I was puzzled.

'Because people are suspicious of us migrants. When I go into the town to do some shopping, it's OK. But if I go into town to party, to have fun, then it's a step too far for them. It will look like I'm trying to mix with them.'

He went on: 'Local people are particularly suspicious that I might have a relationship with an Italian woman – you know, "their woman". That's how they think, if you mix too much with them...'

'How do you know that's how they see it?'

'You see, the people in this town had never seen black people before this camp was set up three years ago,' he said. 'Once, when I was in town, I was asked by local youths in their twenties about my origin and why I was here. When I told them that my cousin in Switzerland is married to a local woman and has three children with her, the local youths were very surprised. It was as if they couldn't believe a cross-ethnic marriage could happen. The concept was alien to them.'

Amat had learned to be cautious with the local youth. Every time they asked him why he was in town, he would reply that he was there just to buy some cigarettes or water. 'I'm careful not to give any impression that I have any business to do with the locals,' he said. The fear of being singled out was the reason why he always preferred to stay in. On New Year's Eve, too.

A few days later, on 30 December 2016, there was great news from Messina: Modou, the 17-year-old Gambian boy, finally got his long-desired transfer to a minors' shelter in Agrigento, although he was not told about where he was going until just before his departure from the Gasparro camp.

When Modou eventually arrived in Agrigento, he still wasn't sure where he was. I was surprised. 'Where are you, exactly?' I asked again.

'Aggregator,' he said.

'Do you mean Agrigento? Is it by the sea?'

'Yes, it is Agrigento.' And Modou was loving it there. 'It's beautiful,' he said. The only thing was that he was missing his friends. It would take time to make new friends.

'But it will come,' I reassured him.

What Modou wanted most was to go to school. He didn't want to waste his youth away in the camps. However, three months after his transfer to Agrigento, he was still waiting to be sent to a school. Finally, in late March 2017, Modou was transferred to another camp, in Licata, also on the southern coast of Sicily. 'It's beautiful,' he said joyfully, just as he had when arriving in Agrigento. This time, at last, he was sent to a school. He was finding the Italian language difficult, but he was trying hard to learn it. Over the weekend, Modou would spend time with his new friends in the camp and play football. He was a great player and one Sunday his team won a trophy in a match with local youths. He often said that his dream was to become a professional footballer, though he wanted to achieve academically, too. Just before Ramadan, I sent him a new schoolbag as a gift. He had never had a schoolbag before and was thrilled. 'I'll do my very best and do well at school,' he said.

On the last day of December 2016, Banta was feeling very anxious. African forces from Senegal and Nigeria were already camping along the borders with Gambia, getting ready to storm into the country and evict the former dictator Yahya Jammeh, who still had support from part of the army and was hanging on to power.

Banta wanted to move his mother and his son out of Gambia. Many Gambians were already heading to Senegal. Some of his family decided to go too, and Banta's sister travelled from Sweden to Senegal, to make sure that they settled in well. She would stay for a while to look after them. However, Banta's mother insisted that she was going to remain at home in Gambia. Home was where she knew and she was not prepared to leave it behind. She was not going anywhere. This was the case with many of the older generation.

A few days later, the dictator Jammeh claimed that he was hanging on to power because 'The judge for appealing against the election results is not in the country' (and would return only in

May). The head of the army was now backing Jammeh. Banta's mother was still in the country, on her own and worried for her safety; in mid-January 2017, Banta asked a friend in the army to keep an eye on her.

To everyone's relief, on 20 January, following days of negotiation, and as the Senegalese army entered Gambia and West African armies threatened joint military action against Yahya Jammeh, he finally ceded power to the newly elected president Adama Barrow and announced his departure (incidentally making off with most of Gambia's gold reserves).

Banta was finally able to concentrate on his work and life in Germany. He had since moved to Mannheim, an industrial city less than 100 kilometres from Stuttgart. Mannheim has a population of 290,000, 44 per cent of whom are non-German. Since 2015, around 12,000 asylum-seekers have been sheltered here, including 2,500 people placed in the former US army barracks, in a ghetto-like quarter away from the rest of the city population.

In Mannheim, Banta found a job, with the help of the Caritas charity organization, as a cleaner, cleaning pubs and old people's homes for five hours a day, five days a week – in a good week, he earned €25, a rate of just one euro per hour. As he had no permit to work, he could only rely on Caritas to find him employment on a zero-hours contract. He didn't know what proportion of his overall wages had been taken by Caritas. Some weeks, several days would pass without any cleaning work at all. He lived in Pyramidenstrasse, a rundown area in the north of town. His rent was paid by Caritas.

When asked what motivated him to move to a new city, he replied: 'To look for greener pastures.'

'Are you happy in this greener pasture?' I asked.

'I can say I'm not very happy... Everyone wants to be near their family,' he said. His sense of being an outsider had been strengthened by the day-to-day reality of living there. It's too expensive to be in Germany, he said. The cost of living had limited his lifestyle, clearly. I saw when I visited that his only relaxation was hanging around the park by the river with other African migrants. He couldn't even afford to sit down for a drink in the beer garden next to the park.

Banta said there was a lot of police control. 'They are always watching you. It's a police state,' he said. The police tended to randomly stop and search African migrants. Banta himself was once watched and followed by several officers, until he decided to approach them before they approached him. 'I went up to them and asked for directions, so they could stop being suspicious of me,' he said, laughing bitterly.

Banta had been missing home badly. He spoke affectionately about his mother and son. But he was only able to afford to call them every now and then. Back in Gambia, not every household has internet access and he couldn't communicate with them on WhatsApp. The price he was paying for earning to support his mother and his son was that he could not choose when he would next see them.

The destinies of his fellow Gambians abroad always concerned Banta and he often shared and discussed their situation with Gambian friends on social media. He sent me videos of Gambian migrants detained in Libyan jails, living an inhuman existence. They had travelled the same route as him, but not been fortunate enough to have managed to escape from Libya. In early April, Banta shared news about 169 fellow Gambian migrants who were released from detention centres in Tripoli and elsewhere, and sent back home to Gambia, arranged by the IOM and the Gambian government. Many of them revealed that they were fed only once a day, and were often beaten and tortured during detention. Some witnessed others being arbitrarily shot dead.

On 20 April 2017, Banta told me that he could not go to work for the next few days. Representatives of the local authorities had come to the neighbourhoods where migrants were living to warn them that they should be particularly mindful of their safety in the next couple of days as AfD members and supporters would be in town for a demonstration from 21 to 23 April. Banta made a recording of the representative's warning and sent it to me. The message said: 'Please don't go near these areas [marked on the card which they were delivering to migrants]. We're telling anyone who's not German to stay close to their flats... These people like Hitler. We will have 4,000 police officers but we don't know if it will be enough [to prevent violence]... We don't want anyone to get hurt or stabbed.'

Mannheim's migrant communities were on alert. AfD was well-known for its violence against refugees and migrants. Its then leader Frauke Petry had notoriously made remarks to the regional newspaper *Mannheimer Morgen* in an interview in late January 2016, that 'German border police must use firearms if necessary to prevent illegal border crossings.'[52] In one of its rallies in Mannheim, Petry's supporters chanted racist slogans and demanded 'concrete proposals to get black Africans to stay in their home countries'. In the state parliament elections in March 2016, AfD gained 23 per cent of the votes in Mannheim's working-class north. Petry's views were seen as too mainstream within the AfD and her approach of working with other parties was rejected at the AfD's party congress in Cologne on 22 April 2017. This move – taken on the same day that Banta and his housemates were kept indoors by the violence of AfD members and supporters in the streets of Mannheim – indicated that the party had decided to move even further to the right ('far far-right').

For Banta and his housemates, many from Gambia and new to the country, the reality of racism and the threat of racial violence in Germany had been a real shock. It was no longer news on a TV screen. This time it was personal. You cannot achieve your goals and fulfil your aspirations in a place where you fear for your personal safety on a daily basis. This is not something you can turn away from. Many of Banta's housemates had decided to leave Germany and return to Italy, where they claimed asylum. 'They have lost faith in Germany,' he said. Banta himself now had serious doubts about this being the kind of country in which he would eventually want his son to live. He told me he had decided that he would be moving to join his sister in Sweden.

In May, after making inquiries about moving to Sweden, Banta told me that the plan was off. 'They only issue three-month tourist visas, which would be no use for work,' he said. He decided that he would return to Palermo next summer, and if he could find work there, he would not be coming back to Mannheim.

'A man has to keep going until he finds the right place to be,' he said.

6

Paris Jungle

Since Jahid and Saeed had waved goodbye to us in Palermo, I had maintained communication with them, although it hadn't been easy. Jahid's uncle had paid for their trip from Palermo to Paris, covering the costs of their forged documents and the transport, including a taxi ride with a Tunisian smuggler who was introduced to the boys by a Bangladeshi contact in Italy. Along with two others, Jahid and Saeed were hidden under the seats at the back of the taxi during the ride, which cost the uncle €250 for Jahid. Before setting off in the taxi from Ventimiglia, they were stopped by an Italian police officer who questioned them but eventually let them go, pointing them in the direction back into northern Italy. It was pure luck that they got away. They were then driven across the border at night, from Ventimiglia to the French town of Antibes, in a black BMW taxi at 190 kilometres per hour. There, they were taken to the nearest train station where they boarded a train to Nice, from where they got on another train to Paris. All in all, the costs added up to €500 ($580). Jahid was indebted before he even arrived in Paris.

Asif's uncle in Palermo sent him on the trip to Paris separately a few weeks later. When he arrived, he stayed overnight on the floor of Jahid's uncle's bedsit with Saeed, but the uncle was not willing to put them up any longer than that. As Asif and Saeed had no relatives in Paris and had nowhere to go, they went to a police station, trying to claim asylum. They were then placed in a hostel for asylum-seeking minors in Paris. However, Asif's destiny was to take a different path when another friend invited him to join him in a shelter in Amiens, 120 kilometres north of Paris. Asif took the decision to leave Paris, as the conditions at the minors' shelter were not good. Saeed decided to stay put. When Asif arrived in Amiens, police immediately sent him to the shelter in town where his friend was. There, he patiently awaited his immigration interview.

When I talked to Saeed on the phone just after Christmas 2016, he told me he was waiting for an immigration interview on 6 January that would determine his status and his destiny. If he did well in the interview, he would be granted asylum in France. If rejected, he would have nowhere to go and possibly, he feared, end up sleeping rough on the street. Despite all the great changes and uncertainty, Saeed still remembered to call me on New Year's Eve and, standing outside his hostel shelter, he joined his housemates in shouting 'Happy New Year!!!!!' to everyone, with the fireworks exploding in the background.

It was freezing cold with temperatures close to zero in early January when we arrived at the Gare du Nord in Paris. Saeed insisted on travelling six stops on the metro to meet us. He had grown his first beard, and looked a little older than the teenager I first met back in Sicily. Most of all, he looked tired and subdued; his light-hearted greetings and teenage humour were absent. Saeed seemed a changed person.

He introduced me to his friend who was also staying in the hostel for asylum-seeking children; the two boys spent most of their time together. Inside the hostel, space was limited and usually four shared a room. The diet was poor: one small piece of cake, juice and coffee for breakfast, salad for lunch which Saeed and his friend said was insubstantial and joked about bitterly, and then a kebab each for dinner. Saeed spent some of his time going to French lessons, but that was all they had to occupy their time. As their movement was restricted – they had to be back in the hostel by 8pm every day and were not permitted to go out in the evening – the absence of any suitable facilities and lack of anything interesting to do in the hostel were serious issues.

Saeed was extremely tense and worried about his interview on 6 January. His life would be decided by that two-hour interview – and it would all depend on whether he could make the officer believe that his case was genuine. He said all he could do now was pray. 'I don't want to end up living in tents, you know, like those people in Jaurès...' Around the Jaurès, Stalingrad and Chapelle metro stations, migrants had been sleeping rough for the previous two years. Even in the depths of winter, I saw people wrapped in blankets, sitting in street corners near Jaurès. The sight of other migrants' homelessness frightened Saeed.

'I will have to move out of Paris if I'm rejected for asylum,' he said, 'because Paris is very tough for us.' He would then begin a life outside the system, for ten long years, before he could possibly qualify to apply for residency. During these ten years, he would have to work without official papers and try to survive the inevitable substandard working and living conditions.

Saeed wanted to come to Britain, but his sister – a close family friend whom he called sister – had told him that it would be impossible to get formal immigration status there. Smiling bitterly, he said, 'I will visit you in England when I get my status sorted in ten years' time.'

Saeed said that, assessing his journey in retrospect, he would have preferred to stay in Sicily than live in France. I noticed that he no longer said 'All is fair and lovely', his amusing old catchphrase in Lampedusa.

He had not seen much of Jahid, because Jahid's uncle never let him visit. The last time he had seen him was when they had met up to say goodbye to Asif before he left for Amiens.

Jahid had kept himself to himself most of the time in the past two months. But the occasional message he wrote on WhatsApp made me think something had gone wrong. In late December he wrote: 'Things are really tough here. I want to go to England.' But when I prompted him to tell me what had happened, he fell silent. Then, during my stay in Paris, Jahid wrote to me again: 'Could you help me to find a sponsor to go to England, please? I'm really unhappy here.'

Then, a couple of hours later I found a missed call from Jahid and called him straight back. 'I'm at the station,' he said, with an urgency in his voice, 'the Gare du Nord.'

I rushed there to meet him and saw him waving to me in the distance, a weary smile on his face. He had just travelled from work and was carrying a heavy bag with drills in it. When asked how he had been, he was unable to speak, and simply kept shaking his head – he did not know where to start. The last three months had brought a huge change; no longer the village boy with a simple T-shirt and a pair of flip-flops, he looked worn out, wrapped in a thin puffer jacket. Most of all, his eyes reflected great sadness.

I asked him where he lived. Reluctantly, he pointed to the right of the station, murmuring, 'Just over there, not far.' I had not realized he was living close to where I was staying, near the Gare du Nord, and wondered why he had not told me.

Over the next couple of hours, Jahid revealed to me the situation he had found himself trapped in over the past two months, and the reason why he could not say where he was living and what he was doing. Jahid had owed €500 to his uncle for the trip and the border-crossing from Italy to France. To pay off the debt he had made Jahid work for no pay, taking him to building sites all over Paris, and making him work as a labourer for 12 hours a day until 10pm. Over a month, Jahid had worked off the debt, yet his uncle had forced him to continue working unpaid, and had said that he would have to do so for another two years.

Jahid described his uncle, a single man who had lived in Paris for years without any papers, as sadistic and controlling – he did not even like him to talk to friends on the phone. He constantly scolded and bullied Jahid. The only opportunity Jahid had to sneak some free time was when he returned to the bedsit on an evening when his uncle was not at work or had left early, as on the day he came to meet me. For the past two months, Jahid had had no social circle, no-one to talk with, and only travelled to and from his uncle's room and work. Before arriving in Paris, he had no idea this was what he was coming to – he had never imagined his own uncle would become his slave master.

Day in, day out, the only person Jahid had to interact with was his uncle, in a tiny bedsit, which contained only a bed and no kitchen or sitting area. They even shared the bed. Jahid was reluctant to reveal the whole picture, but in the end, he was so distressed that he broke down and told me everything. Afterwards he stared at the floor and was unable to talk for several minutes. He was trying to hold back tears. He was proud – but he was broken.

There was not a moment of respite in his life – his uncle was there at work, and even in the same bed when Jahid went to sleep. How could he escape his presence, his control, his smell? 'I often feel like my head is exploding,' Jahid said, burying his head in his hands.

The situation had become so unbearable that he had contemplated running away. Several times, he had travelled far outside Paris, to visit shelters for under-age migrants, to ask if they could take him in. Once, he took the train to Amiens, where Asif was living, hoping that he would be accepted by a shelter so that they could live in the same town. Jahid had walked into the police station, telling them that he needed help and a place to stay. He told them his story as best he could. The police placed him in a hotel room and arranged an interview for him, but when it took place, he had no idea which authorities the two interviewers represented. Everything happened in a flash – and they told him to return to Paris. They insisted that he was over 18. Jahid begged them to listen to him, but they refused.

'I'm too tall. That's why they didn't believe me. They are Christians, but they're very rude. They pushed me out of the door after the interview.'

As Jahid came to meet us straight after work, he had not had time to eat. I ordered a plate of biryani for him and he shovelled it down like he had not eaten for days. He told me that his uncle only fed him once a day, a tiny meal. 'But when I was in the camp in Italy, uncle told me on the phone that he would look after me and cook me nice food,' he said.

Jahid called his sister, who lives in Birmingham and is married to a British man. He wanted to ask if she could apply for asylum on his behalf. But the phone call alarmed and upset his brother-in-law, who seemed desperately worried that Jahid might try to live with them in Birmingham. 'I cannot aid an illegal immigrant,' he said to me on the phone. 'Why don't you ask him to talk to his relatives in London? Ask them to help him.'

We talked some more and then he confessed that Jahid's sister had no formal immigration status herself, therefore it would be impossible for Jahid to rely on her for help.

We walked Jahid home, as far as Rue de Belzunce, where he stopped. He pointed to the corner of the street ahead, 'It's just there.' It appeared he did not want us to go any nearer and, knowing that he feared his uncle finding out that he was talking to me, I didn't insist. He looked so sad as I hugged him goodnight, like a child waving goodbye to his parents. I stood there watching him as he dragged himself along, carrying the heavy drills, and then disappeared into Rue de Maubeuge, where he and his uncle lived.

Midwinter on the streets of Paris

It was two degrees above zero in Paris. Two jumpers and a large poncho weren't enough to keep me warm. As I walked into Boulevard Ney, inhaling freezing cold air as I smoked my morning cigarette, an eight-metre-high inflatable bubble came into view. This was the day centre in front of the city's first official reception centre for refugees, opened only in November 2016.

This construction was an attempt by the authorities to respond to Parisians' objections to the sight of homeless migrants in the city. Over the past couple of years, this destitute population had grown steadily, as migrants came to France in order to reach Britain. Since June 2015, the police had evicted the homeless from around 20 makeshift camps in and around Paris, mainly sheltering under railway bridges around the Jaurès metro and the Jardins d'Eole park near the Stalingrad station. Up to autumn 2016, around 3,800 migrants had been evicted from the streets. 'Eviction' involves simply removing the homeless from public view; no alternative is provided and, with no structures in place to support the migrants, they still have nowhere to go, and are forced to remain on the streets. When I visited in February 2017, at least 1,400 migrants were still sleeping rough in Paris.

This new reception centre on Boulevard Ney was built in a disused warehouse that belongs to the city and the SNCF railway company. It was managed by the Emmaus Solidarity Association, one of the largest charity groups in France, which has been working with the homeless since 1949. The charity was soon to open a second reception centre catering for 350 women and children, in the much more affluent community of Ivry-sur-Seine, to the southeast of the city.

Meanwhile, groups of migrants – mainly from Afghanistan, Sudan and Eritrea – were gathering on Boulevard Ney. There was an overwhelming feeling of frustration and anger in the air, as people looked through the gate anxiously from outside. An 18-year-old boy and his brother from Afghanistan were talking impatiently to others about their situation. They had been waiting for weeks to have an appointment to discuss their asylum application with the Prefecture and wished to get advice at the reception centre about whom they should talk to and how to speed up the process. As a rule, the appointment should take place within three days after an asylum-seeker has expressed the intention to lodge a claim.

Despite the frustration of waiting, the 18-year-old and his brother were among the more fortunate ones here because they were staying with a friend and were not sleeping rough. Most migrants standing outside the gate had not had anywhere to live or sleep for a while. Some had queued there for three days to talk to an advisor in the centre but only 50 migrants could be received each day – and that was just to seek advice and information. In addition, capacity inside was very limited – there were 400 beds there when I visited, but there were thousands outside.

'You have to be here, standing right outside the gate, at 8am, or you'll be too late,' one said. They then crowded around two staff members who came to the gate, asking them questions relating to their own case.

When migrants finally reached the head of the queue, they would be met by social workers, Emmaus Solidarity workers and the OFII (the French Office of Immigration and Integration) who would interview them to pre-assess their needs and determine whether they were eligible for claiming asylum. Those who qualified for claiming asylum would be given a bed there straight away. Then they would be housed for five to ten days before being transferred to 'welcome and orientation centres' (CAOs) for asylum-seekers in other parts of France. Although the city of Paris does not distinguish between economic migrants and refugees, the government does. Therefore, only those deemed to have a valid claim to asylum would be taken to the CAOs. In the month before I arrived, 1,200 men had been housed there, out of whom 774 had left the centre for the CAOs across the country. More had come to take their beds. The demand had been so high that the centre had been forced to think constantly about expanding its capacity.

A young man with a beard was walking around in the crowd with his bedding. His eyes were bloodshot and swollen. It looked as if he had been on a very long and hard journey. He introduced himself as Asil, from Afghanistan. His uncle spent the equivalent of €1,000 to smuggle him out of the country, away from what he described as the dangers from the Taliban. 'I couldn't live there,' he said repeatedly. To his regret, his uncle and his four sisters had remained there. But Asil's wish was to apply for them to join him in France some time in the future.

The toughest part of his journey into Europe was in Bulgaria, he recalled, where he had been arrested and imprisoned for two months. He eventually arrived in Norway – a country that many Afghans believed to be the ideal destination for asylum, due to its reputation as 'a country that respects human rights'. But, when they arrived in Norway, they were often shocked to find the reputation was a myth. 'It's very hard to be granted asylum there,' he said. Many Afghans had therefore left Norway and ended up in France.

Asil said he came to this street corner every day, mainly for food distribution. He had no cash, no mobile phone, no family relations there, and could rely only on charities for basic food provisions to survive. But he also came to this corner for company and to meet fellow migrants from Afghanistan. Their company was what kept him sane. He had been sleeping in a tent under the bridge at Jaurès metro station, not far from the reception centre. He was waiting for the asylum decision, but had no idea when he would be given a bed somewhere.

In France, the asylum reception capacities are very stretched and inadequate, currently unable to accommodate the majority of asylum-seekers in the country. In 2014, there were, in total, 24,418 places in reception centres in France (CADA), which only covered 33 per cent of asylum-seekers, while the country had registered 64,811 asylum applications. In 2015, places in reception centres increased to around 25,500, still far from adequate. When there is no vacancy in a reception centre, asylum-seekers are placed on a waiting list and may be directed to other provisional accommodation. The shortage of bed space has also meant that asylum-seekers have had no alternative but to stay in night shelters or sleep on the street, like those I had seen in Paris in early 2017. This was happening despite the objective of the Ministry of Interior being to make 'regular reception centres the norm and accommodation in emergency centres the exception' by 2017.

Ten other Afghan migrants were staying and sleeping in tents with Asil at the same spot. They looked out for each other. In a strange and, at times, hostile city, they had to stick together. Asil told me he had developed headaches from sleeping out in the cold at night. 'Do you have any medicine?' he asked, frowning and massaging his forehead. I searched my bag and found some painkillers for him, which really pleased him.

'You know, sometimes I get so stressed, I want to slash my wrists and hurt myself,' he said, without any expression on his face. He really didn't look well.

'Shouldn't you go and ask for a doctor in there?' I pointed to the reception centre.

'They can't help me. They say they have doctors, but they can't help.'

Others were sleeping on the other side of the road, under another bridge. 'We're all under bridges,' one man said.

Another middle-aged Afghan looked clearly distressed. 'I have been around this street corner for a month.' He had also been sleeping under the bridge. He came to the centre to wait for it to open its facilities to all migrants at 2pm, when he could go into the reception area, warm up and have a cup of tea and maybe a sandwich. There was wifi there too. The facilities remained open until 8pm every day. He would spend the rest of the time talking with other Afghans outside the gate, because there was nowhere else to go. When I asked him why he didn't go in to try to get a bed in the centre, he replied: 'I don't want to be Dublin-ed.'

The 18-year-old boy who was frustrated about his asylum application butted in, saying: 'This is the Paris Jungle.'

When a couple of staff members appeared at the gate again, I approached them and asked whether they could show me around inside the centre, and they agreed. They were Clem and Lila, in their twenties, enthusiastic and helpful. They led me in through the side entrance, around the dome-shaped day centre, to the main part of the building where many migrants were having lunch in the dining area. Beyond this was a basic wooden structure divided into eight blocks, with rooms housing four people each. We walked through the hall to a donation collection room where clothing and bedding, sent in from across the country – much of it from the south of France – were sorted for distribution. The charity's work depends on this support.

Clem and Lila were concerned about the way under-age migrants, many of those in the queue outside, were treated in the city. Minors who came there for help had been turned down based on random assessment of their age. Clem said that a 13-year-old Eritrean boy had been rejected because the bed space was full. 'The children were confused about why they were rejected. It would have been better if the staff had explained that there were not enough beds,' she said.

The structure was barely coping. Less than half of the migrants who had been received at the centre had actually been given beds there. There was no way of knowing how many migrants had been turned down for possibly making an asylum claim, and on what grounds exactly. But what was clear was that, as the staff revealed, not everyone got a proper interview and therefore not everyone received fair assessment of their eligibility.

'How can the children be expected to carry documents with them to prove their age when fleeing from conflicts and destruction?' Lila said, frustrated. After being rejected, these minors would be given a night at a hostel, but would then have to return to sleeping in the streets.

Clem questioned the role of the state and believed it was not doing its job of protecting under-age migrants. They also had no faith in the media reporting of the true situation of refugees and migrants. Ever since they had been involved in working with refugees, especially in Calais, Clem and Lila had discovered that the reality of the situation was completely different from that portrayed in the French media, which they now saw as a complete distortion and an unjust cover-up. The discovery had made them angry, and had encouraged them to carry on working with refugees. The so-called 'refugee crisis' had never existed. 'Calais refugees only became an issue because politicians needed to get rid of them before the elections,' said Clem. In early 2016, French President François Hollande announced plans to close the Calais camp by the end of the year, as he faced pressure ahead of the 2017 presidential election. The closure of the camp was obviously political; it had long become an electioneering symbol and was exploited by the political right, which blamed migration for the economic decline in the region. Presidential candidates were debating 'long-term solutions to the refugee crisis in northwest France', with parties on the right demanding the overturn of the Le Touquet treaty (signed in 2003) which enabled the UK to undertake its border controls on French soil.

Clem and Lila were also infuriated by the court conviction of the French olive farmer Cedric Herrou, who was sentenced to five years in prison and given a €30,000 fine for helping migrants to cross the border from Italy to France. They were angry with the way ordinary decent people were being criminalized for helping fellow human beings. Cedric Herrou had been unable to ignore the migrants he saw walking the country roads near the border, and had begun to pick them up and host them at his farm near Nice. As he did not have enough accommodation to house the migrants, he took them to an old railway building that had been occupied by NGOs. Herrou said in court: 'I picked up kids who tried to cross the border 12 times.' He was convicted of facilitating the illegal entry, movement and residence of undocumented migrants. Under Article L622-1 of France's immigration law, anyone who 'facilitates or attempts to facilitate the illegal entry, movement or residence of a foreigner in France shall be punished by imprisonment for five years and a fine of €30,000.'

The coldest place in Paris I could think of at this time of year was along the St Martin canal. Walking down from the Jaurès metro in the afternoon, along the canal banks bedding and clothing were stashed away to be used by homeless migrants at night. This was where the police had pulled down their tents the previous winter. Further along the canal was a more affluent part of town, leading to the Bastille and to tourist Paris.

In the evening, the restaurants of Paris are filled with people dining, some enjoying *fruits de mer* that cost around €100 for two.

I watched people eating bouillabaisse (fish soup), dipping their buttered bread into it and licking their lips. You cannot help feeling angry with the obscenity of such inequality. You cannot help thinking how hungry some are, queuing in temperatures below zero for some charity food, only a kilometre away. On the same street corner on Boulevard Ney, migrants stood waiting for the distribution of halal food by kind-hearted local Muslim residents from Iraq.

The next morning, homeless migrants queued again on the street corner, for a breakfast of naan bread and tea, provided by the reception centre. A man in his twenties with ponytails and studious glasses was patiently waiting for his turn. He introduced himself as Sajad. He told me that he was one of the Hazara ethnic group from central Afghanistan, a minority group primarily from the central highland region of Hazarajat. Since the 16th century, the Hazara people have been the target of ethnic cleansing and have suffered continual persecution. Their situation had not changed even after the Taliban were overthrown in 2001. The current government in Afghanistan was continuing systematically to oppress Hazara people and strip them of their basic civil rights.

Sajad was a Hazara soldier for eight years, and had to flee during attacks by the Taliban insurgents. He could not find his family; he did not know where his four-year-old daughter was. He had to leave them behind. Sajad had travelled from Afghanistan, via Iran, Turkey and Greece, to Norway, where he intended to claim asylum. He lived there for over a year, but when his application was eventually turned down, he had to leave the country and travelled to France.

When we met, he had been in Paris for 15 days, and had been fortunate enough to have been given a bed at the reception centre. In early January 2017, he was waiting to be transferred to a hostel in Paris, where he would stay for six months, during which time his asylum claim would be processed.

When I talked with him again a week later, he had indeed been transferred to a hostel in western Paris, along with seven of his friends, with one of whom he shared a room. At least he wasn't alone. He did not want to complain about the limited space he had, because 'It's normal in a life where good things are rare,' as he put it. On 31 January, he was fingerprinted.

Sajad enjoyed spending his time exploring the area; sometimes he played volleyball in the park with his friends. However, he was eager to work, and wondered how he would spend his time waiting in the following weeks and months. Some day in the not-too-distant future, he said, he wanted to be reunited with his family in France. Months later in July, however, Sajad began to feel hopeless as the waiting time seemed to continue endlessly. He was feeling desperately worried for his family and how they could sustain their life without his support.

That morning, at the same street corner on Boulevard Ney, dozens of Afghan men were gathered drinking black tea. Asil was still asleep in the tent and his friend Gul collected his share of the bread and tea for him. Gul, looking half-awake, stood around chatting with his friends, who called him a 'big baby' that everyone had to look after. He was only 17. Everyone was making fun of his newly grown beard. Asil finally appeared after 11am, when the breakfast stand had been put away and the centre staff had left. Gul handed him his bread and tea; this was how his day started – every day; this was how he spent most of his day – every day. This street corner was his world in Paris.

Asil said he wanted to settle here and be able to study eventually. His wish was to study journalism in a French university. As he spoke, nearby the lights of police vans were flashing and just behind him stood several police officers. They simply stood there, constantly making their presence felt.

Solidarity with migrants

Hostility from local communities has always been a problem for newly arriving migrants. Often local objections to asylum housing have been expressed openly and aggressively. In September 2016, the roof of a newly built centre for asylum-seekers in Essonne, at Forges-les-Bains, 45 kilometres southwest of Paris, was burned down overnight, just hours after a demonstration against the centre, which was due to open in October and take in 90 migrants. The new reception centre that was set up in Ivry-sur-Seine also received a substantial amount of hostility from the well-to-do local residents, who were troubled by the sight of vulnerable women and child refugees coming to live in a former factory building in their neighbourhood.

Fortunately, there are many charities and grassroots organizations trying to demonstrate solidarity with refugees and migrants. The response to the lack of sufficient state support structures for refugees and asylum-seekers, including vulnerable and under-age migrants – which is the fundamental unresolved problem in Paris and across the country – has paved the way for the growth of citizen activism.

While the housing shortage persisted, the aggressive police raids enraged many citizens and compelled them to set up voluntary groups to offer the food and shelter needed by homeless migrants. They attempted to fill the gap left by the lack of any state provision.

These citizen activists have continued to provide beds, food and clothes, and to minimize, as much as they can, the level of destitution on the streets of Paris. Since 2015, more than 15,000 migrants present in the Paris area have been offered protection – in terms of wellbeing and personal safety – thanks mostly to the work of these grassroots groups.

A group called Singa has been working with asylum-seekers and refugees in Paris since 2013 and regularly organizes events and workshops to facilitate the socio-economic integration of asylum-seekers. Singa's activists launched the CALM initiative (meaning 'Comme à la Maison', or 'Just Like Home'), aiming to connect families who wish to welcome migrants by offering them accommodation. They had successfully organized housing for periods ranging from a month to a year for asylum-seekers in Paris and across the country.

However, in the past few years, many of these citizen activists have been facing criminal prosecutions as a result of their acts of solidarity. Houssam El Assimi, of la Chapelle Debout collective, for instance, was helping migrants with translation and information on the immigration system. In September 2016, Houssam El Assimi was arrested during a police raid on one of the makeshift camps in Paris. He was charged with 'violence against persons holding public authority' and faced up to three years in prison and a €45,000 fine.

Human rights group Gisti, working to protect the legal and political rights of migrants, documented the increase in the number of these cases of 'crimes of solidarity'. More than 100 NGOs and trade unions signed a manifesto calling for an end to the prosecution of humanitarian activities. The law under which people have been prosecuted was introduced in 1945 to prevent smuggling and was at times used under former president Nicolas Sarkozy to prosecute activists who offered help to migrants. However, things did not improve under the socialist government. In fact, human rights groups said that since 2015, an even wider range of laws had been used to punish those who help migrants.

What next for Jahid and Saeed?

One day Jahid sneaked out of the building site to meet us, as his uncle was not there. Saeed came to the Gare du Nord to see us, too, and it was a nice surprise for Jahid. They embraced several times, conversing in Bengali.

Jahid was eager to run away from his uncle and the life of forced labour. We wanted to report it to the police (although I was worried about how he would be treated), but he insisted that this was not a good idea and refused to co-operate or give any information about his uncle. He feared damaging his family relations and causing harm to his parents, who knew nothing about the miserable life he was leading in France. Apparently, his uncle had been telling lies to Jahid's parents, saying that the boy did not like working and was slow. Jahid did not have the courage to tell his parents the truth, also fearing that he would be thrown out and would end up on the streets. He was new to this country and had no networks of his own to try to find work without any papers. He was a newcomer to the world of the *sans-papiers* and precarious work. He could not survive without the help of an old-timer like his uncle.

Several times during our meeting, Jahid looked down, holding back tears. Apart from reporting it to the police, I had little idea how to get him out of this situation. I didn't even know where he really lived. The chances of him being granted asylum or humanitarian protection in Britain were practically zero, especially as his relatives could not help him with his application. Jahid talked about returning to Italy, but was unsure if he could claim asylum there after the long absence. 'Leaving Italy for France is another of the biggest mistakes in my life,' he said. It sounded familiar – he had said the same about the decision to go to Libya when we were sitting talking on Via Roma in Lampedusa.

Running away was always an option he had in mind. He did it in Libya, in Sicily, and now in Paris he was seriously thinking about it once again. It would appear that, understandably, much of his journey involved escaping from precarious situations, breaking out of entrapment, and his only option was to run away.

Saeed did not do well in the immigration interview. How could he possibly have done well? He was not even given an interpreter who could speak Bengali. Interpretation was from French to English and his English was not good enough to understand the questions and their implications.

Now that Saeed might face a negative decision from the authorities and might have to leave the hostel in Paris, he began thinking up plans with Jahid. Maybe they could travel together to Calais or Dunkirk, he said. There was a great sense of panic. What should they do next? Travel to Calais and see what temporary shelter they could find there? Or try to get a bed in the Dunkirk camp and see what happened? Or find someone to help them cross the sea to Britain?

They both eagerly asked me about Calais and Dunkirk. What was it like there? They were looking for some hope in an utterly desperate situation.

I did not want to encourage them to resort to living in the Calais area or the camp in Dunkirk. I told them that conditions in the former Calais camp were poor and it was maintained by voluntary organizations with only limited resources. Thanks to charity workers, there were six makeshift mosques, a library and a school for children when I visited before its demolition.

Children from the Calais camp

While the Calais camp had existed, a steady supply of donations had kept the residents going. The miserable situation in the camp had drawn much attention from activists across a wide political spectrum to join the effort to organize donations for the day-to-day needs of the migrants. Support for migrants had come from many charities and individuals, such as Sally Kincaid, a Leeds-based activist. Sally became involved after seeing reports about the terrible conditions migrants were living in just across the channel. She became part of the delegation 'We are Wakefield' and joined trips to Calais taking over donations.

'It didn't feel enough just to take well-needed donations. I felt I could do more...' Sally said. 'We took everything, from Eid presents, buying hundreds of pounds' worth of fruit, gas, cooking, medicines, especially for treating teargas, which can be bought over the counter in UK, but not in France... While doing this, I became Facebook friends with many other volunteers, who were supporting refugees but also campaigning for the borders to be opened.'

Later on, Sally and her family went further with their support and provided a home for a teenage migrant who had ended up in northern France. 'On returning from one trip, I was tagged into a Facebook post about a teenager who had managed to get into the UK and was living with a foster parent but was feeling very lonely and isolated. Having spent nearly 11 months living in the Dunkirk camp, always surrounded by people, being on his own was breaking his spirit... In order to take the teenager into our home, we had to go through all the proper checks to become foster parents... Social workers realized that we understood and could appreciate what this child had gone through in order to get to "safety". Once all the processes and checks were completed, he moved into our house just before Christmas.' Other teenagers weren't so fortunate.

In early December 2016, it was found that the UK Home Office was not providing sufficient information to under-age migrants from the demolished Calais camp. In 12 of the reception centres across France where these children are sent, charity organizers and researchers found that the UK Home Office had given insufficient or no information at all to migrants while they were waiting for their applications to be processed. They believed that this was a deliberate tactic of the Home Office to deter migrants from entering Britain. The findings are documented in the report *An Uncertain Future*, by the charity Help Refugees,[53] which reveals that the way the Home Office has dealt with the children has caused great anxiety and in some cases severe mental distress, resulting in incidents of self-harm. Yet there is no mental-health support in place in the majority of these reception centres: only one of these 12 centres provides in-house psychological help.

At a centre in Auxonne, eastern France, a staff worker said that the absence of communication from the UK Home Office, which has six teams of officials touring reception centres in France, was causing distress. The report also documented how one bus carrying 29 under-age asylum-seekers was ready to leave for Britain at the end of October but was cancelled without explanation at the last minute. The children were then dispersed randomly to reception centres across France and had still not been told when they might be taken to the UK.

This situation has led to under-age migrants running away from reception centres and going completely underground. In late November 2016, 44 Eritrean children ran away from a temporary reception centre in Le Havre. Not only had they been anxiously waiting for decisions from the UK Home Office without sufficient information about the likelihood of their applications being accepted, but in addition poor conditions in the centre, such as insufficient food and no clothing, had made it impossible to stay. The centre managers did not listen to their concerns; one of the staff told them, 'If you don't like living here, you could leave.' As it turned out, the centre was receiving only five euros per child per day. It had only been set up to take in the children from the Calais camp; it simply wasn't sufficiently equipped for the purpose of looking after minors.

Most of the minors who ran away from reception centres have returned to northern France, with many going back to Calais, a place with which they are familiar.

Meanwhile, in mid-December, Home Office transfers of unaccompanied minors who were registered in the Calais camp suddenly ended. The Dubs Amendment, launched to help unaccompanied refugee children to come to live in the UK, was no more. This dashed the hopes of many, who were still waiting for a decision. A group of 12 teenagers from Syria, Eritrea and Sudan, aged between 14 and 17, who were sent from the Calais camp to a shelter at the Swiss border in October 2016 and who had had a meeting with UK Home Office officials only four weeks earlier, went on hunger strike against the Home Office's ending of transfers.

Safe Passage estimated that several hundred children from the Calais camp remained in France despite having a legal right to be in Britain. By 9 February 2017, when Britain formally announced the end of the Dubs Amendment, only 350 unaccompanied under-age migrants had been given sanctuary in Britain under the scheme – although immigration minister Robert Goodwill announced two months later that another 130 places for child refugees had been left out of the total number earlier, due to an 'administrative error'. Still a pitiful number. Britain utterly failed to fulfil its duty to offer international protection to the most vulnerable of all refugees.

The closure of the legal route has led to more minors returning to the Calais area to attempt to cross the border in their own way. By the end of December 2016, at least six small settlements in the rural area of the Nord-Pas-de-Calais region had been formed.[54] Many of these minors had had their asylum claims rejected by the UK Home Office earlier that year.

At the same time that minors were returning to Calais, a four-metre-high concrete wall costing £2.3 million ($3 million) was completed, with the aim of separating the former Calais camp from passing trucks. It was built by Vinci, a construction company involved in the multi-million-dollar expansion planned for the Calais port. Sogea, the Vinci subsidiary, was paid by the French government to demolish part of the Calais camp. The money they spent on building the wall to deter migrants would be enough to sustain nearly 300 Syrian refugees in Britain for a year and certainly sufficient to feed thousands of refugees who had been sleeping rough in deep winter in a global city like Paris.

Inside the Dunkirk camp

Many migrants, former residents of the Calais camp, who had returned to northern France and who still aimed to reach Britain, came to the Grande Synthe camp in Dunkirk, 50 kilometres from Calais. This included some of the 1,300 minors who were refused asylum in Britain – they had run away from the reception centres and come to Dunkirk. At the time of my visit in late February 2017, there were 1,000-1,500 migrants there.

Like the Calais camp, Grande Synthe had also become the focus of far-right attention, with the help of hostile media.

In late January 2017, as part of her electoral manoeuvring, Marine Le Pen arrived unannounced at the camp along with several media outlets and attempted to enter it. Standing outside, she tweeted: 'In front of the Grande Synthe Camp, I denounce the crazy immigration policies of successive French governments.' She then said in her tweet: 'We must deport illegals back where they came from and control our national borders, if not the camps will reconstruct themselves.' She boasted an openly anti-refugee policy, and controlling national borders was one of the principal objectives in her election campaign. She was refused authorization to enter by the camp organizers and the regional authorities.

The Grande Synthe camp had changed hands over time. The former camp, which had housed 3,000 migrants, had closed down in December 2015 when the conditions had become appalling. It was replaced by a new camp called 'La Linière', built by the city council and Médecins Sans Frontières, that opened on 7 March 2016. It was initially managed by Utopia 56 and two months later was taken

The ramshackle nature of the Grande Synthe Linière camp in Dunkirk.

over by local authorities and AFEJI, the new management of the camp. The charity workers I met in Paris seemed to think highly of Kesha Niya, a project that has been part of Grande Synthe's Linière camp. It is an internationally funded project run by migrants and volunteers to oversee food distribution and clothing donations. The cooks named themselves 'The Kurdish Brothers' and they produced three meals a day for the 1,000-1,500 residents inside the camp.

Following a 15-minute bus ride from Dunkirk and a couple of kilometres' walk through a vast area of new housing, a migrant whom I met on the way showed me the shortcut, eroded into a thin muddy path by thousands of migrants walking along it day in, day out. Even taking the shortcut, the camp lay on the far side of a motorway, and was situated by the side of a railway line, which disconnected it from the rest of the world.

As I entered the camp, I saw that the living conditions were utterly miserable. Migrants from Iraq, Iran, Afghanistan and other countries – including a few from Vietnam and the Philippines – were housed in tiny wooden sheds of two square metres, three to four people at a time. It was so overcrowded that many Afghan migrants were sleeping in a canteen. There were few facilities apart from the canteen, the community room, and a women's activity room where women and children spent their time.

I met Akram, a man in his late twenties from Iraq. He came here with his family – his two sisters, three children including a nine-month-old, brother-in-law, and the cousin of his brother-in-law. He told me he was here to look after his family and help them make arrangements as they prepared for their crossing to Britain, where they would join his uncle in London. Akram himself had escaped from Iraq long before his family did, during Saddam's rule when his father was in opposition and his family was in danger of persecution. As a minor at the time, he had travelled across continents unaccompanied. He had followed other Iraqis and headed for northern Europe. A year after his arrival in Norway, he was granted asylum and had been living there for nine years.

However, as a refugee, Akram has never felt accepted in Norwegian society. 'People tend to think I'm a criminal or there's something wrong with me,' he said. Since settling in Norway, he had never gone to school. He grew up on the streets. 'But there is plenty to learn out there... All these years, without any schooling, I've learned to speak several languages.' Akram had been concerned about the wellbeing of his family since hearing of their insecure situation in Iraq and subsequent escape to Europe. He had come to the camp to help them and during the two months he had spent there, had been asked to help with interpreting for migrants.

Akram introduced me to another Iraqi man he had befriended who had attempted to board trucks 72 times in the past month. 'The chance of success is so small,' I said to the man, 'Do you still see the point of trying?' He shook his head and said, 'I have to try.' Akram said that any evening, the smugglers might call and inform them that the minibus was ready for a pick-up. They would then have five to ten minutes to get ready for the minibus to pick them up at the camp and drive them to the lorry park. 'One of the smugglers is English,' he said.

Akram said he was prepared to go all the way for his family – he would get on a truck with them if that was what they wanted him to do. He felt that he had nothing to lose and was determined to make sure that his family was safe and well.

He walked me to the shed where his relatives were staying. One of his sisters was particularly distressed with the conditions in the camp, frowning and sighing a lot. Against the wall inside the shed, she had stacked up canned food and biscuits that they brought with them, as if she were planning to stay for a while. She gave a chocolate biscuit to one of her children, a four-year-old, and offered one to me. She said the food was of poor quality and the two sisters had therefore decided to be responsible for cooking for the entire family. She pointed to an old iron stove next to the shed. 'This is where we cook,' she said, with a bitter smile.

To take their minds off the miserable conditions here, the two sisters came with me to the women's activity room, situated in the middle of the camp. At first they were shy, and simply sat in the corner, watching the children play. But after a while the younger sister stood up and walked over to the table to dish out some curry and rice for herself. She started to exchange pleasantries with other women.

Children at large in the Grande Synthe Linière camp.

There were also many single migrants, as well as families, here. I met a 26-year-old Iranian called Hamid, who had been living in the camp for seven long months. Hamid appeared resilient, despite everything that he'd been through and the continuing uncertainty of his future. He told me that in his city of Ahwaz, in southwestern Iran, he had struggled to do two jobs, working as an electrician and a driver, due to the low level of wages. Making a living was very tough and he was anxious to help his parents. He decided to leave Iran to try to earn more and improve the living standards of his family. He travelled from Iran to Turkey, to Greece, and then to Sweden, where he sought asylum. Following nine months of waiting, Hamid received a negative decision. He then had to leave Sweden and decided to come to France, following the footsteps of others who had been refused asylum in Scandinavian countries.

Here in Linière, Hamid had attempted to get into Britain at least every other day. The smuggler would call him at night when the time was right, then he and others would walk up from the camp to a designated location where they would be picked up and driven to where the trucks were parked waiting to go on the ferries. Sometimes, along with others, he would be driven in a minibus to a lorry park in Paris. They would get there about midnight, wait until 2am when no-one was around, then try to get into the park and hide in a truck. Sometimes he would be taken to the lorry park in Calais, other times in Dunkirk. Everything then depended on luck: if there was a truck with unlocked doors, they would quickly get in the back and hide. They would wait until around 4am-5am when the driver came but, so far, Hamid and his friends had always been caught by the driver and been forced to return to the camp. If they managed to reach Britain, then each of them would have to pay the smuggler around £2,500 ($3,250) by money transfer from bank accounts in their home countries.

'There's a very small chance of success,' Hamid said, 'but I've got to try.' Every time he tried to board a lorry, he would take nothing with him but a mobile phone. Every time he walked away from the camp he hoped that it might be the last time he would see it. However slight, there was always the hope that he would reach Britain and start a new life, with a new job, and be able to send money home.

Hamid treated me as a guest in his home, and showed me around politely and attentively. Having lived there for seven months, he was not short of friends who greeted him as he walked past. He pointed out the women's activity room, and introduced me to an English-speaking volunteer, who thought I was a newcomer to the camp. Inside the activity room a dozen or so mothers sat sewing and playing games with their children. A young girl with braided brown hair came up and introduced herself as Tarza, from Kurdistan. 'I live in room number 182,' she said confidently. She was there with her parents. As she was one of the few who could speak English, she spent a lot of her time helping out in the activity room. She was only 14 years old.

Hamid walked with me to the end of the camp, where a path led to the beach in the distance. I tried to lighten up the mood and asked, 'Do you go swimming sometimes?'

He smiled and shook his head, 'No energy!'

We walked past his shed, door number 185. There was nothing inside but bedding. He shared this two-square-metre space with two other people.

The next day, I came across a family of Vietnamese migrants in the camp. One of them, a young woman, told me that she and her brothers and sisters had walked all the way from Vietnam to France over months. They were walking to escape extreme poverty.

The woman had worked as a cleaner in Taiwan for a while, but when the job had come to an end it had been impossible to continue to live there. She and her siblings had decided that they had to do something to change their destiny and had begun their trek to Europe. To date, they had been in the Linière camp for a month, and had tried to board trucks numerous times, without success.

I visited Hamid the following afternoon and he invited me to meet three of his closest friends there. They gave me the only chair they had and we chatted in front of their shed. One of the friends made me a cup of tea with three spoonfuls of sugar, which was a real energy boost. They were all from Iraq. One said he had not actually planned to go to Britain at first – the first time I had heard anyone say this in the camp. He explained: 'I'm waiting for asylum papers for France. It's been taking so long... I decided to come here to join my friends. This is a good place to exchange useful information on immigration issues with others.' Also, clearly, housing in Paris is difficult for migrants who are waiting for their documents and the authorities do not automatically provide housing for asylum-seekers.

Another of Hamid's friends told me that he still had hopes of reaching Britain, because some of his friends had succeeded and this had convinced him that trying to board trucks was not totally hopeless. 'My friends are now working in Glasgow. They're happy there and they're asking me to join them,' he said with an innocent smile.

We went to hear a performance of music, one of the events organized by the volunteers every now and then. Dozens of children were already sitting waiting. A volunteer took the microphone and started singing and rapping, with another volunteer playing guitar in the background. People gathered to watch the show, cheering at times. Halfway through, one of the residents went up and took over the microphone, saying he wanted to sing a song about the camp. Although I did not understand the lyrics, the English words 'camp's no good' came over loud and clear. It made Hamid laugh.

But things were not so much fun for the children. I made a video recording of part of the music performance. To my alarm, when I watched the footage later, back in Britain, I saw that one of the

Afeji volunteers in the foreground approached a boy of four or five years old and started to cuddle and touch him inappropriately. This was someone in a position of care and who had access to children in the camp. I reported the case to the NSPCC, whose staff, following a review of the video footage, said they had circulated the information to all agencies involved, in France and Britain. I also wrote to Afeji, in both French and English, about this incident, and asked them whether they conducted any checks on the volunteers they hired. They never responded to my questions. When I called Afeji's office number, the staff simply put the phone down. This utterly unprofessional behaviour came from an organization that had been paid to manage the camp. While urgent action is needed to rescue approximately 23,000 unaccompanied child refugees stranded in camps known to be unsafe in Greece and Italy, much greater attention also needs to be paid to camps such as this in western Europe, where vulnerable children are at risk of abuse and exploitation at the hands of those who are supposed to provide them with care and support.

Just before midnight the following evening, Hamid received a call from one of the smugglers, telling him to get ready and walk to the pick-up point. At 2am, he and some of his friends boarded one of the unlocked trucks as planned and then waited, hidden inside the vehicle. However, as soon as the driver opened the back of the

Children watching a performance in the Grande Synthe Linière camp.

lorry around 5am, he discovered them. Another abortive attempt.[55]

Two weeks later, in yet another failed attempt to hide in a lorry, this time in Calais, Hamid was arrested and kept in a detention centre for a week, during which he was denied access to a phone. He asked the police officers to allow him to call his mother. They said no. During the week in detention, he was given barely enough to eat. When he was eventually sent back to the camp, Hamid was relieved. 'It's good to be back here; French police are no good,' he sighed.

Such is the existence of so many people housed at Grande Synthe's Linière camp. The period there is transitional and the aim is always to reach the other side of the Channel. They continue to resort to jumping and hiding in trucks. At the end of 2016, a young Kurdish migrant died at the port of Dunkirk when he fell from the lorry in which he was hiding. In March 2017, a 20-year-old Afghan man was found unconscious at the roundabout to the entrance of the Linière camp. He had got on a truck a few minutes earlier, hoping to reach England. But when he realized that the truck was actually heading for Belgium, he and another migrant jumped off. He suffered head injuries, and died a few hours after his transfer from a hospital in Dunkirk to a hospital in Lille.

According to Calais Migrant Solidarity,[56] eight named migrants were killed during 2016 attempting to reach Britain. One was Samrawit, a 19-year-old woman from Eritrea, the victim of a hit-and-run incident on a motorway in Calais on 12 July. In 2015, 24 named migrants were killed when attempting to enter Britain. The deaths are always tragic: Youssuf, a teenager from Sudan, was hit by a car on the motorway on 3 December 2015; Berihu, a 23-year-old man from Eritrea, was run over by a train in the Channel Tunnel on 30 September; on 28 September Omar, an Iraqi, was found crushed to death by falling pallets in the back of a truck; on 24 July, Ganet, a young Eritrean woman, was hit by a car on the A16 – it was reported that she had been gassed in the face by the police before she was hit. In 2014, there were 18 named migrant victims. The list of victims goes on – but these are only the migrants who have been identified and named. The precious lives of these young people have been lost for the sake of maintaining a border regime, yet how many of them have we read or heard about in our media?

The beginning of the year 2017 continued to be marked by the deaths of refugees and migrants – not only when attempting to reach Britain but also during their time in the reception system waiting to come to Britain. On 12 January 2017, Samir, a 17-year-old from Sudan, died of a heart attack at a reception centre in Ameugny in the eastern Saône-et-Loire region. He had travelled via Libya to Italy, and had eventually reached the Calais camp. In November 2016, following the demolition of the camp, Samir had been transferred from Calais to Ameugny. Not long after that, he was informed that his asylum application to Britain had been rejected.

Samir was one of the asylum-seeking minors registered by the UK Home Office at the time. Like other teenagers in the reception centre, he believed that his long, hard journey was soon coming to an end and he would be allowed to settle in Britain.

The autopsy discovered that he had suffered several undetected cardiac arrests, yet the staff at the reception centre were, for unknown reasons, unaware of his heart condition. Samir's death could have been prevented if adequate medical care had been available.

The real story behind the fire in Linière

Back in Grande Synthe's Linière camp, life was becoming more and more difficult, as the police presence was constant and aggressive. Police raids were part of everyday life here. Evelyne Godfrey, of the Campaign to Close Campsfield, visited the Linière camp in August 2016 and reported that the French national police seemed to be controlling access to it day and night. 'The police behaviour we observed at the Dunkirk camp contrasts sharply with reports that have come from Calais.' Raids increased in spring 2017, resulting in clashes between the police and migrants.

With the French presidential election approaching, politicians once again focused public attention on the only state-funded camp in the region. In mid-March, French interior minister Bruno Le Roux said that the Linière camp must be 'progressively' dismantled as soon as possible. He said that the camp was reaching critical mass and could 'act as a magnet for more migrants to come.'[57]

Walking along the streets in the town of Grande Synthe in early

April 2017, it would have been hard to miss the numerous election posters of Marine Le Pen. Her message was clear: her kind of France does not want refugees and migrants. Her supporters there did not care about the parallel world of migrants who had been living in the camp on the outskirts of town, kept away from public view. They did not know what happened to the migrants until they read it in the papers.

On 10 April, riot police went into the Linière camp following a fight between groups of Afghan and Kurdish migrants.[58] The Kurds were the largest group in the camp while Afghan migrants had arrived later and had to sleep in the community canteen as no wooden huts were available. The huts were occupied randomly without the involvement of Afeji, which managed the camp. Severe overcrowding was causing fights to break out among the migrants while political attention, especially as the election approached, was mounting, making its complete closure more likely. To avoid accusations of mismanagement and thus keep its contract for another six months, however, Afeji had decided to reduce the size of the camp by taking down some huts, which only made the housing shortage worse.

According to Hamid and several migrants from Iraq (who weren't involved in the fighting between Afghan and Kurdish migrants that day), it was the heavy-handed approach of the police that led to further clashes between migrants, and which culminated in the fires that broke out.

'The police pushed people to fight each other,' Hamid revealed. He explained: the police came in and asked all the families to leave the site, and kettled all the men inside the camp. The officers blocked both ends of the camp, so the migrants were all trapped inside. Then the police started urging the Afghans to fight the Kurds. 'I saw them pushing the Afghans, saying, "Go, go, go, go fight them!" The police were physically pushing migrants to fight each other, from both ends of the camp. I was very scared and wasn't allowed to get out.'

As the tension was raised by the police, several Afghan men were emboldened and started setting fire to a few of the wooden sheds occupied by Kurdish migrants. 'People were trying to save their huts, but the police stopped them using water to put out the fire. When I tried to put out the fire, the police also stopped me. They didn't let anyone put it out,' said Hamid.

As the blaze went through the camp, he said that the police officers simply stood there, watching huts burning. 'They did nothing. Just watched. The police didn't call the firefighters right until the end, when almost the whole camp was burned down... Then they brought in several firefighters. It was too late.' Hamid's statement was confirmed by all those I talked to later. I also watched the video of the fire he sent me on WhatsApp on the night of the fire, and could not see any firefighters trying to put out the flames. No-one appeared to be helping. As the footage showed, migrants were left startled and helpless; all they could do was try to capture the image of the fire on their mobile phones, to send to their families and friends.

Hamid's closest friend had his hut burned to the ground and lost everything, including his documents, in the fire. Hamid's hut was one of 70 out of a total of 300 huts that survived the blaze.

'The police like this. They like it that the camp is gone,' Hamid said anxiously. He and other migrants were sent to gyms in the local area to spend the night. When asked what his plans were for the next days, he said, still shocked, 'I have no idea. I can only think about this night.'

In the following days, more than 1,000 migrants were sheltered in local gymnasiums. When I went to see Hamid in Grande Synthe, he was placed in the Emile Dufour gym, next to the Anne Frank College, along with 400 other migrants. The building was surrounded by police vehicles. Tension and despair were in the air. Hamid looked exhausted and utterly dispirited. He had been kept awake by his anxiety about the future and had not slept till 7am. The gym had no electricity or other basic facilities, it was overcrowded, with 400 people sharing just two toilets. As the air indoors became stifling due to the lack of ventilation, some migrants decided to take their blankets with them and sleep outside the building. There was nowhere to rest, reflect and work out how to cope next.

Hamid couldn't get over what had happened to the camp. For months, it had been his base in France. It was a social net to fall back on, where he could seek support, advice and friendship, and where he could return to recharge himself after failed attempts to board the trucks. It was where he could find shoulders to cry on. For him, the camp embodied the possibilities and hope for the future, a future that he hoped would be in London. While saddened and distressed, Hamid and his friends now had to plan their next move: they wanted to travel to Belgium. There was a camp near the lorry parks in Brussels where many migrants were staying, he said; they were all aiming to get to Britain. The only worry for Hamid was that, if he went on a truck from Brussels to Calais and got caught in Calais, it would not be easy to return to Belgium.

I asked him if he would consider claiming asylum in France, as pressure was mounting for the migrants to accept being sent to the reception and orientation centres (CAOs). He said he didn't want to stay in France because of the lack of work and the problem of racism. His friend from Iraq told me they had experienced local racism on a daily basis during their time in Grande Synthe: people would shout abuse or make rude hand gestures at them from inside their cars as they drove past.

Anyhow, Hamid did not think he would have any chance in the asylum system. 'It's difficult for Iranians to be given papers here, because they see Iran as neither unsafe nor poor. They think there are no problems in Iran.'

At the same gym, I also met a young Kurdish man called Kiyan, who was deeply traumatized by what had happened. He told me that the Linière camp had become overcrowded, creating a lot of bitterness among the Afghan migrants who had not been given beds like everyone else. Although there was a fight between several Afghan and Kurdish migrants on 10 April, the situation should never have led to the fire that destroyed the camp. Kiyan said that the police had caused the disaster.

> The police came and kept everyone in, except the families. When Kurdish people tried to get out of the camp, the police officers didn't allow it. They suddenly started to teargas us. Everyone was running everywhere. I was scared for my life...

I felt my heart was going to stop beating.

When the Afghan boys started setting fire to our huts, police officers were standing right behind them, laughing! The police just kept laughing and laughing when they saw our huts on fire. They did nothing to stop it. They did not call the firefighters. It was only at the end when the camp was almost burned down that the police informed the fire service. And only five or six firefighters were brought in. How could they possibly put out the fire?

A Kurdish friend of mine was stabbed and suffered serious injuries. He wasn't conscious and we had to get him to a hospital quickly. But when we took him to the gate and told the police, one of the officers lit up a lighter and waved it in my face, sneering. They didn't want to call an ambulance for my friend. Me and several other men had to drag my friend to the hospital, along the motorway. Luckily, we knew someone with a car and he saw us on the motorway. We had already been walking for 15 minutes. He drove my friend to the hospital and he was saved.

The police are brutal. They are like Daesh to us. Before I came to France, I never imagined French police to be so racist. My image of them was very friendly and civilized. I was totally wrong.

Kiyan very much wanted to move back to the burned-out camp because his sole aim was to reach Britain. He spoke good English, he had friends who had done well in Britain, and he had plans to study and work there. But it was not just that he knew more about Britain, it was also that what he had experienced in France convinced him he had to leave.

New jungles

Hamid and his friends took me to the Victor Hugo gym where all the migrant families were given temporary shelter after the fire. As we arrived, we saw several coaches parked there, and police officers surrounding the area. Volunteers had set up a food stall, giving out lunches to migrants.

The authorities had decided to send these families to reception and orientation centres in other parts of the country. People were saying these could be in the south of France; there was a lot of fear and anxiety that they would be sent to a place too far away from the northern shores to ever be able to reach Britain.

On the pavement, a woman was sitting on a blanket, breastfeeding her baby. I recognized her as Akram's sister, whom I had met the last time I visited the Linière camp. She looked sad and nervous, and could barely manage a smile when I greeted her. She simply said that she was worried and unhappy. Her family, like most migrant families from the camp, had little alternative but to accept being sent to reception centres. Some of them had family members in Britain and wanted to join them but, as Britain was refusing to let them in, many families would have to claim asylum in France, even if they did not want to. There was no choice: they simply couldn't sleep rough in the woods like young men did, because they had babies and young children. For Akram's sister, Grande Synthe's Linière camp, with all its problems, was a well-established place where they were able to feed their children and have something to sleep on.

She told me Akram was inside the building. The gym was packed with families, some resting on mattresses, others looking stressed as they discussed their options. Children were running around, unaware of the uncertain destiny ahead of them. The place was so overcrowded that I couldn't see Akram. Hamid introduced me to a friend of his, from Iraq, who had been living in Britain with his two children for eight years. He had applied for his wife to join him and she was currently in the camp waiting to get to the UK. He was clearly upset by what had happened and had come to see his wife. Sadly, she would now have to accept being transported to a reception centre even though she did not want to, because she simply could not live on the streets. 'I have been waiting for a visa for my wife from the UK Home Office,' the man said. 'I have no idea what will happen to her, to us. I have no idea if my family can be reunited again.'

By the end of the day, 128 people, mostly families, at the Victor Hugo gym had been sent on coaches to the reception centres. The last coach left for Lens. Some families, not wanting to give up the hope of reaching Britain to join their relatives, had decided to walk back to the burned-down Linière camp, and tried to get back in the evening after the fire. The police, however, were now on guard round the clock, so that no-one could return to rebuild the camp. After all, the closure of the camp was what the police had wanted in the first place.

The families who returned were determined, and tried to sleep outside the gate. But, by the end of the evening of 13 April, the police at the entrance to the camp had moved on every family.

I sat with Hamid and his friends on the lawn outside the gym, talking for hours. The uncertainty was wearing everyone down and it was difficult to lighten the mood. While people were being coached to reception centres over the next couple of days, they chose to stay put. Hamid said they needed a rest. At 2pm, charity workers brought food to the migrants.

When I returned after their lunch, things had moved on. Many migrants were walking away from the gym in groups, carrying their bedding and belongings with them. They told me they were going to a new 'jungle', a clearing which they had found in the nearby woods in the Puythouck area half an hour away. Few migrants wanted to stay in the gym to be picked up and shipped out by the coach. Hamid and his closest friend had just walked back from the new 'jungle', and told me that they had decided to go there instead of to Belgium. In such unpredictable circumstances, plans seemed to change by the hour.

Hamid had the company of some 340 other migrants who also decided to move to the new 'jungle'. There, some set up their tents, while others slept in the open air. That evening, they looked for branches to make a fire to cook. The new jungle would be their new base from which they would carry on trying to reach Britain.

However, their plans were disrupted once again. By 9am the next morning, the police, and a large number of riot police officers, had surrounded and circled the woods where the new jungle was to be. Officials from the Prefect's office were on site, too. Hamid arranged to pick me up and take me to the jungle. As I was on my way to meet him, he sent me a map of the place on WhatsApp, and said there was no way he could come outside now because the police were everywhere. The jungle was situated on the other side

The temporary shelter for migrant families in a gym after the Grande Synthe Linière camp was destroyed by fire.

of a lake, a kilometre from the Linière camp, and was a quiet area where many local residents strolled, jogged and rode bicycles. How could the police be present there?

But Hamid was right. When I got there, rows of police vans had blocked the road through the woods. Several armed riot police officers were guarding the area and would not allow anyone in. When I walked round to the other side of the woods, right next to the railway tracks, to try to get into the jungle, I saw two armed police officers peeking into the thick woods and moving slowly towards the location where the jungle was. It was as if the police were playing cat-and-mouse. Such a heavy-handed operation looked more as if they were aiming to catch violent criminals, rather than tired and distressed migrants.

I found a tiny path into the woods, and entered the area from there. There were thin wisps of smoke in the distance through the trees, indicating that there was a small fire and cooking on a stove. I came across two migrants who were gathering wood. They pointed me ahead to the location of the jungle and shortly ahead it came into sight. Hundreds of migrants were there; the clearing was naturally partitioned into two by wild bushes and trees. Some were indeed setting up a fire to make lunch. Others were talking in their tents. Things seemed quiet, almost peaceful. Hamid and his friends greeted me.

Within a few minutes, however, rows of riot police marched in from the front of the woods, and circled the entire site. The officers pushed the migrants from one side of the clearing, moving them all into one big group. Hamid and his friends all quickly picked up their belongings, not knowing what to expect from the officers. Everyone else stood, looking fearful but resigned. They no longer had the strength or will to protest or resist.

I urged Hamid and his friends to leave the woods, to avoid a possibly violent confrontation with the police. 'I should stay with everyone,' Hamid said, looking at the hundreds of migrants now circled by the police. He wanted to stay with the others and face this situation together, instead of leaving on his own.

Just then a middle-aged French man in a light raincoat over a light suit, looking like a local official, came towards me with police officers by his side. 'Leave now!' he said aggressively in French. 'Leave!'

I asked who he represented and he barked: 'No questions! Leave!' I stood there without moving for a minute, as he stood his ground. 'Leave now!' He exchanged words with the officers, pushing me on out of the woods. I said to Hamid that I would see him outside and was then escorted away.

Outside the woods, several coaches were parked, surrounded by the police. Charity groups had also arrived and were handing out baguettes, croissants and fruit to migrants. I saw several of the camp residents whom I had met previously, including Akram's friend from Iraq, who told me that he would never go to a reception centre and would carry on trying to get to Britain. Another young Iraqi said he had only come to see his friends. He had been lucky and had avoided staying in the gym after the fire as he had met a British man who let him stay in his house by the beach for a few days. What would he do or where would he go next? He had no idea.

Forty minutes later, hundreds of migrants were walked out of the woods by the police. Hamid and his friends finally appeared. The police had told them that the coaches were to drive them back to the Linière camp. But few believed it. Everyone knew that the coaches were heading for the reception centres. Hamid and friends decided to walk off on their own. With bags of belongings on their backs, the group of a dozen men started walking towards the bus stop outside the Auchan shopping centre, half an hour away. They were clearly exhausted, emotionally and physically, but tried to keep their morale high. One of them, an Iraqi man in his thirties, said 'Are you all right, mate?' He said he'd learned his English from the British troops in Iraq.

Hamid said the group wanted to head to Calais and camp out near the old 'jungle'. He was not sure that was a good idea, knowing how heavy the police presence was in the Calais area. But he followed the group of friends as everyone wanted to stay together. As they reached the bus stop for Calais, their plan changed again: they had received news that another gym, known as the Moulin gym, had opened to house migrants temporarily. It was in the vicinity of the previous gym, so not far away, and Hamid urged the others to go there together. 'Let's go there, sit down and have a rest,' he said. And then they could make plans for the next step.

Their rest turned out to be brief. As soon as Hamid and his friends got to the gym, they were faced with the worry of when it would close and how much time they would have before having to move on again. Kiyan, the Kurdish man I met earlier, had been moved to Moulin too, and said they would have no more than a couple of days before the coaches would come to take them to reception centres. He said to me repeatedly: 'If they dare force me to go there [reception centre] and end my dream, I will end my life.'

Soon enough, all the remaining migrants in the gym were presented with the options of either being transported to places outside Grande Synthe and accept being fingerprinted, or being sent to a detention centre. The result of this ultimatum was that more than 100 migrants had returned to the Puythouck area where they had set up another 'jungle'. Hamid and four of his friends decided to return to their original plan and travel to Belgium. They arrived in Brussels after a long day, by bus and tram, only to find that there was no camp. They had no idea how the information they had been given had become so distorted. Complete strangers to the city and without any cash, they could not find a place to sleep for the night. They went to the train station but it was shut. 'It's cold out here,' said Hamid, walking the streets looking for anywhere to sleep.

According to *Le Monde*, around 1,000 migrants from Grande Synthe's Linière camp had accepted or been persuaded into going to reception centres since the night of the fire. While the French press gave a positive-sounding perspective to their sanitized 'Grande Synthe refugee story', painting a rosy picture of how every state institution – even the police, as the arm of the state – was trying their best to help, the reality was very different for the migrants who had witnessed or experienced police racism and how the state criminalized their camp to the point of its destruction, then driving them out of the area.

Over the following days, Hamid and his friends continued to sleep rough in Brussels. He would not listen to any of my advice about an alternative plan. Even the toughest circumstances could not change his mind about going to Britain. He was, in fact, well justified in carrying on hoping: every week, around 30 people, some of whom he knew, managed to reach Dover on trucks from Zeebrugge. It was a lot easier to cross the channel from the Belgian port than from Calais. 'There's not so much police control in Belgium,' Hamid said. In his second week there, two of his friends had already made it to Britain by lorry. He believed he had a chance.

Meanwhile, other migrants who had left Grande Synthe had decided to go to Germany and Switzerland, their second-choice destinations, the idea of reaching Britain having become more and more improbable. Unexpectedly, when offered the possibility of spending some time in a detention centre, the determined Kiyan yielded to persuasion and was sent to Dijon, the capital city of Burgundy in eastern France, with several other migrants. Here they were given beds in an apartment and were waiting to be fingerprinted. Kiyan tried to come to terms with putting aside his plans to come to Britain, but had started to think about the problems that claiming asylum in France would bring. 'I'm worried about the long wait – they often keep people waiting for decisions for a long, long time,' he said. 'Also, I'm worried whether they would send me to a village where I will know nobody.'

Kiyan's concerns were well founded. The asylum system in France is notorious for the long waiting periods – as well as for the lack of information given to asylum-seekers. All this seemed intended to deter migrants from claiming asylum. When Kiyan was placed in the apartment in Dijon, he was told by social workers that he would have to wait until the end of May to be fingerprinted, after which he would wait around six months to know the result of his claim. A long time, he said, but he was able to see the end of it. He said he could use the waiting time to learn French – he was learning it online as no language classes were offered. We talked daily, and every day he told me that he spent his time either learning French or taking long walks. He sent me a video that he took of the walk along the river, filming a heron wading through the water in slow motion and occasionally looking back at him. He sent me pictures of the quiet town and the ordinary residential streets near him. He had walked around them aimlessly many, many times. He tried not to feel anxious. His friends, however, had not been able to put up with the wait: they did not want to stay endlessly in Dijon, doing nothing, and had headed back to the woods in Grande Synthe.

One night, just after cooking some rice and opening a tin of minced meat, bought with some of his weekly allowance of €28, there was a power cut in Kiyan's apartment and he spent the entire evening alone in the dark. All he could do was think about his future and how he had no control over it. What would happen to him if he was refused asylum after all this waiting?

Then one day in May, Kiyan sounded distressed when we talked. 'The social [worker] told me that they might have to send me back to Italy because I gave my first fingerprints there,' he told me. He felt betrayed. 'They told me to come to Dijon. They said I could claim asylum and stay here. Now they have changed their minds and want to send me to Italy!' It now looked as if his friends who had lost faith in the asylum system and headed back to Grande Synthe were the sensible ones after all.

'If they are going to force me back to Italy, I will return to the jungle,' Kiyan said. He did not stay to find out their decision. The long wait in solitude had worn him out. For him, there was nothing much worse than being penniless and not having any control over his life. One day at the end of May, Kiyan called me from a train station in Paris. He'd left Dijon. He said he was waiting for someone to take him to the lorry park. 'I will try to get on a lorry from here. See you in London.' I have not heard from him since.

Forced labour and desperation

In Paris, I asked Jahid if I could offer some help and at least give him some cash for the trip he was thinking of taking – at this point he had not decided where he was running away to. He refused. 'I don't want money. I'm already grateful for your friendship,' he said.

Dave and I saw him off at La Chapelle metro station. He had to return to the building site before his uncle found out that he was absent. I felt helpless leaving him in that state but I knew he could not wait any longer. In desperation, I got in touch with Clem at the reception centre on Boulevard Ney for advice. I told her that Jahid's situation was a case of forced labour. She said Jahid could come in to the centre and they would see if they could give him a bed. Following our conversation, she had informed the centre about his situation and they had reported it to the police, as they are obliged to in such cases concerning minors. Later that afternoon, she said that accommodation would be given as soon as Jahid went to the police about his situation of forced labour. He would be looked after as an under-aged victim. Unfortunately, when I informed Jahid about this, he once again refused to go to the police. 'My parents are talking with my uncle now and sorting out the problem. Everything's fine now,' he said. I knew it wasn't true and could see that his fear had overcome everything.

Clem called me the next day, telling me that Jahid should visit the reception centre, and that the police would be present when he visited. I continued trying to persuade him to seek protection at the centre but he was fearful and hesitant. After work, around midnight, he texted me, saying that he was feeling confused about what to do. He said that if his uncle was arrested, it would cause huge problems for his family. But he was finding it unbearable to carry on living with the uncle and work without any pay. I explained to him that he had every right to seek protection and he would be given it.

'What about my sister? I want to be with my sister,' he said.

I had to explain to him again that it would not be possible to be reunited with his sister in England at this stage, as she had no formal immigration status herself. 'The British government has stopped taking in children,' I told him. 'Please go to the reception centre on Boulevard Ney tomorrow. Please.' He suddenly went offline. His uncle must have returned home.

Jahid was in a state of severe confusion. He said sometimes he felt like he was going mad. One of the reasons he was wary of going to the reception centre on Boulevard Ney was because a 16-year-old boy had told him that he had been refused the chance to claim asylum even though he was an under-age migrant. 'He even looked like a child and they still refused him. What chance do I have? I'm too tall for them to believe my age,' he said anxiously.

More bad news: Saeed's asylum claim was refused. They did not believe his story. He sent me the letter from the authorities, in French, which I translated into English. The letter was extremely brief; it outlined his story, without even mentioning his experience in Libya, or Lampedusa. It was impossible to know whether this was due to the quality of the interpreting during the interview. After this rejection, Saeed was transferred to another hostel, to wait for an interview for his appeal against the decision.

One night after Jahid returned from the building site, he wrote to me: 'I'm not OK.' 'Send me pictures of Lampedusa, please,' he asked. Pictures of our time on the island gave him some comfort. He said he wanted to get out of Paris. Someone told him that Toulouse might be a good place because it had shelters for minors. He was going to travel on his own to Toulouse and try it out. 'I need to leave any time soon; I need to get free from my uncle,' he said. I suggested that we could go with him, and immediately enquired about a shelter for minors in Toulouse. When I spoke to them, they asked Jahid to call them himself, to book an appointment.

That evening, he sent a message saying 'My head's not working well now'. Then he called me on WhatsApp. 'Why is it that every step I took on this journey turned out to be the wrong one, and made my situation worse than before, each time? Should I never have left home?' he said, his voice shaking.

I tried to reassure him, but he was not taking my words in.

'Can we prepare for my phone conversation with the shelter?' he asked. He wanted to go through all the possible questions that the shelter staff might ask him. He had already experienced being rejected by other shelters when he had arrived on their doorsteps and was desperate to avoid giving the wrong answers again. So I went through all the possible questions with him, one by one. Why did he leave home? Why did he leave Libya? And why did he leave Italy? He rehearsed the answers with me for approval. I felt like a mother preparing his homework with him.

However, when the time came the following afternoon, Jahid was so nervous that he decided not to make the call. He gave up the opportunity, which upset me deeply.

Asif, Jahid and Saeed: in and out of limbo

Asif got in touch with me on WhatsApp. Asif believed that he had done well in an interview with the shelter and that things were moving forward for him. It was such a relief to hear from him: this was the first time he had got in touch with me since going to live in the minors' camp. I had expected bad news about his case because Saeed's claim had been rejected: after all, they had taken the same trip and told the same story to the immigration interviewers, but their destinies were now a world apart. I was overjoyed with Asif's news. Following the successful interview, he was, naturally, feeling much more relaxed about life. He had taken many selfies posing like the carefree teenager that he should be. He had done something new to his hair; it looked well combed and a bit more curly. He had started to look after his appearance – like a proper youngster growing up. Asif would be all right from now on – I truly believed that. The quietest of the three Bangladeshi boys, Asif was the first who managed to stay in the system – or so I thought at the time.

I met him again in Amiens in February 2017. He appeared truly content: he was settling well there and trying his best to adjust to living in France. The shelter opened the door at 9am every day and the teenagers could then go out. Asif went to school every morning between 10am and 12 noon, and spent the rest of the day socializing with other teenagers in the shelter. They went to the cinema – Asif developed a liking for American action movies and sat in the cinema watching films dubbed into French which he did not understand. He and his friends also played football in the park, or just talked and hung out. The 20 teenagers there, half of them boys, the other half girls, had come from Morocco, Eritrea, and elsewhere. There was plenty of space, Asif said. He shared his bedroom with a 16-year-old boy from Pakistan.

The teenagers shared their social space and they were like a big family. I could see there was genuine solidarity and friendship among them. When an Eritrean housemate walked past him, Asif greeted and embraced him. The boy was 16 years old and was one of Asif's best friends there. A young girl from Morocco also walked past and greeted him warmly, asking where he had been as she had not seen him for a few hours.

Despite being happy where he was in Amiens, Asif had yet to recover from the past, from the traumatic journey that he would never be able to forget. Sometimes he woke in the middle of the night, after a bad dream about the boat trip across the

Mediterranean. He dreamed about standing in the middle of the tiny boat with dozens of others, frightened at the waves that were rocking their boat.

Dave and I walked him back to his shelter just before 7.30pm when it would close. The teenagers would not be permitted out again until 9am the next day. Asif's educator opened the door for him and began to ask him where he'd been. I could see that he was receiving good care there.

In three months, Asif would have the opportunity to move to a shared apartment where he would have his own room. He was really looking forward to it, to an independent life. He said he would carry on living in Amiens.

One day, Jahid did run away. He finally did it. He had mustered his courage and run away from his uncle – never to return. He went to live in a shared room with four young men from Bangladesh, in a two-room apartment in the Gare du Nord area. It was such a relief to know that he had managed to free himself and was at least safe and no longer under his uncle's exploitative control. However, despite my persistent requests, Jahid would not talk to or visit any more shelters for minors because of his previous bad experiences. Then one night, he told me he was coming to England.

'What do you mean?'

'One of my uncles from France has just arrived there. Someone got him over there. I'm going to try the same.' Someone had requested €5,000 ($5,800) to smuggle him to England which meant he would be in heavy debt if he reached Dover, let alone the risk to his safety during the journey.

'Please don't do it. It can be very dangerous,' I warned him.

'I've no choice now. I want to be with my sister. I don't want to live in the dark here any more,' he said.

Jahid revealed that, in order to pay for the rent at the shared flat, he had walked around the streets near the Gare du Nord where there were Bangladeshi and Indian restaurants, going door to door asking for work. A Bangladeshi restaurant owner had given him a job as a kitchen porter, cutting vegetables and meat for one euro per hour, for a minimum of 12 hours a day, every day of the week. His wages were barely sufficient to pay for his rent and afford food, let alone thinking about sending any cash home. No-one should have to accept and tolerate such a hellish existence.

However, I did not want Jahid to put his safety at risk by coming to Britain via a smuggler, becoming indebted and so possibly trapped in bonded labour. 'If you claim asylum in France, you'll be in the system,' I continued with my persuasion, 'and eventually you'll be able to come to England to be with your sister.'

'The shelters won't accept me,' he replied. He seemed so convinced that there would be no exception for his case.

A few days later, without any notice, Saeed was sent to an overcrowded camp for minors in Metz, near the border with Germany. He would be given an appeal interview there. At the camp, most migrants were Africans; Saeed was one of the only two boys from Bangladesh, which made him feel isolated and alone. He was not permitted to go out of the camp and was not told how long he would have to stay there. Every day, he prayed by his bedside for his freedom – there was no-one he could turn to.

After many days of fraught persuasion, in February 2017, Jahid finally agreed to let me take him to a shelter. As he wanted to be near Saeed, I asked the Paris reception centre worker Clem for advice on the shelters in Metz. She kindly directed me to a children's shelter in suburban Metz which she contacted and was certain that they had bed space. When we met Jahid at the Gare du Nord he brought one small cotton bag with him – that was all his luggage, after months of being in Europe since the autumn of 2016. He looked exhausted, probably not having recovered from the previous night's work in the restaurant kitchen. He had told his flatmates that he would not be returning. By the end of this day he would have to be accepted in the shelter or all was lost.

The train journey to Metz took two hours, during which Jahid talked about how much he wanted to be granted leave to remain in France. He had come to terms with the fact that he wouldn't be able to join his sister in England for the time being. He wanted to become documented in France, to go to school, learn the language and receive training for a job. He knew that if he failed to be granted protection, he would surely descend back into the exploitative world of undocumented labour and return to the dark days of having to accept a €1-per-hour job. And he would not be able to return to visit his parents in Bangladesh.

Thinking of the consequences of a failed attempt to get Jahid into a shelter, I felt extremely tense and nervous as I knocked on the door of the children's centre in Metz. It was fortunate that the person who opened the door was an approachable, sympathetic nurse. She listened to me as I explained Jahid's situation, and welcomed us in. She confirmed that a space was available and that Jahid could stay. She introduced us to the director of the shelter, who greeted us politely. It felt like this would be a homely place for Jahid. As I looked around I saw that the centre was surrounded by a large green area, and it seemed to be situated in a safe neighbourhood. I felt relieved that we had come to the right place.

To follow the correct procedures, Jahid had to visit the local police station where he would be interviewed and registered. However, the attitude of some of the police officers was a sharp contrast to the caring professionals at the children's centre. A female officer came to question Jahid, requesting ID from him. She looked him up and down, hostile and suspicious, and did not demonstrate the slightest sympathy in dealing with minors in a vulnerable position. She did not appear to have been trained in working with migrants and refugees.

'Why is he here, if he's got you?' the officer demanded.

'I don't live in France. I'm not able to look after Jahid,' I replied. But she repeated the question three times. Each time I repeated my answer, my voice raised a little higher.

Eventually, she went out of the room to talk to her superior and came back, saying, 'He needs to wait here.'

'For an interview?' I asked.

'Yes,' she replied and asked me to leave the police station.

'I can't wait with him?'

'No, you need to leave,' she answered firmly.

'When should I come back to pick him up?'

'No, you don't come back. We take him,' she said.

'You will take him to the children's centre?' I wanted to be sure. She nodded.

As it turned out, Jahid waited at the police station from 5pm to

1am, without any of the officers informing him how long he had to wait or what was happening. No-one interviewed him or even talked to him. He just sat on his own in the reception area for the entire evening. At one point, an officer came to search him and his bag. At 1am, they drove him to the children's centre.

In the morning, the battery of Jahid's phone was flat. I didn't know where he was and believed that he must still be at the police station. I returned there and the officers on duty told me that they had no idea who Jahid was because they had no record on their system about him having been there the previous evening. His name was not on their books. His registration was not logged. So what was the purpose of his long wait in the police station?

Dave and I stood outside in panic. Where was Jahid? Had the police sent him out into the street alone at 1am with a flat phone battery and no one to help him? Then a text message came through from him – he was at the minors' shelter.

When we visited him there, Jahid told me he had immediately fallen asleep after the long day – even though he did not have a bed, but had been given a mattress on the floor in a hall, with 15 other under-age migrants from Afghanistan, Bangladesh, Gambia, Somalia and Côte d'Ivoire who had recently arrived at the centre. The space was stretched, as more people were arriving all the time. But Jahid reassured me that, following an interview in a few weeks' time, he would be given a bed in a room shared with just one other person. For now, at least, he was well protected and had been allotted an educator from whom he could seek advice on a daily basis. He had turned a corner – he no longer had to live under debt bondage or endure forced labour or exploitation.

Soon after that, I received bad news from Saeed: he had been refused an asylum appeal and told to leave the camp the day after. He said that there were only two options left for him at that point – either to live on the streets, or to join Asif in Amiens. He did not have the time to wait for me to find him temporary accommodation in Paris, and chose to travel to Amiens immediately. There, he was placed in a minors' shelter and then a room in a hostel. He had no idea what the authorities would do with him.

Meanwhile, things had taken a bizarre turn for Asif, whom I

believed had settled down in the system and was all set to live in an apartment. Totally unexpectedly, since the minors' shelter had changed its manager, he was transferred from the shelter, not to an apartment but to a room in a hostel, as it happened, next door to Saeed. Such an abrupt and unexpected change was a mystery to Asif and, with no explanation, he was thrown back into a state of uncertainty; he felt utterly confused, not having understood what he was told in French and not having received any information in English, either spoken or written. Later, he realized that the change of circumstances was because the authorities did not believe he was a minor. He was now awaiting an age assessment test which would include measuring the circumference of his wrist. When I visited Asif at the end of July 2017, he appeared to have lost weight. He told me that he was trying to lose weight to appear thinner and younger. He had also had the entitlements such as language lessons taken away from him and had not received the state support of €45 per month that he had received in the shelter. He had never been so distressed.

In March 2017, Jahid was given an interview at the children's centre. Not only were an interviewer and a translator present, but also a psychologist, for the purpose of detecting any 'suspicious' body language from Jahid in case he was making up his story. Jahid was very intimidated by the interviewer's aggressive questioning, but he tried to remain calm. A few weeks later, he was informed that he had passed his interview. He was sent to live in a shared apartment in town that accommodated 300 other under-age migrants. He had no idea what this actually meant for his immigration status in France or if the decision was final. But, for the moment, Jahid was ecstatic. He had been given a room of his own – his own room, for the first time in his life! An educator continued to look after his needs. Excited, Jahid told me that he would be starting school the following week. He was full of hope. He felt that he was on a path to a new life – and one that he could determine himself.

In the following months, Jahid was really enjoying school and eagerly learning the language. French words started to appear in his messages. Then one day, he told me: 'I'm learning French so much that I think I'm losing my English. With the way it's going, you'll have to speak French to be able to understand me when we next meet.'

Sometimes though, Jahid would tell me how alone he felt. 'All the boys I know from Bangladesh are staying in another camp,' he told me. He met up with them in town and in the local mosque. He sent me pictures of them having Iftar dinner together.

One evening in late May, Jahid was joyful as a result of further good news: he had received a two-year work contract with a Pakistani restaurant in Metz. He would be working part-time for no pay, but with 'some pocket money', for three weeks a month and going to school on the fourth week.

I was puzzled – this did not sound like good news to me. 'This is how it works here for people like me,' Jahid explained, 'I must work free and the tax goes to the state, for two years, and after that, I'll get the "immigrant card".'

'And what will happen after you receive the card?' I asked.

'I will eventually become a formal immigrant in France,' he said, sounding so hopeful.

When I visited him again at the end of July, Jahid wasn't so sure about the promise of a contract. Many minors have been promised the same and been let down at the last minute, only to realize that the 'game of the system' is to delay them until they reach the age of 18, so that the state is no longer responsible for their protection. They then have to apply for asylum as an adult and are easily subject to rejection. Jahid was told by other minors that educators were simply 'spying' on them to find an opportunity to reassess their age. Few seemed to trust the adults who were in charge of their care. Jahid feared that he would end up like the others who had been failed by the system. 'They're doing everything they can to get rid of us. I have a 50-50 chance of surviving.'

The migrant death toll continues to rise– to all our shame

On 14 January 2017, at least 190 migrants drowned in the Mediterranean Sea between Libya and Italy after a boat sank in rough conditions. Only four people survived.

On 3 February, over 1,300 migrants were rescued in 13 separate operations in the Mediterranean.

On 24 March, more than 200 migrants were drowned in two sinkings off Libya.

In the first three months of 2017, at least 559 people died or went missing en route to Europe, according to the International Organization for Migration (IOM).[59]

Over the Easter weekend, 8,360 people were rescued in one of the largest rescue operations carried out in the Mediterranean in recent years.[60]

By July 2017, more than 2,207 people had lost their lives crossing the Mediterranean.

'Lampedusa counts the dead,' said Alberto Biondo, the activist from Palermo. He wrote:

> The sea doesn't discriminate. It knows no racism, but swallows everything we offer it. And the Lampedusans will cry, and continue to count and gather the dead. The dead who have no common denominator save for being brought down by this system: fishermen who brave the waves to be able to live, to feed their own families, and migrants searching for freedom, and to feed their families in turn. 2017 has begun just as 2016 ended, with death upon death, with the daily murder of young men, women and children. A massacre without end.
>
> Around 3am at night on 14 January, 61 people arrived on the island, including 14 women, 4 children and two cadavers, as well as a third corpse of a young migrant who did not manage the final step of the voyage, and died on arriving at the island. The final part of the journey was made on a Coast Guard motorboat on which there was no chance to lie down, and thus those already debilitated by an inhumane exhaustion were unable to bear it and, as has already happened in other situations, died on the island.
>
> At the end of a long day 250 people have arrived on the island, and three bodies... With all our hypocrisy we even celebrated the Global Day for Migrants and Refugees, a day marked by the death of still more innocent victims. Another massacre took place in the Mediterranean Sea when a large boat went down off the Libyan coast. At the time of writing, only eight bodies have been recovered, and

four survivors, who have said that there were 190 people on board, swallowed up by the sea.

Britain and the EU's refusal to open up legal routes for those seeking refuge and betterment has continued to create a huge demand for people smugglers on much more dangerous routes. The EU's operations to combat smuggling have doubtless driven the use of smaller and less safe boats for the sea crossing, overloaded with at least 150 people each time. A new report, by the MEDMIG[61] project, titled *Unravelling the Mediterranean Migration Crisis*, concludes that smuggling is driven, rather than broken, by European policy. 'The closure of borders seems likely to have significantly increased the demand for, and use of, smugglers – who have become the only option for those unable to leave their countries or enter countries in which protection might potentially be available to them,' said Dr Franck Duvell, from the Centre on Migration Policy and Society at the University of Oxford.

According to the IOM, over 25,000 migrants have died in their attempt to reach or stay in Europe since 2000. These deaths would be entirely avoidable if legal routes were made available. For those who have undertaken the journey and arrived in Europe, their hardship is still not over – as the stories of many migrants told in this book show. As demonstrated, the EU and its institutions have maintained and even profited from the misery of refugees and migrants.

The truth is that there has been no 'refugee crisis' or 'migrant crisis', as the mainstream media would like to have us believe. Media misrepresentation has been one of the main reasons why a large section of the general public in the Western world does not understand the reality of and background to people crossing borders and seeking refuge, international protection and betterment of their lives. The crisis we are actually confronted with is created by Europe's border regime.

The media should instead highlight the causes that compel people to move: wars and conflict, and the massive inequality, created by the system in which we live, are the motivating forces that push people to cross borders. We need to expose the falsehood of the distinction between 'refugees' and 'economic migrants', a distinction invented by the state. Abject poverty is often born out of colonialism and the resulting conflict; political instability produces poverty and sustains economic inequalities. Nick Dearden, director of Global Justice Now, has said: 'Migration is bringing those of us in Europe face to face with the reality of the brutal and unjust world our leaders have constructed.'

Somali-Canadian journalist Hassan Ghedi Santur observes[62] that, in addition to Europe's destructive colonial legacies, more recent Western military machinations have also contributed significantly to current migration patterns. Beyond the West's destruction of Iraq, Santur points out that 'Many European countries continue to sell billions of euros' worth of weapons to various countries in Africa and the Middle East where violence has compelled thousands to flee.' He cites the revelation in 2016 that Britain had signed off on arms exports worth $4.1 billion to Saudi Arabia during the first year of its bombardment of Yemen. Instead of reflecting on its own role in causing the displacement of people, Santur said, Europe persists with the notion that Europeans are somehow the real victims of a 'refugee crisis' that has seen untold numbers of human beings risk their lives to extricate themselves from political and/or economic oppression.[63]

'We are told that the principles of free movement, solidarity between members and respect of human rights are at the foundation of the EU. But the value of these principles is dramatically undermined if they are only extended to a privileged minority who arbitrarily hold a particular passport,' says Nick Dearden. In other words, 'freedom of movement' set out by the EU is a principle for the Global North only.

Alex Scrivener, policy officer Global Justice Now, says: 'It's unacceptable that people from rich countries are free to go almost anywhere in the world while people from the Global South are denied freedom of movement, even when they are fleeing war and extreme poverty. A right that only exists for the rich is not a right at all. There's one rule for "expat" Europeans and North Americans and another for the rest of the world. This is apartheid on a global scale. We need to move towards free movement for everyone.'

This apartheid on a global scale allows Europe and North

America to extract resources from the Global South while shutting their doors to people fleeing the unbearable consequences of the system they created.

Following the drownings, Alberto Biondo said: 'The Lampedusans will cry as they have always done. They have always taught us how to welcome the dead, in a town in perennial mourning, forgotten by everyone, the system winning out once again. Why does it win with such ease? Probably because... we abandoned the struggle for the rights of everyone, and have confined ourselves to looking after our own standard of living... we abandoned the idea of freedom and prefer to be "controlled" by politicos and look after our own backyard. We are slaves to a system which has anaesthetized us.'

Afterword

This book has highlighted the plight of many migrants trapped in a European asylum system that is plainly not fit for purpose. Yet, for all their failings, the countries through which I have travelled in my research all accept more refugees than the US, Australia and Britain, where many readers of this book live.

Across the Atlantic in the United States, the political climate has hardened for refugees and migrants. Trump has been the latest embodiment of anti-migrant, anti-refugee racism against which tens of thousands of people worldwide have rallied since he became president. His initial executive order barring citizens of Iran, Iraq, Libya, Somalia, Sudan, Syria and Yemen from entering the US for 90 days, and banning Syrian refugees indefinitely, came alongside his order to build the wall along the border with Mexico and the hiring of an extra 15,000 border guards and immigration officers.

This is no anomaly for the immigration regime of the US. In effect, this is the emboldened escalation of anti-migrant, anti-refugee policies of previous administrations. Under Bill Clinton, the 1,100 kilometres of heavily militarized wall across the border with Mexico had already begun. Obama talked of 'Putting more boots on the Southern border than any time in our history' and added 20,000 more border police in 2015, an increase from the 9,000 border police in 2000. Over the past two decades, the state machine for mass deportations has been consolidated with the federal government using local police and prisons as a key tool. The 'Secure Communities' programme under Obama linked an FBI database comprising fingerprints collected by local law enforcement bodies to Immigration and Customs Enforcement. During his administration, millions were deported. Now this machine has been inherited by Trump and is being enlarged and strengthened by his administration.

Trump started his presidency with the immediate 'Muslim ban'. Not only have none of the countries targeted produced a single terror attack in the US since 1975, but also, more important still, all seven countries have been devastated by US wars and military actions which created endless conflict, endemic poverty and millions of displaced people.

The ban applied to these countries was a direct inheritance from the Terrorist Travel Prevention Act of 2015 under Obama, where the same countries were already named. While diplomats and politicians signed a petition against Trump's Muslim ban, they should be aware that his policy is not 'un-American' but a heightened continuation of policies that were already well in place before him. As Arun Kundnani, author of *The Muslims are Coming: Islamophobia, Extremism, and the Domestic War on Terror*, said in the US media, Trump is saying out loud what the US establishment and political culture have been producing and reproducing all along. His policy corresponds to the many policies that have already been in place for some time. 'We already rounded up thousands of Muslims within the US and deported them simply because they are Muslim. We already have put every mosque in New York City under surveillance by the New York Police Department simply because they are mosques. We've had politicians across the board asking that no Syrian should be able to come as a refugee, just because they were from Syria. We already had 1.2 million people on the terrorism watch list...' Kundnani said.

On 6 March 2017, Trump passed an 'Executive Order Protecting the Nation from Foreign Terrorist Entry into the United States', suspending travel from the same targeted countries, except Iraq, and halting the resettlement of refugees. Under this ban, the US government would conduct a 'worldwide review to identify whether additional information will be needed from each foreign country' to determine whether nationals from the particular country are a 'public safety threat.' Without the required information from these countries, migrants and refugees would be permanently denied entry to the US. The order also allowed submission to the President of names of additional countries by the Secretary of State and Attorney General, which means the banning of any country is completely under the President's control. Meanwhile, US military intervention against Syria continues, while the refugees this creates are banned entry.

Trump is not unique in the Western world in terms of regressive policy towards refugees and migrants. Australia's politicians beat him to it years before. They do not accept refugees full stop: they do not allow anyone who tries to reach the country by boat to settle there. They insist that the policy aims to dissuade migrants from attempting the dangerous sea crossing from Indonesia (note the same language adopted by British prime minister Theresa May when Britain refused to take part in Mediterranean rescue operations). Instead, Australia detains asylum-seekers in camps outside the country – in Nauru and Papua New Guinea, whose governments are paid to maintain them. These camps are notorious for their appalling conditions, and migrants are kept for an indefinite period of time, waiting for their asylum claims to be processed. Their fate is sealed even before the asylum application begins: Australia simply doesn't take them.

Australia eventually reached an agreement with Obama that the US could resettle up to 1,250 asylum-seekers detained in those Australian-funded camps in the Pacific, in return for the resettlement by Australia of refugees from El Salvador, Guatemala and Honduras. Trump at first backtracked on the deal before ultimately agreeing to abide by it. The precondition is that the asylum-seekers will be subjected to 'extreme vetting'. No-one yet knows what that means.

In Britain, Conservative prime minister Theresa May refused to condemn Trump's policies from day one of his presidency, even while the anti-Trump movements unfolded. It was hardly likely she would criticize his stance given her own track record of attacking the most vulnerable groups of people in society. Shamefully, as one of the wealthiest industrialized countries, Britain imposes the most appalling treatment on asylum-seekers and refugees – far worse than most of its European counterparts.

Over the years, I have witnessed so many asylum-seekers living without sufficient support yet prohibited from working – a life in desperate limbo which has pushed them to descend into the world of exploitation and forced labour. I have seen asylum-seekers who have not received a penny after working for months on a building site, and without any means of demanding their wages. I have known people who were badly injured or disabled in unsafe workplaces because their asylum status did not allow them to work openly. I have known people who lost their friends and family members who were asylum-seekers and died tragically while working in Britain. When Theresa May became prime minister and proclaimed her 'mission' in front of 10 Downing Street, that she would '...make Britain a country that works for everyone', she was certainly not thinking about the asylum-seekers and refugees whom she and her government have exploited, penalized and marginalized.

The intention of the Conservative Party is to make Britain as asylum-free and migrant-free a country as possible. In 2015, in her notorious Tory conference speech, then Home Secretary Theresa May maintained that asylum seekers should not even be allowed into Britain before their claims were assessed. She also demonized asylum-seekers by claiming that a significant number of them were 'foreign criminals'.

Those who have ended up in the asylum system in Britain have always had to survive on sub-standard state support and endure appalling living conditions in which they often find themselves trapped, in shelters managed by private companies whose primary interest is to fill their pockets. In 2012, transnational security companies G4S and Serco, as well as others such as Jomast[64] and Clearsprings, were given the largest-ever contract for housing asylum-seekers by the Home Office under Theresa May, awarding them £1.7 billion ($2.2 billion) under the COMPASS contract (Commercial and Operational Managers Procuring Asylum Support Services), which came into operation in February 2012. This 'upgrading' of Britain's asylum market consolidated the country's system of deterrence, by which the already-poor asylum housing fell further below standard. It ensured that living conditions for asylum-seekers would remain among the worst in Europe. Yet, at the Tory party conference in 2015, May set out further plans to make life even more unbearable for asylum-seekers, plans intended to make Britain an even less welcoming destination for them. Her record since then proves that she meant this literally.

During that conference, she vowed to introduce strengthened 'safe return reviews', held when a refugee's temporary stay of protection in the UK comes to an end, or if there is an improvement in the conditions of their own country. Under the 'strengthened' review, the government can now reassess an individual's need for protection, rather than offer settlement in Britain.

Consequently, asylum-seekers who have overcome all the hurdles to be granted refugee status, will – after five years – face a review to determine whether they can be safely returned to the country from which they have claimed asylum. In other words, despite recognition of their status, they will live under constant threat of deportation. May has devised the procedure to act as a further deterrent to anyone seeking refuge in 'civilized' Britain.

Britain is also known for its practice of detaining asylum-seekers and migrants. It is the only country within the EU[65] to allow indefinite detention, described as the 'black hole at the heart of British justice', whereby detainees are held without legal charges, time limit or proper access to legal representation. Britain was able to do so by opting out of the EU Returns Directive, which sets a maximum detention time limit of 18 months – already a lengthy period. More than 30,000 people are sent to Britain's detention centres every year, where they endure poor treatment, lack of medical care and in many cases racism from the staff. In Yarl's Wood detention centre, in particular, which I have visited many times, I have observed that abusive practices are reported to all levels of authority, within the centre and all the way to the Home Office, yet are completely ignored. So inhumane are the conditions that even a sane person could be driven to commit suicide. In Dover detention centre, I used to visit a Chinese man who was detained for more than a year, during which period he witnessed other detainees attempting suicide while he himself struggled with indefinite incarceration. He was asked to work for one pound ($1.30) per hour, whenever required, helping in the kitchen and cleaning, throughout the period of his detention. He was literally on a zero-hours contract. He laughed bitterly about the irony of the situation. 'I was never allowed to work outside, as an asylum-seeker. But in here, I'm asked to work – and on a Chinese wage.'

According to Migration Observatory at the University of Oxford, Britain has one of the largest networks of immigration detention facilities in Europe, with a capacity that has extended to 3,500 places. In 2016, asylum detainees accounted for around 46 per cent of all detainees. In the case of many asylum detainees I have known over the past two decades, life in detention is equivalent to a jail sentence without knowing how long it will be.

The Tory government not only refuses to participate in the reception of refugees and accept its fair share of the international responsibility for refugee protection, it goes further by disregarding the basic rights of vulnerable people who are seeking humanitarian protection, including children seeking family reunion. In early 2017, Theresa May's government abandoned the Dubs Amendment and refused to bring any more unaccompanied asylum-seeking children into Britain (see chapter 6). What happens to these children? They live in the woods at Calais and Dunkirk. They sleep rough on the streets of Paris. Some, tragically, are killed in accidents when jumping on to trucks in an attempt to come to Britain.

Just before midnight on 31 March 2017, a 17-year-old Kurdish Iranian asylum-seeker, Reker Ahmed, who had arrived unaccompanied a few months before to seek sanctuary in Britain, was brutally attacked by a group of up to 20 people in Croydon. Their only motivation for kicking and beating him was that he was an asylum-seeker. Given the serious injuries caused to his head and spine, Ahmed was very lucky to have survived. The racist attack on him was set against the background of state violence – consistent attacks on asylum-seekers and refugees by government policies – and mainstream media racism. The demonization of asylum-seekers and refugees has been going on for years. These government policies, combined with a hostile media, have without any doubt caused much misery for asylum-seekers and strengthened racism, resulting in the increase of hate crime. Far-right activity against refugees and migrants also grew in this context. In July 2017, *Daily Mail* columnist Katie Hopkins joined the European far right in attempting to disrupt the work of rescue boats in the Mediterranean. Their argument that rescue action by NGOs and charities was a 'pull factor' falls in line with government thinking in Britain and across Europe. To stop racist violence and anti-refugee, anti-migrant far-right activity happening again, we need to resist discriminatory state policies, call out racism in the media, and ensure that the very circumstances that breed racial violence are eradicated.

Effective resistance against anti-migrant, anti-refugee racism will have to come from collective action. It worked in the protests against the Byron burger chain in London in 2016, when unionized migrant workers were supported by local trade unionists. It worked, briefly, in the strike by the New York Taxi Workers' Alliance at JFK airport, where unionized migrant workers were united in opposing Trump's Muslim travel ban. It is struggles such as these that will challenge and finally debunk misguided social perceptions, prejudices and myths about refugees, asylum-seekers and migrants.

Endnotes

1. This is documented in my book *Chinese Whispers: The True Story Behind Britain's Hidden Army of Labour*. Penguin, 2008.
2. Most presidential candidates in France wanted to renegotiate the 2003 Le Touquet accords by which France agreed to allow Britain to conduct border checks on French soil.
3. Soon after Macron became president, the government announced an 'action plan' in July, to 'systematically' deport 'illegal economic migrants' and cut the processing time for asylum requests. Macron has described the French asylum system as 'completely overwhelmed' with 40 per cent of asylum-seekers living on the streets. The country received 85,000 asylum requests in 2016. Macron's approach is to deport as many as possible.
4. See *Dangers of Detoxication*, nin.tl/NFdetox
5. Macedonia, Croatia and Slovenia – three of the countries that lie between Greece and the preferred refugee destinations in northern Europe – all announced on 9 March 2016 that their borders were now closed. Several hundred thousand asylum-seekers have used this route to reach countries such as Germany since 2015.
6. British authorities were reluctant to support such search-and-rescue operations in the Mediterranean and argued that it would act as a 'pull factor', 'encouraging more migrants to make the dangerous journey'.
7. See 'Operation Sophia: Tackling the refugee crisis with military means', nin.tl/OpSophia
8. Council Decision (CFSP) 2015/778 available at: nin.tl/EUCouncildecision
9. Under the Dublin Regulation, migrants must claim asylum in the first country of arrival in the EU, the country where their fingerprints are taken.
10. Rome is 1,200 kilometres away from Lampedusa by ferry and train.
11. See Amnesty International report: nin.tl/AmnestymigrantsItaly
12. See nin.tl/ECrelocationdata
13. He is the main character in *The Optician of Lampedusa* (2016) by Emma Jane Kirby.
14. According to ISMU (Istituto per lo Studio della Multietnicità), the majority of the unaccompanied minors come from Africa, especially from Eritrea (3,714; 15.4% of the minors arrived in 2016), Gambia (3,119; 12.9%) and Nigeria (2,932; 12.1%). Around 90,000 unaccompanied children claimed asylum in Europe in 2015. However, as the European Commission found (in 2013), as many unaccompanied children applied for asylum in the EU as did not. This is still the case today.
15. In the same month, the then French Minister of the Economy Emmanuel Macron warned that, should Britain vote to leave the EU in June 2016, the border control arrangements that allow British immigration officials to operate in Calais might be threatened, and that as a consequence the Calais Jungle might transfer to Britain.
16. Since June 2015, the police have evicted migrants from around 20 such makeshift camps around Paris – some from under railway bridges around

the Jaurès metro station and Les Jardins d'Eole park near the Place de Stalingrad, others from along the Quai d'Austerlitz by the Seine.

17. The population of Palermo urban area is estimated by Eurostat to be 855,285, while its metropolitan area is the fifth most populous in Italy, with around 1.2 million people.

18. The Sicilian Mafia, also known as *Cosa Nostra* ('Our thing'), is a criminal organization in Sicily. The basic group is known as a 'family', 'clan', or *'cosca'* in Sicilian. Each family claims sovereignty over a territory, usually a town or village or a neighbourhood, in which it operates its rackets. Its members call themselves 'men of honour', although more often the public refers to them as 'Mafiosi'.

19. According to the refugee association La Cimade, the regions that have reception centres offering beds in France are: Brittany – 30 centres, fewer than 1,000 beds; Normandy – 25 centres, fewer than 1,000 beds; Hauts de France – 29 centres, more than 1,000 beds; Grand-Est – 64 centres, more than 1,000 beds; Pays-de-la-Loire – 36 centres, fewer than 1,000 beds; Centre-Val-de-Loire – 29 centres, fewer than 1,000 beds; Bourgogne-France-Compté – 31 centres, fewer than 1,000 beds; Nouvelle-Aquitaine – 59 centres, more than 1,000 beds; Auverne-Rhone-Alps – 47 centres, more than 1,000 beds; Occitane – 71 centres, more than 1,000 beds; Provence-Alpes-Cote-D'Azur – 29 centres, fewer than 1,000 beds.

20. According to the UK Home Office, nearly 70 per cent of all local authorities house fewer than 10 asylum-seekers, while 174 councils – 45 per cent of the total – are currently not accommodating any at all.

21. helprefugees.org.uk/dubs

22. This was on 27 October 2016.

23. At the central station square, I also met two 18-year-old boys from Gambia. They were living in a camp for minors named Ciclamino, one hour away by train from Palermo. They had been in the camp for one year and were still waiting for their asylum documents. One of them said that his documents had actually been sent to the camp, but the management was withholding them for unstated reasons. The two boys did not want to spend time in the camp because the room was small and shared among four. They preferred to spend the daytime hanging around in Palermo, but there was little they could do apart from going to the language school.

24. Cooperativa BeFree, Inter/rotte. Storie di tratta, percorsi di resistenza (Inter/rupted, Stories of trafficking, paths of resistance), April 2016, Rome.

25. Study on Migrants' Profiles: Drivers Of Migration And Migratory Trends. Available at: nin.tl/IOMprofiles

26. C.A.R.A. di Mineo, Centro di Accoglienza per Richiedenti Asilo, is a temporary centre to house asylum seekers.

27. In Italy, an asylum claim can be lodged either at the border police office or within the territory at the provincial police station (*Questura*), where fingerprinting and photographing are carried out. The police authorities send the registration form and the documents concerning the asylum application to the Territorial Commissions or Sub-commissions for International Protection (*Commissioni territoriali per il riconoscimento della*

protezione internazionale, CTRPI) located throughout the national territory, the only authorities competent to conduct the substantive asylum interview. By law, the interview before the Territorial Commissions should be carried out within a maximum of 30 days from the date the claim and related documents are received.

28. See nin.tl/Eurostatasylum

29. 'Mafia Capitale' refers to a scandal involving the government of the city of Rome, in which crime syndicates misappropriated money destined for city services. A police investigation by Rome's chief prosecutor, Giuseppe Pignatone, revealed a network of corrupt relationships between certain politicians and criminals in Rome (though in July 2017, the court judgement decided that there was no implication of Mafia association). The scheme took advantage of the recent arrival of migrants, with one of the group's associates boasting that they made more money from the new arrivals than they did from drug trading. The criminal organization also used its connections to secure lucrative public contracts, before accepting payments for substandard or non-existent services. Arrest warrants were issued in December 2014, followed by dozens of arrests. Among those investigated and arrested were the president of Rome's council and the head of the city's public-housing division.

30. Centro di Identificazione ed Espulsione (centre for identification and expulsion).

31. Antonio Mazzeo described the management of the asylum reception system in Messina: 'A good part of the financial resources "invested" by the state in Messina for the management of migrants was given to a consortium led by the company Senis Hospes of Potenza, with the participation of Cascina Global Service SRL and the Consorzio Sol Co, both non-profit co-operative societies. According to expenditure data from the prefecture, in the two years of 2013-14 a total of €2,654,633.13 was paid out to the consortium. (The amount awarded was actually €873,536). Specifically, the association led by Senis Hospes was entrusted with "the management of reception services" in the period between 1 January and 31 March 2014 (amount paid €431,295.23), an operation extended again from 1 April to 20 June 2014 (€539,225.79) and a second time the following July (€169,044.84). According to the tendered contract, the triad of Senis, Cascina and Consorzio Sol Co took on the provision of every migrant with food, pocket money of €2.50 a day, a hygiene kit, and healthcare. In exchange, they received €24.33 each day for each person "hosted" in the tent city and the former barracks at Bisconte. When, on 17 July 2014, the prefecture opened a new competition to find a "new" management body for the provision of assistance to asylum seekers (from 1 August to 31 December 2014) it was yet again the Senis Hospes consortium which beat the competitors and obtained for its services the payment of €1,391,217.33. The "reception" contract was renewed up to last May [2015], when the Senis Hospes, Cascina and Sol Co group ceded the Pala Nebiolo and Bisconte centres to the relatively unknown "social co-operatives" ARCA and Medical of Trapani, which presented a better deal of €23.98 per day per migrant in the latest tender.'

32. This is to register an asylum claim. The police authorities cannot examine the merit of the asylum application.

33. At the end of the 2000s, the foreign-born population of Italy was from: Europe (54%), Africa (22%), Asia (16%), the Americas (8%) and Oceania (0.06%).

34. MSF report accessible at nin.tl/OutofSightMSF

35. Similarly, while conducting his research for the *Out of Sight* report, De Mola found that the average resident living in 'irregular housing' situations had been inside the country for six years.

36. In 2015, Eritreans accounted for the largest group of people applying for asylum in the UK, with 3,726 applications.

37. Association des Flandres pour l'éducation des jeunes inadaptés.

38. Ilvo Diamanti: nin.tl/otherSalvini

39. 'The latest reports of "slave markets" for migrants can be added to a long list of outrages [in Libya],' said Mohammed Abdiker, IOM's head of operations and emergencies in April 2017.

40. See Britain's involvement in funding some of these detention centres: nin.tl/UKfundingLibyancentres

41. Also, the rate of rejected asylum-seekers increased. Around 80,000 people either left voluntarily or were deported in 2016, twice as many as in 2015.

42. See *Living in Insecurity: How Germany Failed Victims of Racist Violence*, Amnesty International, 2016, pp 41-2.

43. See above, pp 46-7.

44. The NPD, founded in 1964, is a far-right party. It calls itself a patriotic organization and openly lists British fascist leader Oswald Mosley among its former supporters. Its policy opposes 'the rising flood of migrants', the 'devastating consequences of globalization and multiculturalism' and calls integration 'genocide'. It writes in its manifesto that 'Germany must remain the country of Germans.' Some of its members have been convicted of Holocaust denial or incitement. The party holds a single seat in the European Parliament, but is not represented in the German Bundestag and won just 0.1 per cent of the vote in the last national election in 2017.

45. For Instance, the Clausnitz attack. In February 2016, a racist mob of more than 100 attempted to stop the bus that was driving 20 refugees to their new shelter in the village of Clausnitz, Saxony. The mob was chanting 'We are the people' and 'Go home', terrifying the new arrivals, including children. The attack was led by an AfD supporter named Frank Hetze, whose brother, also an AfD member, turned out to be the director of the shelter to which the migrants were being driven.

46. Amnesty International, op cit, p 47.

47. Amnesty International, op cit, p 48.

48. See the Antonio Amadeu Foundation report *Hate Speech against Refugees in Social Media*, published in 2016, nin.tl/HateSpeechAAS

49. Amnesty International, op cit, p.46.

50. Ibid, p.14.

51. As the Amnesty International report points out, on 14 October 2015, the German Federal Parliament established another Committee of Inquiry

focusing on two particular aspects of the cases that remained unclear: the role played by paid informants within the far-right scene, including the information that they may have had regarding the NSU; and the support that the three members of the NSU may have received from other individuals. The inquiry followed concerns that the authorities had received information about the NSU before November 2011. 'Since the 1990s, dozens of members of the far-right scene have been co-operating with intelligence services in several states as informants. It remains unclear to what extent those informants provided the authorities with reliable information on the three members of the NSU as well as on their supporters. In particular, some of the informants, especially in Thuringia, were very close to far-right groups in which the three members of the NSU were active in the 1990s.' To date, no inquiries had identified the specific authorities responsible for the failures in this aspect of the investigation of the murders.

52. At this time, the polls showed that the AfD had 11-per-cent electoral support, which made it the third-strongest party in Germany.

53. Help Refugees was founded in the late summer of 2015, after a group of friends decided to send a van of donations to Calais. It soon became one of the main suppliers of aid to northern France. Since the closure of the Calais camp, the charity's main focus has shifted to Greece, where about 50,000 refugees – 40 per cent of them children – have been stranded in camps with degrading living conditions.

54. See the report in *The Independent*, nin.tl/secretFrenchcamps

55. According to the police, around 300 migrants a day are being turned back at the ports of Dunkirk and Calais, and at the entrance to the Channel Tunnel.

56. See https://calaismigrantsolidarity.wordpress.com/deaths-at-the-calais-border/

57. His comments came as regional authorities were due to sign an agreement between the state, the town of Grande Synthe and the association that ran the camp, to extend its use for a further six months from April 2017.

58. Soon after the fire, the Wikipedia page for Grande Synthe was updated and a contributor wrote: 'The camp was destroyed in fighting between ethnic factions.' This was far from being the whole truth.

59. This compares with around 350 deaths in the first three months of 2016. More than 20,000 migrants arrived in Italy in the first three months of 2017, compared with fewer than 19,000 arrivals in Italy in the first three months of 2016.

60. The WatchTheMed Alarm Phone network was involved in two emergency cases and could observe first-hand both the inadequacy of rescue efforts by EU authorities and the important and crucial contribution of NGOs in preventing deaths at sea. See details: nin.tl/AlarmPhone

61. The MEDMIG project is led by the Centre for Trust, Peace and Social Relations at Coventry University, in collaboration with the University of Birmingham (UK), the University of Oxford (UK), ELIAMEP (Greece), FIERI (Italy), People for Change Foundation (Malta) and Yasar University (Turkey).

62. See his e-book *Maps of Exile*, published by Warscapes Magazine, 2017. See review by Belen Fernandez, a contributing editor at Jacobin magazine: nin.tl/MapsofExilereview

63. 65 million men, women and children were forced from their homes by war and persecution in 2015, leaving one in every 113 people a refugee, internally displaced person or asylum-seeker at the end of that year, according to the UN in 2016. Meanwhile, contrary to the idea of a 'refugee crisis' in the eyes of Europe, developing countries are hosting 80 per cent of refugees, according to UNHCR's 2010 Global Trends report. Pakistan, Iran and Syria have the largest refugee populations at 1.9 million, 1.1 million and 1 million respectively. Pakistan also has the biggest economic impact with 710 refugees for each US dollar of its per-capita GDP, followed by Democratic Republic of the Congo and Kenya with 475 and 247 refugees per dollar respectively. By comparison, Germany has 17 refugees for each dollar of per capita GDP.

64. In early 2016, Jomast was criticized for creating apartheid in Britain by painting the doors of houses where asylum-seekers live red, potentially identifying their status and location: nin.tl/reddoorapartheid

65. From 2011-16, the known capacity of detention camps identified by Migreurop (a network of activists and researchers from Europe, Africa and the Middle East) has totalled 47,000 places.

Index

Page numbers in *italic* refer to illustration captions.